THE INTERNATIONALISATION OF RETAILING

Edited by
Gary Akehurst and Nicholas Alexander

FRANK CASS
LONDON • PORTLAND, OR

First published in 1996 in Great Britain by
FRANK CASS & CO LTD
Newbury House, 900 Eastern Avenue
London IG2 7HH, England

and in the United States by
FRANK CASS
c/o ISBS
5804 N.E. Hassalo Street, Portland, Oregon 97213-3644

ISBN 0-7146-4648-2 (cloth)
ISBN 0-7146-4174-X (paper)

British Library Cataloguing in Publication Data

Internationalisation of Retailing
I. Akehurst, Gary II. Alexander, Nicholas
381.1

Library of Congress Cataloging-in-Publication Data

The internationalisation of retailing / edited by Gary Akehurst and
Nicholas Alexander.
    p. cm.
"First appeared in a special issue ... The Service industries
journal, v. 15, no. 4" — T.p. verso.
Includes bibliographical references and index.
ISBN 0-7146-4648-2 (cloth). — ISBN 0-7146-4174-X (paper)
1. Retail trade. 2. International trade. I. Akehurst, Gary,
1955–   . II. Alexander, Nicholas, 1962–   .
HF5429.I549   1995
381'. 1—dc20   95–40589
                                                         CIP

This group of studies first appeared in a Special Issue of *The Service Industries Journal*,
Vol.15, No.4, published by Frank Cass & Co. Ltd.

Printed in Great Britain by Antony Rowe Ltd, Chippenham, Wilts.

THE INTERNATIONALISATION OF RETAILING

Contents

The Internationalisation Process in Retailing

GARY AKEHURST and NICHOLAS ALEXANDER

INTRODUCTION

This special issue of *The Service Industries Journal* focuses on the internationalisation of retailing. Traditionally, retailing has been regarded as a localised commercial sector composed of small-scale operations. Undoubtedly, small retail operations remain an important element in the retail structure of developed economies, but in the 1990s large retail operations rank among the largest business enterprises in these economies.

Increasingly, major retail operations are developing international operations. If major retailers are to remain important commercial entities, they are no longer able to remain within the boundaries of their domestic market. For such organisations, international retailing is no longer simply an option; it has become a necessity. Retailers who fail to make the transition from national to international retailer face a bleak future of marginalisation. International operations provide retailers with opportunities for concept development, for sourcing and for operational development, which are not available to the purely domestic retailer. International markets provide valuable growth opportunities and allow for information gathering as a result of commercial experience. The internationalisation process, however, is not sufficiently understood.

For a considerable period of time retailers have operated in international markets; indeed, the international trader or retailer has a longer history than is often recognised in the retail literature. Nevertheless, in recent decades the apparent convergence of markets and the increased internationalisation of other business sectors has led to fundamental changes in the environment in which retailers operate. As within the national environment retailers have lagged behind the growth and development of the manufacturing sector, their suppliers, so in the global market retailers have also been slow to respond to developments in the manufacturing sector. Large retailers have come to dominate distribution channels in the domestic market, but beyond the national market they have been less influential. The internationalisation of retailing, the pace of which has quickened in recent years, is redefining channel relationships and the economics of distribution on a global scale.

SUBJECT DEVELOPMENT

Research Environment

Research activity in the area of international retailing has increased dramatically in the last ten years. This has been the product of both the academic and commercial environments. Considerable development has occurred as far as research within universities is concerned: retailing has become firmly established as a subject area in its own right. This development in retail studies, and the increase in retail research units, has coincided with a growth in the number of retail operations engaging in international activity. In the 1990s international retailers and the internationalisation of retailing have attracted, and continue to attract, considerable research interest.

The development of retailing as an academic discipline in Europe has followed that in the United States. Likewise, the study of international retail activity in the European environment has chronologically, and to some extent intellectually, followed developments in the United States. It is tempting to extend this analogy and to suggest that international retailers in Europe have followed the example of US international retailers. However, such an assertion would be ahistorical. The early international expansion of US retailers such as Sears Roebuck and Woolworths is well recognised [Fritsch, 1962; Truitt, 1984; Wood and Keyser, 1953; Woolworth, 1954]; the international expansion of European retailers, however, has been less well recognised, and yet European retailers have long contributed to the international exchange of retail concepts and operations. Hollander [1970], for example, notes that European retailers, alongside US retailers, were instrumental in developing retail structures in Latin America in the first decade of the twentieth century. Nevertheless, at certain times within more recent phases of international development, US retailers have been a more dynamic force within the global environment than their European counterparts.

Commercial Environment

In the post-1945 environment, US retailing did achieve a particularly high profile internationally, as retailers from both Japan and Europe looked to the US for inspiration and example. In Europe, for instance, Sainsbury's was instrumental in introducing the supermarket to post-war Britain in the early 1950s. Alan Sainsbury, joint-general manager of J.Sainsbury, the UK grocery retailer, visited the US in 1949 and was impressed by the alternative approach to grocery retailing that the self-service system represented [Boswell, 1969]. The first self-service Sainsbury store was opened in the

UK in 1950. Likewise in Japan, Sueko Suzaki, the founder of the retail operation Kotobukiya, recognised the influence of US products, brands and tastes on Japan during the late 1940s and 1950s. In consequence, imported goods from the US began appearing, and an American ambience was established, in her stores [Tanner, 1992].

The expanding US economy of the 1950s and 1960s supported a rapidly developing retail structure which was in advance of European [Gomez, 1963] and Japanese [Tanner, 1992] structures. The international expansion of US operations was more pronounced and, because of the innovative qualities of retailing in the buoyant US market, they were more influential internationally. Consequently, much of the early business literature on the subject of international retailing was the product of research carried out in the United States [Fritsch, 1962; Gomez, 1963; Hollander, 1968, 1970; Wood and Keyser, 1953; Yoshino, 1966]. This literature was important in establishing the parameters of later study. Hollander's [1970] work in particular remains an important reference point for the study of international retailing.

The 1960s and 1970s, however, saw a fundamental change in the development of international retailing. A renewed interest was shown by European retailers in the international environment. As a result of fundamental developments in their domestic markets European retailers were increasingly prepared to expand internationally. Sustained economic development in their domestic markets had enabled European retailers to reconstruct or construct their domestic operations. By the 1960s the larger of these operations had reached a stage in their domestic development where limited growth opportunities in the domestic market were increasingly apparent. In developed European markets, increasingly concentrated retail structures [Akehurst, 1983, 1984] were encouraging retailers to look beyond their national markets. Thus, in the late 1960s and early 1970s, as Burt's [1991, 1993] findings show, there was a period of intense international retail activity by European retailers.

Expanding Literature

Alongside this development in European operations, there was also a growing European literature on international activity [Dunn, 1962; Jackson, 1973; Jackson and Winton, 1975; Jefferys, 1968, 1973; Jefferys and Knee, 1962; Knee, 1966; Langeard, 1974]. However, ironically, a major impetus for the study of internationalisation was the result of a downturn in retail activity and international operations. The economic uncertainty of the mid-1970s to the early 1980s led to restricted opportunities for international growth, but there were significant large-scale developments in North

America by European retailers who sought to escape the unattractive conditions of European markets [Kacker, 1985]. Therefore, this period saw a continued development of interest in the international or comparative retail dimension on both sides of the Atlantic [Ball, 1980; Dawson, 1976, 1978, 1979, 1982a, 1982b; Dunn, 1962; Goldman, 1981; Martenson, 1981; Siegle and Handy, 1981; Truitt, 1984; Waldham, 1978; White, 1984]. European retailers' interest in the US market was to prove a stimulant to research.

A decade ago, the literature on international retailing was limited in quantity. The publication of Kacker's [1985] study of internationalisation was to herald increasing interest in this issue. From the mid-1980s there was a rise in the number of international retail actions. In this period it was not only the US and European retailers who began to emerge in greater numbers but also the Japanese retailers. Nevertheless, the 1980s were the decade of European internationalisation. In these years integration within the European community was to play an important role in facilitating cross-border activity. While retailers may be at great pains to play down the significance of the European Union [Alexander and Morlock, 1992] and Hallsworth [1992] is justified in asking whether the Single European Market is anything more than a contextual rather than a contingent factor in the development of international operations, European socio-economic and regulatory integration has certainly facilitated internationalisation.

Retail Revolution

Some commentators may seek to place particular stress on the last ten years of international retail development: 'It is clear ... that cross-border retailing in Europe is overwhelmingly a phenomenon of the 1980s and the late-1980s in particular' [CIG, 1991: 3]. While the last ten years have been important for internationalisation, they have been simply the culmination of a long period of development. Push factors have continued to encourage internationalisation but the influence of pull factors has also increased in these years. The organisational development of large retail operations has facilitated functional specialisation within retailing, which in turn has contributed to retailers' improved capacity to exploit international opportunities. For example, the development of formalised marketing functions within major UK retail operations in the last twenty years [Piercy and Alexander, 1988] has provided UK retailers with a far more sophisticated planning procedure than was previously evident within international retail marketing strategies.

International retailing is not a new development in the sense that retail operations have only recently begun to internationalise, but it is a new development in that the retail operations operating in international markets today have, for the most part, only been in the host environment for a short period of time. For example, of the 196 non-domestic retailers operating in Belgium where the date of market entry is known, only 31 entered the market before 1980 and only 5 before 1970 [CIG, 1994]. Likewise, of the 135 non-domestic retailers operating in the UK, only 12 were operational before 1980, only 2 before 1970. While companies will have withdrawn from markets over the years, and retailers who entered these markets at an early date may not be included in these calculations because of uncertainty as to the date of market entry, the figures show that, in most instances, those retailers operating in international markets today have only entered the market in the last fifteen years. This increased commercial interest in the international environment has stimulated academic interest.

Recent Research

In the last ten years there has been a dramatic increase in the interest shown in international retailing. If for a time the literature was no more than a trickle, by the late 1980s it had become something of a torrent [Alexander, 1988; Arbose, 1985; Bunce, 1989; Burt, 1984, 1986, 1989; Conners *et al.,* 1985; Davies, and Treadgold, 1988; de Somogyi, 1986; Gibson, 1989; Ho and Sin, 1987; Kacker, 1988, 1985, 1986a, 1986b; Kaynak, 1988, 1985; Knee, and Walters, 1985; Leunis, and François, 1988; Lord *et al.,* 1988; Martenson, 1988, 1987; Mitton, 1987; OXIRM, 1989a, 1989b; Pellegrini, 1992; Sanghavi, and Treadgold, 1989; Salmon and Tordjman, 1989; Tordjman, 1988, 1986; Treadgold, 1989, 1988; Treadgold and Davies, 1988]. International operations were an exciting developing aspect of retail activity.

By the early 1990s the literature on international retailing had built up into a flood of academic output, with an increasing variety of international retailing issues being considered, as a representative sample of the literature will illustrate [Alexander, 1990a, 1990b, 1994a; Alexander and Marsh, 1993; Alexander and Morlock, 1992; Brown and Burt, 1992; Burt, 1991, 1993; Burt and Dawson, 1991; Clarke-Hill and Robinson, 1992; Davies and Jones, 1993; Davies and Whitehead, 1993; Davies, 1993a; Dawson, 1993; Exstein and Weitzman, 1991; Fernie, 1992; François and Leunis, 1991; Fulop, 1991; Hallsworth, 1990, 1992; Hamill and Crosbie, 1990; Kacker, 1990; Lane and Hildebrand, 1990; Laulajainen, 1991, 1992; Laulajainen *et al.,* 1993; McGoldrick and Ho, 1992; OXIRM, 1990; Pellegrini, 1992, 1994; Pellow, 1990; Reynolds 1992; Robinson and Clarke-Hill, 1990; Segal-Horn and Davison, 1992; Sparks, 1990; Sternquist and Kacker, 1994; Tordjman and Dionisio, 1991; Thompson and Knox, 1991; Treadgold,

1990a, 1990b; Whitehead, 1992; Williams, 1992a, 1992b; Wrigley, 1993]. The issue was being considered in greater depth and by a greater number of academics than it had been two decades earlier when another period of commercial activity had stimulated interest.

This interest in international issues does not appear to be abating. At recent international retail conferences in Europe and North America, the depth and variety of interest in this area has been much in evidence through the papers presented [Alexander, 1992, 1993a, 1993b, 1994a, 1994b; Babb and Lascu, 1994; Burt and Sparks, 1993, 1994a, 1994b; Chen and Sternquist, 1994; Cheung, 1994; Davies, 1993b, 1994; Dupuis and Tissier-Desbordes, 1994; Erickson, 1994; Gascoigne, 1994; Hallsworth, 1994; Loker *et al.*, 1994; McGoldrick and Fryer, 1993; Morganosky, 1993, 1994; Mulder, 1993; Reynolds, 1994; Rinehart and Zizzo, 1994; Robinson and Clarke-Hill, 1994; Spannagel, 1993; Staines and Fernie, 1994; Sternquist and Runyan, 1993; Williams, 1994].

However, the literature has focused on international retailing as if it had a separate entity; increasingly the study of international retailing is becoming blurred as, by its very nature, retailing is becoming international. To study a major retail firm in the 1990s is to study the operations of an international retail operation.

Hence the internationalisation process demands separate consideration from the functional development of international operations, although the latter will inform the former. The internationalisation process is both narrower and broader than the study of international activity or the consideration of characteristics of international operationalisation. It is the study of contextualised change over time. Thus the global environment may not simply be taken to be the retail environment, but the broad economic and social environment. Also, the intellectual framework should not be taken to be the retail framework, but a broader intellectual framework influenced by developments within the wider service sector, the international business literature and established economic theories.

A BROADENING AGENDA

The development of international retail operations and the growth in research on internationalisation has important implications for the study of retailing but also for the study of international business.

The horizon of early retail literature was essentially that of the nation-state. Retailers studied were usually confined within national boundaries. That is not to say that consideration was not given to developments on a wider canvas, as Jefferys and Knee's [1962] study of European retailing exemplifies, but that even within such literature retailing was defined in terms of national structures. The literature was more concerned with comparisons than integration. The study of retailing was national rather than international in nature. In the 1990s, as more retailers develop international operations, the research agenda is changing. Some retailers, such as Benetton and IKEA, may no longer be thought of in terms of their market of origin as they are defined both by, and within, the global environment. Such organisations are influenced by an international organisational and operational structure. Thus, when retail academics call for new studies on an international level [Whitehead, 1992] the implication should be that retailing must redefine itself within international perspectives, rather than that new research must develop in tandem alongside those studies which have already been undertaken on companies operating on a national basis by researchers with a culturally defined agenda.

The development of international retail operations and international business theory challenges perceptions of established and proposed theories of international trade and business development. Increasingly, it is no longer credible for theories of international business to ignore the experience of retail organisations. As Dawson [1994: 269] notes, '...Dunning does not deal explicitly and in his substantial study of 1993 in effect ignores...' examples from retailing to describe ownership specific advantages. Dawson suggests his own examples, which might be used to support Dunning's eclectic paradigm [1981, 1988], but also states that 'Dunning's three factors approach ... provide a possible framework for considering the internationalization of retail operations but, perhaps more importantly, they serve to highlight the considerable differences between DFI decisions in retailing and manufacturing sectors' [Dawson, 1994: 270]. As classical and neo-classical theories of international trade were challenged because they failed to accommodate both the changing nature of international trade and developments in economic thought, so theories of international business must accommodate the experience of service sector operations such as retailers. Nevertheless, before the international experience of retail organisations is incorporated into the wider interpretations of international business, such experiences must be better understood on their own terms and in respect of other service sector developments.

CONTRIBUTIONS

The articles published in this volume cover a wide variety of issues which are part of the internationalisation process, and help to set the agenda for future research. They offer conceptualisations of internationalisation: Simpson and Thorpe consider strategic issues and provide an analytical framework; Bailey, Clarke-Hill and Robinson propose a taxonomic structure within which retail alliances may be placed; and Myers discusses the need for a reappraisal of the internationalisation process itself. Articles focus both on the internationalisation of individual retailers and on groups of retailers: Sparks considers the development of the 7–Eleven convenience store; Davies and Fergusson examine the activities of Japanese retailers; while Chen and Sternquist discuss the characteristics of Japanese international retailers. Articles consider particular aspects of internationalisation: Fernie studies distribution issues, while Hallsworth, Jones and Muncaster consider planning issues. Markets and market structure are also discussed: Burns and Rayman consider the US and Canada; Davies and Flemmer study Denmark and Spain; and Drtina the Czech Republic.

In the 1990s there are three regions of the world where the internationalisation process is progressing quickly: North America, Europe and advanced markets of the Pacific Rim. These global regions are discussed by the collection of articles in this volume.

The role of the North American market is considered by Burns and Rayman, by Hallsworth, Jones and Muncaster and by Sparks. Historically, the US market has been a source of innovative retail operations. Burns and Rayman discuss the conditions which have helped to make the US a source of international retail operations, through an analysis of the socio-economic environment in Canada and the US and the development of cross-border retailing. Innovation in the US has led to the internationalisation of operations, as the case of the Southland Corporation illustrates. The 7–Eleven convenience store concept, however, was to prove so attractive that Ito-Yokado were eventually successful in their bid to acquire the operation, having initially been the Japanese licensee. Sparks considers the organisational developments which led to this example of reciprocal internationalisation. The influence of US retailers has been considerable, as noted above, but it has somewhat declined as both European and Japanese retailers have moved into the international arena in greater numbers. Hallsworth, Jones and Muncaster's article shows that the innovative US retailer is still active in the international environment and challenging established structures in international markets.

Several articles in this volume consider internationalisation within the European Union. The international retail alliance is one aspect of the integration of European retail structures. Bailey, Clarke-Hill and Robinson consider the taxonomical issues involved in interpreting the levels of involvement that these alliances represent. The need to understand the internationalisation process is a theme which is taken up and developed in Myers' article. Myers considers the changing nature of internationalisation within an integrating Europe. The determinants of the process of integration within environments such as the European Union are changing rapidly. This article empirically tests European retailers' perceptions of this environment. The issue of integration is considered on the consumer level by Davies and Flemmer. Integration at a retail structural level is facilitated by a number of socio-economic and cultural factors which are reflected in consumer behaviour. Davies and Flemmer's article highlights and explores empirically an important area for future research. Drtina's article raises the issue of retail development of European markets which have operated under a completely different economic system to those in western Europe. While it may be some time before the markets that were once part of the communist bloc enter the European Union, some of them are emerging rapidly and provide an opportunity for eastward expansion. The Czech Republic is one of these markets and, as Drtina notes, European and US retailers have already shown considerable interest there.

Japanese retailers are now playing a role in the internationalisation process. Three essays, by Davies and Fergusson, by Chen and Sternquist, and by Sparks, consider the development of Japanese retailers. Davies and Fergusson consider the international activities of these retailers, while Chen and Sternquist compare the characteristics of Japanese retailers who have expanded internationally and those who have remained domestic operations. Davies and Fergusson's study presents information which is crucial to understanding the internationalisation process. Such data series are a valuable contribution to the study of the process of change. Chen and Sternquist, through the use of discriminant analysis, have profiled fifty-three Japanese companies and identified the characteristics of domestic and international operations. This research approach provides an insight into the conditions which lead to international actions and hence the motivations which lie behind the process. In contrast, Sparks focuses on the process of reciprocal internationalisation through the experience of one operation, 7–Eleven convenience stores, and two organisations, Ito-Yokado and the Southland Corporation.

Collectively, these papers represent a state-of-the-art consideration of the internationalisation process. The contributors, based in North America and Europe, bring a variety of perspectives to the consideration of this issue.

REFERENCES

Akehurst, G., 1983, 'Concentration in Retail Distribution: Measurement and Significance', *Service Industries Journal*, Vol.3, No.2, pp.161–79.
Akehurst, G., 1984, ' "Checkout": The Analysis of Oligopolistic Behaviour in the UK Grocery Retail Market', *Service Industries Journal*, Vol.4, No.2, pp.189–242.
Alexander N., 1988, ' Marketing the UK's Retail Revolution Post-1992', *Quarterly Review of Marketing*, Vol.14, No.1, pp.1–5.

Alexander, N., 1990a, 'Retailers and International Markets: Motives for Expansion', *International Marketing Review*, Vol.7, No.4, pp.75–85.

Alexander N., 1990b, 'Retailing Post-1992', *Service Industries Journal*, Vol.10, No.2, pp.172–87.

Alexander, N., 1992, ' "First with the Most": Marketing and Retailing the American Dream', *The Americanisation of Culture and the End of History*, Conference Paper, American Studies Centre, University of Wales Swansea, 15–18 Sept..

Alexander, N., 1993a, 'Internationalisation: Interpreting the Motives', *International Issues in Retailing, ESRC Seminars: Research Themes in Retailing*, Manchester Business School / Manchester School of Management, 15 March.

Alexander, N., 1993b, 'UK Retailers' Changing Attitude to European Expansion', *7th International Conference on Research in the Distributive Trades*, Institute for Retail Studies, University of Stirling, 6–8 Sept..

Alexander, N., 1994a, 'Isoagora: Retail Boundaries in Free Trade Areas', presented at *Retailing: Theories and Practices for Today and Tomorrow, The Fourth Triennial AMS/ACRA National Retailing Conference*, 22–24 Oct., Richmond, Virginia.

Alexander, N., 1994b, 'NAFTA and The EC: UK Retailers' Strategic Response', *Recent Advances in Retailing & Services Science Conference*, Banff – Alberta, 7–10 May.

Alexander, N. and H. Marsh, 1993, 'Evaluating International Retail Options', *Department for Management Studies, University of Surrey*, Working Paper, 1/93.

Alexander, N. and W. Morlock, 1992, 'Saturation and Internationalization: The Future of Grocery Retailing in the UK', *International Journal of Retail & Distribution Management*, Vol.20, No.3, 1992, pp.33–9.

Arbose, J., 1985, 'The Folksy Theories that Inspire Lifestyle Merchant IKEA', *International Management (UK)*, Vol. 40, No. 11 (Nov.), pp.51–4.

Babb, H. and D. Lascu, 1994, 'Eastern Europe in Transition: Exploring Polish and Romanian Retailing Practices', *Retailing: Theories and Practices for Today and Tomorrow*, Special Conference Series Volume VII, R. King (ed.), The Academy of Marketing Science and The American Collegiate Retailing Association, pp.154–57.

Ball, R., 1980, 'Europe's US Shopping Spree', *Fortune*, 1 Dec., p.82–8.

Boswell, J., 1969, *JS 100, The Story of Sainsbury*, J.Sainsbury Ltd.

Brown, S. and S. Burt, 1992, 'Conclusion – Retail Internationalisation: Past Imperfect, Future Imperative', *European Journal of Marketing*, Vol.26, No.8/9, pp.80–4.

Bunce, M., 1989, 'The International Approach of Laura Ashley', in ESOMAR Proceedings, *Adding Value to Retail Offerings*, Edinburgh, 24–26 April 1989, pp.101–16.

Burt, S., 1984, 'Hypermarkets in France: Has The Loi Royer had any Effect?', *Retail and Distribution Management*, Vol.12, No.1 (Jan./Feb.), pp.16–19.

Burt, S., 1986, 'The Carrefour Group – the first 25 years', *International Journal of Retailing*, Vol.1, No.3, pp.54–78.

Burt, S., 1989, 'Trends and Management Issues in European Retailing', *International Journal of Retailing*, Vol.4, No.4, monograph.

Burt, S., 1991, 'Trends in the Internationalisation of Grocery Retailing: The European Experience', *International Review of Retail, Distribution and Consumer Research*, Vol.1, No.4, pp.487–515.

Burt, S., 1993, 'Temporal Trends in the Internationalisation of British Retailing', *International Review of Retail, Distribution and Consumer Research*, Vol.3, No.4, pp.391–410.

Burt, S. and J. Dawson, 1991, 'The Impact of New Technology and New Payment Systems on Commercial Distribution in the European Community', *Commission of the European Communities, DG XXIII, Series Studies, Commerce and Distribution*, 17.

Burt, S. and L. Sparks, 1993, 'Comparing Retail Margins: A Preliminary Analysis', *7th International Conference on Research in the Distributive Trades*, University of Stirling, 6–8 Sept., pp.563–73.

Burt, S. and L. Sparks, 1994a, 'Capital Construction in Food Retailing: An International Comparison', *Recent Advances in Retailing & Services Science Conference*, Banff – Alberta, 7–10 May.

Burt, S. and L. Sparks, 1994b, 'Understanding Retail Grocery Store Format Change in Great Britain: The Continental European Dimension', *Retailing: Theories and Practices for Today and Tomorrow*, Special Conference Series Volume VII, R. King (ed.), The Academy of Marketing Science and The American Collegiate Retailing Association, pp.139–43.

Chen, Y. and B. Sternquist, 1994, 'Japanese Multinational Retailers: Are They Different from Those Who Stay at Home', *Retailing: Theories and Practices for Today and Tomorrow*, Special Conference Series Volume VII, R. King (ed.), The Academy of Marketing Science and The American Collegiate Retailing Association, pp.158.

Cheung, C., 1994, 'Globalization of Japanese Major Retailers and Stages of their Global Strategic Management', *Recent Advances in Retailing & Services Science Conference*, Banff – Alberta, 7–10 May.

CIG, 1991, *Cross-Border Retailing in Europe*, London: The Corporate Intelligence Group.

CIG, 1994, *Cross-Border Retailing in Europe*, London: The Corporate Intelligence Group.

Clarke-Hill, C. and T. Robinson, 1992, 'Co-operation as a Competitive Strategy in European Retailing,' *European Business and Economic Development*, Vol.1, No.2, pp.1–6.

Conners, S., A. Samli and E. Kaynak, 1985, 'Transfer of Food Retail Technology into Less Developed. Countries', in A. Samli (ed.), *Technology Transfer*, Westport: Quorum, pp.27–44.

Davies, B. and P. Jones, 1993, 'The International Activity of Japanese Department Stores', *Service Industries Journal*, Vol.13, No.1, pp.126–32.

Davies, G. and M. Whitehead, 1993, 'The Legislative Environment as a Measure of Attractiveness for Internationalisation', *International Issues in Retailing, ESRC Seminars: Research Themes in Retailing*, Manchester Business School/Manchester School of Management, 15 March.

Davies, K., 1993a, 'Trade Barriers in East and South East Asia: The Implications for Retailers', *International Review of Retail, Distribution and Consumer Research*, Vol.3, No.4, pp.345–66.

Davies, K., 1993b, 'The International Activities of Japanese Retailers', *7th International Conference on Research in the Distributive Trades*, University of Stirling, 6–8 Sept., pp.574–83.

Davies, K., 1994, 'Internationalization of Retailing: The Examples of East and South-East Asia', *Recent Advances in Retailing & Services Science Conference*, Banff – Alberta, 7–10 May.

Davies, R. and A. Treadgold, 1988, 'Retailing Internationalisation: Trends and Directions', *Coopers & Lybrand, The European Centre for Public Affairs and OXIRM Briefing*, London, July.

Dawson, J., 1976, 'Control Over Larger Units in France The Loi Royer and its Effects', *Retail and Distribution Management*, Vol.4, No.4 (July/Aug.), pp.14–18.

Dawson, J., 1978, 'International Retailers', *Geographical Magazine*, Vol.51, No.3, pp.249–9.

Dawson, J., 1979, 'Retail Trends in the EEC', in R. Davies (ed.), *Retail Planning and the European Community*, Farnborough: Saxon House, pp.21–49

Dawson, J., 1982a, *Distribution in Europe*, London: Croom Helm.

Dawson, J., 1982b, 'A Note on the Law of 29 June 1975 to Control Large Scale Retail Development in Belgium', *Environment & Planning*, A 14, pp.291–6.

Dawson, J., 1993, 'The Internationalization of Retailing', *Department of Business Studies, University of Edinburgh, Working Paper Series* No.93/2.

Dawson, J., 1994, 'The Internationalization of Retailing Operations', *Journal of Marketing Management*, Vol.10, pp.267–82.

de Somogyi, J., 1986, 'Retail Planning for the Next Ten Years', *Retail and Distribution Management*, Vol.14, No.5, pp.9–13.

Dunn, S., 1962, 'French Retailing and the Common Market', *Journal of Marketing* (Jan.), p.20.

Dunning, J., 1981, *International Production and the Multinational Enterprise*, London: Allen and Unwin.

Dunning, J., 1988, 'The Eclectic Paradigm of International Production: A Restatement and Some Possible Extensions', *Journal of International Business Studies*, Vol.19, pp.1–31.

Dupuis, M. and E. Tissier-Desbordes, 1994, 'Trade Marketing and Partnering: A European Approach', *Retailing: Theories and Practices for Today and Tomorrow*, Special Conference

Series Volume VII, R. King (ed.), The Academy of Marketing Science and The American Collegiate Retailing Association, pp.134–8.

Erickson, G., 1994, 'Retailing Entry into Eastern Europe: The Matter of Technological Leaps', *Retailing: Theories and Practices for Today and Tomorrow*, Special Conference Series Volume VII, R. King (ed.), The Academy of Marketing Science and The American Collegiate Retailing Association, pp.147–9.

Exstein, M. and F. Weitzman, 1991, 'Foreign Investment in US Retailing: An Optimistic Overview', *Retail Control* (Jan.), pp.9–14.

Fernie, J., 1992, 'Distribution Strategies of European Retailers', *European Journal of Marketing*, Vol.26, No.8/9, pp.269–85.

François, P. and J. Leunis, 1991, 'Public Policy and the Establishment of Large Stores in Belgium', *International Review of Retail, Distribution and Consumer Research*, Vol.1, No.4, pp.469–86.

Fritsch, W., 1962, *Progress and Profits: The Sears Roebuck Story in Peru*, Washington DC: Action Committee for International Development.

Fulop, C., 1991, 'The Changing Structure of Hungarian Retailing: Prospects for Foreign Retailers', *Journal of Marketing Management*, Vol.7, No.4, pp.383–96.

Gascoigne, R., 1994, 'The Development of the Deep Discount Sector in Grocery Retailing', *Recent Advances in Retailing & Services Science Conference*, Banff – Alberta, 7–10 May.

Gibson, C., 1989, 'Consumer Trends in the EEC – How can Retailers Respond?', in *Responding to 1992: Key Factors for Retailers*, Harlow: Longman Group, pp.23–34.

Goldman, A., 1981, 'Transfer of a Retailing Technology into Less Developed. Countries: the Supermarket Case', *Journal of Retailing*, Vol.57, No.2, pp.5–29.

Gomez, H., 1963/64, 'Common Market Benefits: Will the European Retailer Utilize Them?', *Journal of Retailing*, Vol.39, No.4, pp.1–8, 56.

Hallsworth, A., 1990, 'The Lure of the USA: Some Further Reflections', *Environment and Planning*, A22, pp.551–8.

Hallsworth, A., 1992, 'Retail Internationalisation: Contingency and Context?', *European Journal of Marketing*, Vol.26, No.8/9, pp.25–34.

Hallsworth, A., 1994, 'British Retailing – The Institutional Context', *Recent Advances in Retailing & Services Science Conference*, Banff – Alberta, 7–10 May.

Hamill, J. and J. Crosbie, 1990, 'British Retail Acquisitions in the US', *International Journal of Retail and Distribution Management*, Vol.18, No.5, pp.15–20.

Ho, S. and Y. Sin, 1987, 'International Transfer of Retail Technology: The Successful Case of Convenience Stores in Hong Kong,' *International Journal of Retailing*, Vol.2, No.3, pp.36–48.

Hollander, S., 1968, 'The Internationalisation of Retailing: a foreword', *Journal of Retailing*, Vol.44, No.1, pp.3–12.

Hollander, S., 1970, *Multinational Retailing*, East Lansing, MI: Michigan State University.

Jackson, G., 1973, 'Planning the Move to the Continent: Questions that Must be Asked', *Retail and Distribution Management*, Vol.1, No.6, pp.14–16.

Jackson, G. and T. Winton, 1975, 'British Food Retailers: No Rush to the Continent', *International Association of Chain Stores Quarterly Review*, Vol.17, Oct..

Jefferys, J., 1968, 'Large Scale Retail Firms in Europe: Their Characteristics, Relative Importance and Future Developments', *British Journal of Marketing*, Vol.2, No.4, pp.268–72.

Jefferys, J., 1973, 'Multinational Retailing: Are the Food Chains Different', *CIES Quarterly Review*, Vol.8, No.3.

Jefferys, J. and D. Knee, 1962, *Retailing in Europe: Present Structure and Future Trends*, London: Macmillan.

Kacker, M., 1985, *Transatlantic Trends in Retailing*, Connecticut: Quorum.

Kacker, M., 1986a, 'The Metamorphosis of European Retailing', *European Journal of Marketing*, Vol.20, No.8, pp.15–22.

Kacker, M., 1986b, 'Coming to Terms with Global Retailing', *International Marketing Review*, Vol.13, No.1.

Kacker, M., 1988, 'International Flow of Retailing Know-How: Bridging the Technology Gap in Distribution', *Journal of Retailing*, Vol.64, No.1, pp.41–67.

Kacker, M., 1990, 'The Lure of US Retailing to the Foreign Acquirer, *Mergers and Acquisitions*, Vol.25, No.1, pp.63–8.

Kaynak, E., 1985, 'Global Spread of Supermarkets: some experiences from Turkey', in E. Kaynak (ed.), *Global Perspectives in Marketing*, New York: Praeger.

Kaynak, E., (ed.), 1988, *Transnational Retailing*, New York: Walter de Gruyter.

Knee, D., 1966, 'Trends Towards International Operations Among Large-scale Retailing Enterprises,' *Rivista Italiana di Amministrazione*, Vol.2, pp.107–11.

Knee, D. and D. Walters, 1985, *Strategies in Retailing: Theory and Application*, Oxford: Philip Allen.

Lane, H. and T. Hildebrand, 1990, 'How to Survive in US Retail Markets', *Business Quarterly*, Vol.54, No.3, pp.62–6.

Langeard, E., 1974, 'Corporate Strategy of Mass Distribution Firms within the European Environment', in D. Thorpe (ed.), *Research into Retailing and Distribution*, Farnborough: Saxon House, pp.125–47.

Laulajainen, R., 1991, 'Two Retailers Go Global: The Geographical Dimension', *International Review of Retail Distribution and Consumer Research*, Vol.1, No.5, pp.607–26.

Laulajainen, R., 1992, 'Louis Vuitton Malletier: A Truly Global Retailer', *Annals of the Japan Association of Economic Geographers*, Vol.38, No.2, pp.55–70.

Laulajainen, R., A. Kazutoshi and T. Laulajainen, 1993, 'The Geographical Dimension of Global Retailing', *The International Review of Retail, Distribution and Consumer Research*, Vol.3, No.4, pp.367–90.

Leunis, J. and P. François, 1988, 'The Impact of Belgian Public Policy upon Retailing: The Case of the Second Padlock Law', E. Kaynak (ed..), *Transnational Retailing*, New York: Walter de Gruyter, pp.135–53.

Loker, S., L. Good and P. Huddleston, 1994, 'Entering Eastern European Markets: Lessons from Kmart', *Recent Advances in Retailing & Services Science Conference*, Banff – Alberta, 7–10 May.

Lord, D., W. Moran, T. Parker and L. Sparks, 1988, 'Retailing on Three Continents: The Discount Food Operations of Albert Gubay', *International Journal of Retailing*, Vol.3, No.3, pp.1–54.

McGoldrick, P. and S. Ho, 1992, 'International Positioning: Japanese Department Stores in Hong Kong', *European Journal of Marketing*, Vol.26, No.8/9, pp.61–73.

McGoldrick, P. and E. Fryer, 1993, 'Organisational Culture and the Internationalisation of Retailers', *7th International Conference on Research in the Distributive Trades*, Institute for Retail Studies, University of Stirling, 6–8 Sept.

Martenson, R., 1981, *Innovations in Multinational Retailing: IKEA on the Swedish, Swiss, German and Austrian Furniture Markets*, Gotenburg: University of Gotenburg.

Martenson, R., 1987, 'Culture Bound Industries? A European Case Study', *International Marketing Review*, Vol.4, No.3, pp.7–17.

Martenson, R., 1988, 'Cross-cultural Similarities and Differences in Multinational Retailing', in E. Kaynak (ed.), *Transnational Retailing*, New York: Walter de Gruyter.

Mitton, A., 1987, 'Foreign Retail Companies Operating in the UK: strategy and performance', *Retail and Distribution Management* (Jan/Feb.), pp.29–31.

Morganosky, M., 1993, 'International Direct Marketing: A Perspective by U.S. Retailers', *7th International Conference on Research in the Distributive Trades*, University of Stirling, 6–8 Sept., pp.527–33.

Morganosky, M., 1994, 'Retailers' Expansion into International Markets: An Analysis Based. on Organizational Stages', *Retailing: Theories and Practices for Today and Tomorrow*, Special Conference Series Volume VII, R. King (ed.), The Academy of Marketing Science and The American Collegiate Retailing Association, pp.126–30.

Mulder, N., 1993, 'International Comparisons in Distribution: Value Added., Labour Productivity and Purchasing Power Parities in Brazilian and US Wholesale and Retail Trade', *7th International Conference on Research in the Distributive Trades*, University of Stirling, 6–8 Sept., pp.544–53.

OXIRM, 1989a, 'Foreign Retailers in the USA', *OXIRM Fact Sheet*, Sept.

OXIRM, 1989b, 'Europe's International Retailers', *OXIRM Fact Sheet*, Dec.

OXIRM, 1990, 'International Retailers in Europe', *OXIRM Fact Sheet*, Sept.

Pellegrini, L., 1992, 'The Internationalization of Retailing and 1992 Europe', *Journal of Marketing Channels*, Vol.1, No.2, pp.3–27.

Pellegrini, L., 1994, 'Alternatives for Growth and Internationalization in Retailing', *The International Review of Retail, Distribution and Consumer Research*, Vol.4, No.2, pp.121–48.

Pellow, M., 1990, 'Physical Distribution in International Retailing', *International Journal of Retail and Distribution Management*, Vol.18, No.2, pp.12–5.

Piercy, N. and N. Alexander, 1988, 'The Status Quo of Marketing Organisation in UK Retailers: A Neglected. Phenomenon of the 1980s', *Service Industries Journal*, Vol.8, No.2, pp.155–75

Salmon, W. and A. Tordjman, 1989, 'The Internationalisation of Retailing', *International Journal of Retailing*, Vol.4, No.2, pp.3–16.

Sanghavi, N. and A. Treadgold (eds.), 1989, *Developments in European Retailing*, Yeovil: Dower House.

Siegle, N. and C. Handy, 1981, 'Foreign Ownership in Food Retailing', *National Food Review*, Winter, pp.14–16.

Reynolds, J., 1992, 'Generic Models of European Shopping Centre Development', *European Journal of Marketing*, Vol.26, No.8/9, pp.269–85.

Reynolds, J., 1994, 'Managing Local Markets Across Europe: Issues for Retailers', *Recent Advances in Retailing & Services Science Conference*, Banff – Alberta, 7–10 May.

Rinehart, S. and D. Zizzo, 1994, 'The Canadian and U.S. Retailing Sectors: Important Changes over the last 60 Years', *Recent Advances in Retailing & Services Science Conference*, Banff – Alberta, 7–10 May.

Robinson, T. and C. Clarke-Hill, 1990, 'Directional Growth by European Retailers', *International Journal of Retail and Distribution Management*, Vol.18, No.5, pp.3–14.

Robinson, T. and C. Clarke-Hill, 1994, 'Competitive Advantage Through Strategic Retailing Alliances – An European Perspective', *Recent Advances in Retailing and Services Science Conference*, Banff – Alberta, 7–10 May 1994.

Segal-Horn, S. and H. Davison, 1992, 'Global Markets, the Global Consumer and International Retailing', *Journal of Global Marketing*, Vol.5, No.3, pp.31–61.

Spannagel, R., 1993, 'Small and Medium Enterprises in Retailing in Germany – Strong in the West, Weak in the East', *7th International Conference on Research in the Distributive Trades*, University of Stirling, 6–8 Sept., pp.584–660.

Sparks, L. 1990, 'Spatial–Structural Relationships in Retail Corporate Growth: A Case Study of Kwik Save P.L.C.', *Service Industries Journal*, Vol.10, No.1, pp.25–84.

Staines, H. and J. Fernie, 1994, 'A Taxonomy of European Grocery Market Structures', *Recent Advances in Retailing & Services Science Conference*, Banff – Alberta, 7–10 May.

Sternquist, B. and R. Runyan, 1993, 'Coercion and Reciprocal Actions in Distribution Systems: A Comparison of Japan and the United. States', *7th International Conference on Research in the Distributive Trades*, University of Stirling, 6–8 Sept., pp.554–62.

Sternquist, B. and M. Kacker, 1994, *European Retailing's Vanishing Borders*, Westport Connecticut: Quorum.

Tanner, D., 1992, 'Kotobukiya Co., Ltd.', A. Hast, D. Pascal, P. Barbour, J. Griffin (eds) *International Directory of Company Histories*, Vol. V, Detroit: St James Press, pp.113–114.

Thompson, K. and S. Knox, 1991, 'The Single European Grocery Market: Prospects for a Channel Crossing', *European Management Journal*, Vol.9, No.1, pp.65–72.

Tordjman, A., 1986, 'A Comparative Study of Distribution in Six Countries: Methodological Problems and Results', *ESOMAR Conference Proceed.ings on Retail Strategies for Profit and Growth*, Brussels, 4–6 June, pp.13–57.

Tordjman, A., 1988, 'The French Hypermarket Could it be Developed. in the States?', *Retail and Distribution Management*, Vol.4, No.2, pp.3–16.

Tordjman, A. and J. Dionisio, 1991, 'Internationalisation Strategies of Retail Business', *Commission of the European Communities, DG XXIII, Series Studies, Commerce and*

Distribution, 15.

Treadgold, A., 1988, 'Retailing Without Frontiers', *Retail and Distribution Management*, Vol.16, No.6, pp.8–12.

Treadgold, A., 1989, '1992: The Retail Responses to a Changing Europe', *Marketing and Research Today*, Vol.17, No.3, pp.161–6.

Treadgold, A., 1990a, *The Cost of Retailing in Continental Europe*, London: Oxford Institute of Retail Management, Longman.

Treadgold, A., 1990b, 'The Developing Internationalisation of Retailing', *International Journal of Retail and Distribution Management*, Vol.18, No.2, pp.4–11.

Treadgold, A. and R. Davies, 1988, *The Internationalisation of Retailing*, London: Oxford Institute of Retail Management, Longman.

Truitt, N., 1984, 'Mass Merchandising and Economic Development: Sears Roebuck & Co in Mexico and Peru', in S. Shelp *et al.* (eds), *Service Industries and Economic Development*, New York: Praeger.

Waldham, C., 1978, *Strategies of International Mass Retailers*, New York: Praeger.

White, R., 1984, 'Multinational Retailing: A Slow Advance?', *Retail & Distribution Management*, Vol.12, No.2, pp.8–13

Whitehead, M., 1992, 'Internationalisation of Retailing: Developing New Perspectives', *European Journal of Marketing*, Vol.26, No.8/9, pp.74–9.

Williams, D., 1992a, 'Motives for Retailer Internationalization: Their Impact, Structure, and Implications', *Journal of Marketing Management*, Vol.8, pp.269–85

Williams, D., 1992b, 'Retailer Internationalization: An Empirical Inquiry', *European Journal of Marketing*, Vol.26, No.8/9, pp.269–85

Williams, D., 1994, 'Motives for International Retail Expansion: A Comparative Analysis', *Recent Advances in Retailing & Services Science Conference*, Banff – Alberta, 7–10 May.

Wood, R. and V. Keyser, 1953, *United. States Business Performance Abroad; The Case Study of Sears, Roebuck de Mexico, S.A.*, Washington DC: National Planning Association.

Woolworth, 1954, *Woolworth's First 75 Years: The Story of Everybody's Store*, New York, Woolworth.

Wrigley, N., 1993, 'The Internationalisation of British Grocery Retailing', in R. Bromley and C. Thomas (eds.), *Retail Change: Contemporary Issues*, London: UCL Press.

Yoshino, S., 1966, 'International Opportunities for American Retailers', *Journal of Retailing*, Vol.43, No.3, pp.1–10,76.

A Conceptual Model of Strategic Considerations for International Retail Expansion

EITHEL M. SIMPSON and DAYLE I. THORPE

Expansion into global markets is a dominant issue influencing most retailers' plans for strategic growth. However, internationalisation is not a viable alternative for every retailer. This paper discusses four independent elements that are considered as preconditions that should take precedence in the global expansion decision-making process. These elements comprise the PLIN Model.

INTRODUCTION

The trend toward the globalisation of business is well underway, with the area of international retailing emerging as an important theme. Certain forces at work in the domestic market have influenced many retailers to consider entering foreign markets as a viable strategy for growth. These forces include maturity in the home market, enhanced communication technology, financing opportunities, lowered barriers to free trade and the changing face of retailing through mergers and acquisitions [Kaynak, 1993; Spain, 1993; Treadgoid, 1990; Walters, 1994].

'Thinking globally' has been a message communicated to US retailers for the past several years through trade, popular and academic literature, and many retailers have responded accordingly. For example, Grabowsky [1989:5] has encouraged retailers to begin identifying their company's niche in the international marketplace. Peters [1988:122] has advised every firm with over $2 million in revenues to 'examine international market-creation opportunities now'. Other experts in the field of international business see this internationalisation movement as the most important force affecting retailing today, emphasising that every retailer will eventually be involved in some capacity [Doocey, 1992; Miller, 1994; Shern, 1993; Sloan and Graham, 1990; Treadgold, 1990].

During the last decade Levitt [1986] predicted that even the smallest company in the smallest town would be subject to the effects of global competition and referred to the expanding global marketplace as the 'new society' [Levitt, 1986: xxiii]. Similarly, Root [1987:2] recommended that 'all business firms whether small or large, domestic or international, must strive for profits and growth in a world economy'. By 1992 Doocey [1992] reported that more and more American retailers were branching out into foreign markets, with Europe as the primary target. Supporting the Doocey report is an Ernst and Young survey [Shern, 1994:38] showing that 85 per cent of all restaurant chains have operations outside the US, with 38 per cent of speciality retailers and 21 per cent of general merchandise mass merchants as 'globally active'.

However, concern has also been expressed as to whether or not global expansion is an appropriate strategy for every firm. Feigenbaum [1993: 4A] reported that many opportunities exist for US retailers to expand abroad, but indicated that, 'most should stay home'. Furthermore, Quadt [1990:7], president of International Advantage, recognised that the new economic environment may offer opportunity for US companies, but asked the question: 'How do you decide whether overseas marketing is right for your company and your product lines?'. Even Joseph Antonini, chief executive officer of KMart, has wondered what it will take to succeed in the global marketplace [Antonini, 1991]. Miller [1994] warned there are no clear signs that global expansion initiatives will translate into success for every retailer; and Kotler [1988] alerted retailers that international expansion is one decision that should not be taken for granted.

STATEMENT OF PURPOSE

Based on these various commentaries, it is apparent that an investigation of retail expansion strategies should address the issue of the appropriateness of international expansion for all retailers. Therefore, the purpose of this paper is to present the elements that were found as important and characteristic of retailers who have successfully expanded into foreign markets.

Since the literature suggests that not all retailers should expand into the global marketplace, there may be existing preconditions uniquely inherent in and characteristic of the successful global retailer. If such preconditions exist, then it stands to reason these should be considered before making the decision to expand into the international marketplace. Thus, the premise of this paper is that not all retailers should expand into the global market. However, if particular preconditions exist, then the retailer may consider international market entry as a viable strategy for growth opportunity.

CONCEPTUAL MODEL

As a result of competitive pressures to enter international markets during the

1980s, retailers were forced to re-evaluate their current positions and future strategies [McCammon, Kasulis and Lesser, 1980]. A decade later Kaynak [1993] asserted that the trend toward globalising all firms creates competitive forces that must be reckoned with in order to remain viable.

Differential Advantage

According to Williams [1991], specific differential advantages are key elements which a firm can exploit in its pursuit of customers and profits for successful long-term performance. One differential advantage the retailer should examine is its potential for distinctiveness that may offer business opportunity in an overseas market. Moreover, how consumers view these distinctive differences or lack of differences would serve to answer several additional questions posed by Cort, Diener and Dominguez [1980] and Berman and Evans [1992]. First, where is the retailer relative to the competition; in what direction should the retailer plan to move; does the retailer have unique characteristics in the marketplace, and are these advantageous to the customers; or, should the retailer mirror the competition? The complete examination of differential advantages would define a retailer's general merchandise mix, strategic planning methods, market segmentation delineations and store positioning strategies.

In a speech before a national retailing symposium in Florida, Joseph Baczko, international executive for Blockbuster Entertainment Corporation, told American retail companies to concentrate on local operations rather than take advantage of opportunities in overseas markets, because only a small percentage of firms can succeed. Baczko's criteria for success include a proven, well-developed store concept, a commitment to expanding abroad and financial resources to cover unexpected costs [Feigenbaum, 1993: 4A]. According to Baczko, speciality chains that focus on a single merchandise category and have brand-name recognition are the retail formats that meet his criteria. 'These stores will come closer to succeeding because they focus on a narrow group of products, which makes it easier to adjust to local tastes and fill gaps in international retailing' [Feigenbaum, 1993: 4A].

Differential advantage implies that retailers set themselves apart from their competitors, and allows the individual company the opportunity to develop a degree of monopolisation within its competitive environment. By focusing on certain elements such as product, image and niche, differential advantage can be more easily achieved [Kotler, 1976: 239]. Williams [1991] confirmed the importance of emphasising specific differential firm advantages as vital to long-term success in international markets. The importance of these three elements, product, image and niche, is highlighted, as well as a fourth element, customer segments [Williams,

1991]. Two other sources confirm the consumer element by indicating the differences created by the differential advantage strategy should be easily recognised and perceived as a benefit by the customer base [Samli, 1989; Treadgold, 1991].

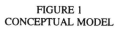

FIGURE 1
CONCEPTUAL MODEL

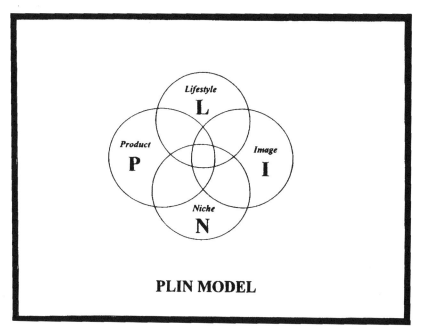

The PLIN Model

After reviewing the literature, four elements appear to exist that are unique and inherently common to those speciality retailers who have successfully expanded into international markets. The following explains the elements that we posit as necessary not only to differentiate speciality retailers within the domestic market, but to provide the basis upon which these retailers can employ international expansion as a viable growth strategy. We conceptualise these elements as 'The PLIN Model' (see Figure 1). Our model includes as the four elements: Product, Lifestyle, Image, and Niche, which we define as follows.

Product: a category, classification, and/or mix of *unique* merchandise that allows the retailer a point of differentiation from all other general merchandise categories and from the merchandise offerings of competitors.

Lifestyle: the compatible match between the company's unique store environment,   merchandise, and sales and promotional efforts, *and* the characteristic lifestyle patterns, behaviours, and needs and wants of a *distinctive* group of targeted consumers.

Image: the attribute that is formulated in the mind of the consumer, representing a composite picture about the status and personality of the company. Some factors that stimulate this mental image include: (a) a unique and immediately recognisable company name, (b) brand-name and/or private label merchandise that are unique, easily recognised, and commonly associated with the company name, and (c) an organisation that is an established and dominant leader in the company's own domestic market.

Niche: a marketing strategy viewed as a component necessary for establishing a differential advantage within the field of competitors. Niche retailers are positioned in the marketplace in such a way that they fill a gap in the competitive environment. The retail business and the merchandise offered fit a portion of the broader consumer market that represents a unique and reachable consumer segment.

These four elements appear as inherently and characteristically common among only those speciality retailers who have been first successful in differentiating themselves within their domestic marketplace, and then within the international marketplace. When reviewing the extant literature, a curious attribute of these variables becomes apparent. Any distinction or differentiation among these elements is ambiguous, at best. Therefore, we suggest that the elements have the property of interdependence, as demonstrated by the overlapping of circles, illustrated in Figure 1. Thus our claim is that all four elements must exist simultaneously, are interdependent and are preconditions necessary to create a differential advantage for speciality retailers in the foreign marketplace.

BACKGROUND

The objective for the literature review was to identify particular factors, concepts and/or variables as common precursors to the decision to expand into international markets. Characteristics of those retailers designated as successful in their international operations were also sought. The four elements listed in the PLIN Model as Product, Lifestyle, Image and Niche, emerged predominant and characteristic of those retailers who were found to   position and differentiate themselves successfully within the international as well as the domestic marketplace. Each element is discussed below.

Product

A study by Alexander [1990] examined the European Community (EC 1992) expansion project and its effect on retailing. He determined that expansion opportunities across borders were based primarily on product lines and product distinctiveness. Similarly, Williams [1991] found that retailers who were already operating in international markets attached great importance to their product. In fact, one retailer succinctly stated: 'Ultimately our success depends upon our products' [Williams, 1991:5]. In another study that focused on the business expansion philosophy of the Laura Ashley organisation, Treadgold [1991:17] found that 'uniqueness in the product-offer makes entry into foreign market much easier'.

Further support for using product distinction as a tool for global expansion was given by Crawford, Garland and Ganesh [1988]. Product characteristics were used as part of their research of market segmentation. Certain product characteristics were discovered as acceptable to the global consumer, suggesting a demand homogeneity, which in turn would constitute a global trade segment. However, all of these researchers agree that unique product distinction alone is not enough to guarantee success for the globally expanded retailer.

Lifestyle

Patterns in which people live and spend time and money have been defined as lifestyle [Kelly, 1955]. Lifestyles are also derivatives of personal value systems and consumer decisions. Retailers seeking to differentiate themselves within a market may appeal to a consumer by providing merchandise that is reflective and/or compatible with that consumer's lifestyle. Dawson [1985] found that the lifestyle concept has become a constitutive force in retailing. He also concluded that an high degree of company differentiation can lead to a successful monopolisation of the market. Examples to support this claim were highlighted by Antonini [1991]. He recognised the success of such 'lifestyle marketers as IKEA, Bennetton, and Toys 'R' Us, [who] have hit upon formulas that successfully span the world...' [Antonini, 1991:5].

Image

In order to discover new forms of competition, retailers can evaluate the consumer perceptions of store attributes and their differentiation [Bates, 1989]. Ring, King and Tigert [1980] examined consumers' perceptions of store image to support the need for unique retailing characteristics. The concepts of consumer perceptions and retail position were used in the study focusing on aggressive department stores. To achieve their purpose, Ring *et al.* [1980] first established a positioning analysis from the retailers' point of view rather than from the customers'. In comparing these two analyses, it was found that almost 60 per cent of the consumer sample failed to classify, or position, the department stores in the same manner as the retailers. This suggests the department stores did not have distinct images in the minds of consumers.

This image homogeneity is not restricted to the Ring *et al.* [1980] sample. Even the retailing giant, Sears, has been guilty of this lack of distinction from the customer's perspective. In the late 1970s, Sears' fashion image resembled discount mass merchandising, while their price structure was that of traditional department stores, resulting in general customer confusion [Blackwell and Talarzyk, 1983]. After a re-examination of strategies, Sears has repositioned the company in the consumer's mind [Moin and Auerback, 1992; Patterson, 1993]. By analysing domestic consumer perceptions, retailers begin to understand the need for a distinct company image. After determining their company image at the domestic level, retailers can then judge how the same image will fit into an international market.

Niche

Understanding the consumer market and segmenting it to reach a specific, narrow consumer group is considered 'Niche' marketing [Salmon, 1989]. Mason, Mayer and Ezell [1991: 668] further elaborate on the concept by describing it as a 'strategy whereby a retailer carves out a narrow position in the marketplace that offers an high potential (for success and profits), and then specialises in meeting the needs of the consumers in that segment'.

Blackwell and Talarzyk [1983] studied expansion and differentiation by combining retailing attributes which were important to consumers. They concluded that a well-programmed store could produce a natural appeal for a specific target market. To achieve this appeal, the store needed to present a product selection, atmosphere, personnel and price range which fit the consumer psychographic and demographic profile. This totality in marketing execution is yet another way to define niche retailing [Lewison, 1994; Levy and Weitz, 1995]. Throughout the literature one can find listings of various US-based speciality and discount retailers who have already successfully entered the foreign markets of Europe, Asia, Central and South Americas, and other parts of North America (e.g., McDonalds, Pizza Hut, Hallmark Cards, Toys 'R' Us, the Gap, Circle K, 7–Eleven, Bed Bath and Beyond, Wal-Mart and KMart). The lists also include a number of 'foreign' retailers entering the US market, as well (e.g., IKEA, Benetton,

Laura Ashley, The Body Shop, and Marks & Spencer). The marketers who remain successful represent innovative and niche forms of retailing that can be differentiated within their domestic competitive environment [McGee, 1987; Davies and Brooks, 1989; Walters, 1994].

IMPLICATIONS

This paper posits that when a retailer is considering global expansion, an application of the PLIN Model must take precedence in the decision-making process. At this time, the retailer should determine if all four PLIN elements, Product, Lifestyle, Image and Niche, are evident and established as a collective differential advantage within their domestic marketplace. If all of these elements are clearly manifested and confirmed by management, the speciality retailer could then consider expanding beyond US borders. If just *one* of these elements does not differentiate the retailer at the domestic level, a speciality retailer may wish to delay or simply not choose global expansion as a viable growth strategy for international business expansion. Application of the PLIN Model as a framework to guide the strategic decision to expand into foreign markets may reduce the likelihood of an ill-fated, costly decision. At the same time, applying the model may increase the likelihood of a managerial decision leading to a successful, profitable operation in international markets.

REFERENCES

Alexander, N., 1990, 'Retailing Post 1992', *Service Industries Journal*, Vol.10, No.1, pp.172–87.

Antonini, J.E., 1991, 'Trends in Retailing for the Nineties', *Retail Control* (Dec.), pp.3–7.

Bates, A.D., 1989, 'The Extended Specialty Store: A Strategic Opportunity for the 1990's', *Journal of Retailing*, Vol.65, No.3, pp.379–88.

Berman, B. and J.R. Evans, 1992, *Retail Management: A Strategic Approach*, 5th edition, New York: Macmillan.

Blackwell, R.D. and W.W. Talarzyk, 1983, 'Life-Style Retailing: Competitive Strategies for the 1980s', *Journal of Retailing*, Vol.59, No.4, pp.7–27.

Cort, S. J., B. J. Diener, and L.V. Dominquez, 1980, *An Empirical Analysis of Competitive Structure in Retailing: The Case of Men's Clothing*, Chicago: American Marketing Association.

Crawford, J.C., B.C. Garland, and J. Ganesh, 1988, 'Identifying the Global Pro-Trade Consumer', *International Marketing Review*, Vol.5, No.4, pp.25–33.

Davies, G.J. and J.M. Brooks, 1989, *Positioning Strategy in Retailing*, London: Paul Chapman.

Dawson, J.A., 1985, 'Retail Research: Studies in Lifestyle', *Retail and Distribution Management*, Sept./Oct., pp.38–9.

Doocey, P., 1992, 'Euro-Retailing: Developers Flirt with Emerging Markets', *Stores*, July, p.76.

Feigenbaum, N., 1993, 'US Companies Warned on Overseas Expansion', *Journal of*

Commerce and Commercial, 18 May, p.4A.

Grabowsky, L., 1989, 'Globalization: Reshaping the Retail Marketplace', in L. Berry (ed.), *Retailing Issues Letter*, Nov., pp.1–6.

Kaynak, E., 1993, *The Global Business: Four Key Marketing Strategies*, New York: International Business Press.

Kelly, G.A., 1955, *The Psychology of Personal Construct*. Vol 1., New York: W. Norton & Co.

Kotler, P., 1976, *Marketing Management: Analysis, Planning, Implementation, and Control*, 3rd edition, Englewood Cliffs, N.J.: Prentice-Hall.

Kotler, P., 1988, *Marketing Management: Analysis, Planning, Implementation, and Control*. 6th edition, Englewood Cliffs, N.J.: Prentice-Hall.

Lewison, D.M., 1994, *Retailing*. 5th edition, New York: Macmillan.

Levitt, T., 1986, *The Marketing Imagination*. New York: Free Press.

Levy, M. and B.A. Weitz, 1995, *Retailing Management*, 2nd edition, Chicago: Irwin Press.

Mason, J.B. , J.L. Mayer and H.F. Ezell, 1991, *Retailing*, 4th edition, Homewood, IL: Irwin Publishing.

McCammon, B.C., J.J. Kasulis and J.A. Lesser, 1980, 'The New Parameters of Retail Competition: The Intensified Struggle for Market Share', in *Competitive Structure In Retailing Markets*. Chicago: American Marketing Association Proceedings, pp.108–18.

McGee, J., 1987, 'Retailer Strategies in the UK', in Gerry Johnson (ed.), *Business Strategy and Retailing*, Chichester, Great Britain: John Wiley & Sons.

Miller, C., 1994, 'Overseas Expansion Hot, but Caution Urged, *Marketing News*, 31 Jan., pp.1,11.

Moin, D. and J. Auerback, 1992, 'Saks' Martinez Makes Move to Sears Group', *Women's Wear Daily*, 11 Aug., pp.1, 15.

Patterson, G.A., 1993, 'Sears will Re-Establish Base in Malls, Target Middle-of-the-Road Merchants', *Wall Street Journal*, 27 Jan., p.A8.

Peters, T., 1988, *Thriving on Chaos: Handbook for a Management Revolution*, New York: Alfred A. Knopf.

Quadt, S., 1990, 'To Market Overseas or Not: How to Decide', *Marketing News*, 9 July, p. 7.

Ring, L.J., C.W. King and D.J. Tigert, 1980, 'Market Structure and Retail Position', in *Competitive Structure In Retailing Markets*, Chicago: American Marketing Association Proceedings, pp.149–60.

Root, F., 1987, *Foreign Market Entry Strategies*, Lexington, MA: D.C. Heathe & Company.

Salmon, W. J., 1989, 'Retailing in the Age of Execution', *Journal of Retailing*, Vol.65, No.3, pp. 368–78.

Samli, A. C., 1989, *Retail Marketing Strategy: Planning, Implementation and Control*, New York: Quorum Books.

Shern, S.M., 1993, 'American Retailers Setting Global Goals', *Ernst & Young's Retail News*, Summer, p.1.

Shern, S.M., 1994, 'Going Global', *Chain Store Age Executive*, Feb., pp.38–9.

Sloan, P., and J. Graham, 1990, 'International Intrigue: As Domestic Sales Lag, U.S. Retailers Probe Foreign Markets', *Advertising Age*, 19 Jan., pp.S1–2.

Spain, K.M., 1993, 'How to Assess and Enter International Markets', *Ernst & Young's Retail News*, Summer, pp.2–3.

Treadgold, A., 1990, 'The Developing Internationalization of Retailing', *International Journal of Retailing and Distribution Management*, Vol.18 March/April, pp.4–11.

Treadgold, A., 1991, 'Dixons and Laura Ashley: Different Routes to International Growth', *International Journal of Retail and Distribution Management*, Vol.19, No.4, pp.13–19.

Williams D. E., 1991, 'Differential Firm Advantages and Retailer Internationalisation', *International Journal of Retail and Distribution Management*, Vol.19, No.4, pp.3–12.

Walters, D., 1994, *Retailing Management: Analysis Planning and Control*, London: Macmillan.

Towards a Taxonomy of International Retail Alliances

JAYNE BAILEY, COLIN M. CLARKE-HILL and TERRY M. ROBINSON

International alliances in retailing are a fairly new phenomenon. A range of relationships is being formed between retailers in order to take advantage of new opportunities and to counter the threats created by the internationalisation of retailing. This paper proposes a taxonomy of the range of alliances being formed between and among retailers, giving evidence from the UK retail sector to support the taxonomy. A comprehensive identification of UK retailer presence in international alliances is presented, along with a discussion on the potential advantages that accrue from membership of an alliance. We conclude by highlighting further issues for discussion.

INTRODUCTION

The term 'alliance' is fairly new in the literature and is applied to *independent* organisations which are co-operating and forming partnerships and coalitions based on mutual needs. 'Strategic alliances' can be distinguished by those alliances taking place in the context of a company's long-term strategic plan [Devlin and Bleakley, 1988]. Whilst there has been extensive discussion in the literature on how alliances work through the analysis of numerous case histories, there has been little work in developing a general definition of what constitutes an alliance within the context of retailing. However, the existence of horizontal co-operation between retailers is not new and has existed, for example within the Co-operative movement, for many decades along with the early development of voluntary chains. What is new is the acceleration of such horizontal co-operation through institutionalisation and internationalisation. There is a significant body of literature on the international nature of retailing [see, for example, Burt, 1989; Burt, 1991; Treadgold, 1988; Treadgold, 1989; Treadgold, 1990] but this has concentrated more on motives for internationalisation rather than on the mechanisms involved in international retailer activity.

Kanter [1989], among others, has suggested that co-operative relationships are of escalating importance to firms that are seeking to improve their competitive advantage. Co-operative relationships may take a variety of forms and may occur at different points in an organisation's value chain. Relationships among firms can be placed on a continuum ranging from infrequent arms length transactions to closer long-term relationships and to fully integrated relationships involving mergers and acquisitions [Stafford, 1994]. Typically, strategic alliances represent the middle ground of this continuum whereby partners receive *mutual* benefits from the relationship and have freedom of exit from the relationship [Murray and Mahon, 1993]. The focus of discussion in this study is to concentrate on alliances that are horizontal, and which in many instances involve companies that *may* be seen as competitors. Vertical alliances, usually supplier/manufacturer alliances, are specifically excluded from our study. The relationships that we are studying are horizontal, between and among retailers.

Various definitions of alliances have been given:

An alliance is an on going formal business relationship between two or more independent organisations to achieve common goals. [Sheth and Parvatiyar, 1992]

A strategic business alliance is a long term business agreement between two or more companies to pool, exchange and/or integrate specified company resources for achieving some agreed objectives. [Hung, 1992]

Alliances are coalignments between two or more firms in which partners hope to learn and acquire from each other technologies, products, skills and knowledge that are not otherwise available to their competitors. [Lei and Slocum, 1992a]

Giving a retail perspective, Dawson and Shaw [1992] describe an alliance as: 'co-operation between two or more retail companies whereby each partner seeks to add to its competencies by combining some resources with those of its partners'.

The above definitions show that alliances have a strategic purpose, i.e. they are created in order to realise certain corporate objectives. However, alliances may also have an operational focus in that they are formed to support the various functions of the businesses involved. In terms of retailing, alliances have traditionally been very operational in nature, for example in supporting buying functions. However, strategic issues are becoming more evident in retail alliances as more retail alliances continue to be formed. Therefore, retail alliances are often both operational and strategic in nature with multiple goals.

AIMS OF THE PAPER

European retailing literature in recent years has focused on the process of internationalisation, and more recently on the identification and scope of retail alliances. This paper concentrates on three important issues which have not yet been addressed, namely:

- A more detailed and extensive classification of alliances in retailing, including a classification within a wider definition of the term.
- The extent of actual retail alliance presence within those classifications.
- The potential advantages that accrue from alliances in retailing.

INTERNATIONAL RETAILING ALLIANCES – A PROPOSED TAXONOMY

International retail alliances that currently exist take many forms. These coalitions range on a continuum from the 'loose' to the 'tight' in terms of the degree of commitment and the existence of organisational infrastructures that bind the partners.

The Institute of Grocery Distribution in the UK [1992] has identified four types of alliances which have developed over recent years: *The Buying Group*, where members co-operate in purchasing, allowing them to increase their leverage with manufacturers; *The Development-Based Alliance*, an agreement between retailers to co-operate on a specific project – often entry into a national market; *The Skills-Based Alliance* where retailers share knowledge and expertise with others; *The Multi-Functional Group*, which combines the element of the other three, and where individual members would gain strategic advantages by sharing expertise such as information technology and systems [Buckley, 1994]. Whilst this taxonomy is useful in classifying some of the alliances, it does not give a full picture of the extent of horizontal interrelationships between retailers. What follows is an extended taxonomy which takes in what we believe to be the full range of relationships.

We propose a way of defining retailing alliances that captures the full range of relationships in existence. We propose an eight stage hierarchy within the 'loose to tight' continuum, where relationships become more established and exit barriers from the alliance increases due to high disengagement costs. At the 'loose' end of the continuum, we define alliances in terms of 'loose affiliations', and at the 'tight' end of the continuum, we define alliances in terms of full mergers with retained identity of partners. Six stages of the taxonomy are substantiated by studies from the body of literature available on alliances concerning classification of alliance types [James, 1985; Lei and Slocum, 1992b; Stafford, 1994; Sheth and Parvatiyar, 1992]. An area of contention, however, is whether the full or partial acquisition constitutes an alliance *per se* [Murray and Mahon, 1993; Sheth and Parvatiyar, 1992]. Traditionally, discrepancies have arisen in terms of whether these types of relationship can be viewed as collaborative. However, evidence from the retailing sector suggests that full or partial acquisition does exhibit some collaborative tendencies in that the acquired company often retains its own identity or autonomy and has an ability to collaborate on an independent level. Although the assumption has yet to be empirically tested, in retailing it would seem appropriate to include these two classifications in the overall 'alliance' description.

The proposed hierarchy is illustrated in Figure 1 below and developed in the narrative that follows.

FIGURE 1
A HIERARCHY OF ALLIANCE TYPES

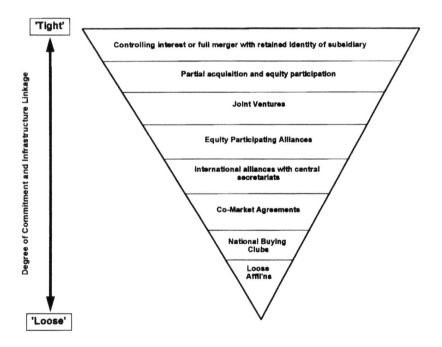

METHODOLOGY

The research presented in this study comprises the first stage of a long-term project on international alliances in retailing. There exists little data on the number of UK retailers involved in international alliance activity, therefore the first stage of the project concerned identifying the population of international retail alliances. In order to ascertain which UK retailers were involved in alliance activity and to categorise the relationships in terms of the taxonomy presented, a search of secondary data sources, e.g., Press, CD-ROM, company reports, market reports, was undertaken. This was supplemented by a short questionnaire mailed to all large UK retailers enquiring about any 'alliances' they may have. Alliances of particular interest were direct relationships that involved two or more retailers. Specifically, those relationships representing the middle ground of the taxonomy, namely co-marketing alliances, buying groups, alliances with central secretariats, formal alliances involving equity participation and joint ventures. Partial and full acquisitions were omitted as the inclusion of these classifications in the 'alliance' description has yet to be empirically tested. The research was centred around the UK population of 'large' retailers, measured in terms of turnover. The research has sought responses from retailers with turnovers of over £20m with a list being generated from the Corporate Intelligence Group's Retail Rankings report [1994a] and the Lotus One Source On Line Database [ICC On Line]. Approximately 220 retailers have been targeted, with 97 completed questionnaires received to date (response rate of 44 per cent). Annual report and accounts were also requested from public companies in order to search for alliances involving equity participation. The information received so far has confirmed/revealed that 16 retailers are involved in direct relationships with foreign retailers, excluding full and partial acquisitions. Other sources, market reports, directories and research bodies, for example, revealed a further 24 retailers involved in alliances. It was anticipated that alliance activity would become less apparent as turnover decreased and, for the purposes of the research, the 'cut-off' point of a turnover of £20m was deemed to be sufficient.

Retailers included in the research were UK domiciled groups, including mail order and cash and carry operators, whose principal business was retailing. Also included in the study were retailers partially owned by foreign groups. Exclusions from the study were: retailers of services, e.g., financial services; fast food retailing; and the retail of petrol and associated products. However, certain retail groups associated with the oil companies operate shops on petrol station forecourts and, in this respect, it was felt necessary to include these retail groups in the search.

INDICATIVE FINDINGS

Loose Affiliations

These are defined as organisations whose primary function is to act as a focal point for a number of members. Essentially these are trade bodies engaged in research and dissemination of market data as well as political lobbying. Also within this category we would include 'task forces' set up by retailers with specific objectives to achieve. Examples of 'task forces' include: the examination of in-store security at both local and national levels; the analysis of trends in music hardware and software which would impact on range policy; and retailer to retailer arrangements to share the distribution costs in the supply of goods to stores in remote locations. Examples of national trade bodies include the Retail Consortium (UK), the Institute of Grocery Distributors (UK), the Conseil National du Commerce (France) and the Hauptgeminschaft des Deutschen Einzelhandels (Germany). On an international level, there is a Europe-wide trade body entitled CECD (Confédération Européene du Commerce de Détail) [Eurostat, 1993] and the CIES Business Forum, which is a body representing the interests of food and food retailing world-wide. National bodies, such as the Retail Consortium, have links with foreign trade associations in order to facilitate the exchange of information between retail members operating in like markets.

The National Buying Club

These are defined as buying organisations, that exist for the benefit of their members, predominantly within one nation-state, whose main purpose is the procurement of merchandise and maximisation of purchasing power. Often members of buying clubs compete with each other in the same market. Typically this form of alliance has been in existence in France for many years, Paridoc for instance. UK examples include Nisa Today's, a buying club representing the interests of 750 independent UK convenience store retailers, and Tiger, a buying club representing the interests of independent electrical retailers. Shaw *et al.* [1994], in their study of the characteristics and functions of retail buying groups, reported that there were 27 national buying groups operating in the UK in 1991. By definition, buying clubs are national in nature. However, this does not preclude them from becoming members of international alliances. For example, Tiger is a member of an European alliance 'Euronics' and Nisa Today's is a member of the European Marketing Distribution (EMD) alliance. Euronics and EMD are more formal types of alliance where the buying function is one of a number of areas of activity. Discussion of retailer presence in these types of alliance follows.

Co-Marketing Agreements

Co-marketing alliances are a form of working partnership that are defined by Anderson and Narus [1990] as 'the mutual recognition and understanding that the success of each firm depends in part on the other firm'. Bucklin and Sengupta [1993] suggest that such alliances are contractual relationships undertaken by firms whose respective products are complements in the marketplace, and are intended to amplify and/or build user awareness of benefits derived from these complementarities. They involve co-ordination among the partners in one or more aspects of marketing.

The Bucklin and Sengupta definition must be slightly adapted from the high-technology sector on which the research was based into the retailing context. This entails a broader definition of the word 'product' to encompass retailing skills and competencies, retail formats, brand values and space assets. Thus this definition is wider in scope, encompassing a range of co-marketing activities whereby one retailer joins with one or more partners for the specific purpose of engaging in some form of marketing activity. A co-marketing agreement may often be a precursor to the relationship developing into a joint venture.

Examples of such co-marketing agreements include business format franchising, e.g., Benetton, Tie Rack, Sock Shop, Vision Express, Body Shop, Toys 'R' Us, French Connection, GUS' Burberrys, Mulberry, Storehouse. Marks & Spencer's co-marketing activities are in the form of the operation of shops within shops and licensing agreements (and possible joint ventures) with partners in Spain and Hungary. Marks & Spencer also has what it describes as franchising agreements in Portugal, Greece and the Nordic countries [The European Retail Digest, 1994]. Austin Reed has licensing agreements in the US and Japan. Monsoon has a number of licensees abroad, in Norway, Malaysia, New Zealand for example. Dixons' PC World has a distribution arrangement with Vobis (Germany) for the exclusive supply of Vobis computers to Dixons' stores. Most of the Burton Group's foreign ventures have been in-store concessions, within the Spanish department store Galerias Preciados, for instance, and it also has a small number of franchised outlets [Corporate Intelligence Group, 1994b]. Sears is another shop-within-shop operator, e.g., its Olympus concessions in Galerias Preciados [The European Retail Digest, 1994]. Other concession operators are Alexon, Falmers, Country Casuals, GUS' Burberrys, Mulberry, Pringle of Scotland. The most recent retail group to enter into a co-marketing agreement is Asda with Promodes of France, although the exact nature of the relationship has yet to be identified.

International Alliances with Central Secretariat

These are retail groups which form an international alliance and create a central secretariat for the purpose of co-ordinating operational activities – buying, branding, expertise exchange and product marketing. The distinguishing feature here is the existence of a formal centre, often in a neutral location, to act as a focal point for the group. To date, the range of activities performed by the centres is limited and excludes order processing and central payments, but over time these roles are likely to take a more strategic focus with the development of pan-European retailer brands. Table 1 illustrates the number of current European alliances comprising UK members which have been identified to date:

TABLE 1
INTERNATIONAL RETAIL ALLIANCES AND UK MEMBERS

Name of International Alliance	UK Member
Associated Marketing Services (AMS)	Argyll Group
Association Commerciale Internationale (ACI)	John Lewis
Buying International Group Spar (BIGS)	Spar Landmark
Coopération Européene de Marketing (CEM)	Booker
* Euro Buro	John Heath
* Euro–Activ	Image Group
Euronics	Tiger (UK Buying Group)
European Marketing Distribution (EMD)	Nisa Today's (UK Buying Group)
Intercoop/NAF	CWS and CRS
International Group of Department Stores (IGDS)	Selfridges
* International Sports Retail Group	Stag
SEDD	J. Sainsbury
Spar International	Spar Landmark

*: These alliances have been identified by the Oxford Institute of Retail Management [1993] but have yet to be classified into the appropriate category.

The CEM is understood to have been officially disbanded due to the recent departure of its main member, Edeka, to the AMS alliance (to take up membership in 1995). However, remaining members, of which Booker is one, are known to wish to continue the co-operative relationship [IGD European Fact File, 1994].

SEDD was formed in April 1994 and is a new alliance which we believe falls into the international alliance category. Although at present it does not have a central secretariat, it is anticipated that it will follow this format. SEDD is the mnemonic of its constituent members (J. Sainsbury, Esselunga, Docks de France and Delhaize).

Intercoop and NAF are two complementary alliances which deal with the differing business needs of the Cooperative Wholesale Society and Cooperative Retail Service. It is understood that Intercoop and NAF have recently established links with an European alliance, Deuro Buying [IGD European Fact File, 1994].

As mentioned earlier, two UK national buying groups are also members of pan-European alliances. Nisa Today's, which represents the interests of independent convenience store retailers, is also involved in the EMD alliance in order to take advantage of pan-European developments. Similarly, Tiger, which represents the interests of independent electrical retailers, is also involved in Euronics, which comprises other European electrical retailers.

Equity Participating International Alliances

These types of alliance involve two or more members each of which has an equity stake in its partners, and the alliance is formally constituted. The only known current example of such an alliance is the European Retail Alliance (ERA). There are three members: Argyll Group (UK), Casino (France) and Ahold (Netherlands). A characteristic of this alliance is that it is a majority shareholder in a looser buying alliance (as above), namely the AMS. The rationale for such an alliance is to achieve wider and more strategic goals than the operational focus of a buying alliance [Robinson and Clarke-Hill, 1993b].

Joint Ventures

Harrigan's [1988] definition of joint ventures as being 'business agreements where two or more owners create a separate entity' can be said to apply equally well to retailer joint ventures as to those in other industrial sectors. They involve one or more partners joining together to create a new identity with specific purpose. Table 2 illustrates the number and type of joint ventures identified to date:

TABLE 2
JOINT VENTURES COMPRISING UK RETAILERS

UK Retailer	Partner	Equity Split (respectively)	Purpose
Courts	Neal and Massy (Trinidad)	75:25	Market Entry and Development
J. Sainsbury	G.I.B. (Belgium)	75:25	Formed Homebase, the UK DIY Chain
Kingfisher	Staples (US)	N/A	Formed Staples The Office Superstore (UK)
Liberty	Ryohin Keikaku (Japan)	N/A	For the opening of 'Muji' stores in the UK
Littlewoods	Gostiny Dvor (Russia)	N/A	Opening of Department Store in St Petersburg
Marks & Spencer	Cortefiel (Spain)	70:30	Formed Marks & Spencer Espana
Marks & Spencer	Demexco (Austria) and 'S' Modell (Hungary)	N/A	To Open Pilot Store in Budapest
Monsoon	Regn (Iceland)	N/A	Unknown
Next	The Limited (US)	78:22	Market Entry i.e. US and UK
Sears	Groupe Andre (France)	50:50	Market Entry and Development
Virgin Megastores	Blockbusters (US)	N/A	For the Opening of Stores Abroad
Virgin Megastores	Marui (Japan)	N/A	For the Opening of Stores Abroad
Vision Express	Latmedteknica (Latvia)	60:40	Formed Medtech Express Ltd
Vision Express	Optika (Russia)	60:40	Formed the Lenam Joint Stock Society

Source: Information collected from Corporate Intelligence Group [1994b] and The European Retail Digest [1994].

An examination of Table 2 reveals that joint ventures are being formed to enter new markets (in either geographical and/or new trading format terms) or to help develop existing international and domestic markets. Joint venture partners can contribute the required cultural and/or retailing expertise and experience gained in their own markets to aid overseas partners in their markets. For example, Sears has a joint venture with

Groupe Andre to develop Andre Deutschland and Sears Hoogenbosch (the market leader in Dutch footwear). Both companies possess a detailed knowledge of their product (footwear) and have an implicit knowledge of the cultures prevailing in their own domestic markets. This knowledge has provided both retailers with the opportunity to expand their shares of the footwear markets in Germany, the Netherlands, Belgium and Luxembourg to account for some 422 outlets. The success of the venture has prompted the companies to develop a retail clothing network which, in 1992–93, had 19 outlets [Corporate Intelligence Group, 1994b].

Kingfisher's joint venture with the US retailer Staples has enabled it to enter the office stationery and supplies retail market in the UK as a result of an inward transfer of skills in trading format knowledge. Similarly, Sainsbury's joint venture with G.I.B. provided Sainsbury with the opportunity to enter the UK DIY market. Whilst these joint ventures have been formed to adding different trading formats to existing portfolios, many others have been concerned with expanding existing formats into new geographical markets. For instance, Marks & Spencer is relying on the market knowledge of Cortefiel in order to establish itself in the Spanish market. Next has recently opened two stores in the United States, with the guidance of The Limited, and it is understood that The Limited has plans to establish its Bath and Body Works shops in the UK market [Pratley, 1994].

MULTIPLE ALLIANCES

The use of the various methods outlined in the taxonomy must not be seen as mutually exclusive. Retailers may, and often do, pursue multiple alliance strategies and strategic goals. In the case of J. Sainsbury, the company entered into a joint venture with GB Inmo of Belgium in order to enter the UK DIY market and also recently announced the formal alliance with a central secretariat namely SEDD. Along with these alliances the company is also involved in trade associations and owns Shaws supermarkets in the US. Recently, Sainsbury also took a 16 per cent stake in Giant Food (US). Thus, one retailer is pursuing several separate 'alliance' strategies simultaneously. A similar situation can be seen in the case of Marks & Spencer with their co-marketing and joint venture activities in Europe and the Far East.

In some instances, notably among smaller retail groups, a 'nested' hierarchy of alliances may occur, operating at both national and international levels. An example is the UK domestic buying club of NISA which in turn is a member of the larger European alliance EMD. Table 3 below illustrates the numbers of UK retailers involved in transnational alliance types, identified to date:

TABLE 3
TRANS-NATIONAL RETAIL ALLIANCES WITH UK MEMBERS

Type of Alliance	Number of Alliances with UK Members
Co-Marketing Arrangements	19
International Alliances with Central Secretariats	11*
Joint Ventures	11
Unclassified	3

* includes one equity participating alliance, and one alliance that is yet to create a central secretariat.

At present the web of alliances we are observing is relatively simple, but it is likely to become more complex as uncommitted retail groups either join existing alliances or form new ones, as in the recently announced alliance between Asda and Promodes, for instance. Current alliance activity beyond the lower level alliances in the taxonomy is likely to limit the potential for retailers to expand in to new international markets in which their partners' are based. Put simply, members do not compete in each other's domestic markets. For example, Dansk left the AMS alliance when its discount retailing subsidiary, Netto, began trading in the UK in competition with the Argyll Group's discount operation.

The issue of the advantages that can accrue to member retailers within different forms of alliance still remains unresolved and this is discussed in the next section.

BENEFITS FROM ALLIANCES

Previous empirical work on international alliances with central secretariats [Robinson and Clarke-Hill, 1993a], and on equity participating international alliances [Robinson and Clarke-Hill, 1993b], identified alliance motivations as having both operational and strategic orientations. Some of the advantages of alliance membership we have identified apply to the full range of alliances in our taxonomy. Since our research is not yet complete, we have not classified alliances in terms of their strategic or operational benefits, but we can identify the following advantages:

- *Common voice in the trade/political arena* (Loose Affiliations, i.e., trade associations)
- *Situation specific and short-term advantages* (Loose Affiliations, i.e., task forces)
- *Buying economies/buying power/countervailing power relationships with manufacturers* (Buying Clubs, International Alliances with Central Secretariats)
  Alliances often act in an advisory capacity on decisions regarding supplier selection. In the case of the AMS, strategic motives were present in the change of suppliers as members attempted to move towards a pan-European supply network [Robinson and Clarke-Hill, 1995]. Alliances help create networks between members in areas such as price intelligence, price bargaining and centralised order processing. BIGS is currently partially operating a centralised payment system [Robinson and Clarke-Hill, 1995].

- *Brand/Image transfer and development of pan-European retailer brands* (International Alliances with central secretariats, Co-Marketing Agreements, Equity Participating Alliances)
  In the membership of the ERA, the Argyll group is developing own-label lines with Casino, and the French chain is also introducing some of its own brands into selected Argyll stores [Corporate Intelligence Group, 1993]. Similarly, Esselunga, the Italian supermarket chain, was noted as carrying selected Sainsbury own-label products in some of its stores prior to the creation of the formal alliance, SEDD [Corporate Intelligence Group, 1993]. Spar International is involved in a pan-European branding programme, designed to be flexible and to allow each country to adapt the products to its particular market while maintaining a unified brand image [IGD European Fact File, 1994].

- *Trading format skills* (International Alliances with Central Secretariats, Equity Participating Alliances, Joint Ventures)
  Spar International has its own working parties to investigate areas such as management and store design [IGD European Fact File, 1994].

- *Procurement in specific product areas* (Buying Clubs, International Alliances with Central Secretariats)
  It is likely that the SEDD alliance will move towards the centralised purchasing of own-label products, tertiary brands and fresh produce [IGD European Fact File, 1994].

- *Promotional skills* (International Alliances with Central Secretariats, Equity Participating Alliances, Co-Marketing Alliances)
  The EMD is involved in marketing and co-ordinating international

promotional campaigns, from actual Europe-wide price promotions to the organisation of European presentations [IGD European Fact File, 1994]. EMD's co-operation with branded goods suppliers means that Euro promotions can be developed to meet the needs of the national markets. BIGS also intends to organise Europe-wide sales promotions.

- *Systems and technology skills* (International Alliances with Central Secretariats, Equity Participating Alliances)

   Nisa Today's connection with the EMD is enabling UK members to acquire the latest technology, such as scanning lanes, at the right price [Woodcock, 1993]. SEDD members aim to exploit opportunities in information technology [IGD European Fact File, 1994]. BIGS aims to take advantage of its members' experiences in the fields of logistics, packaging and distribution, and to support joint developments with manufacturers [IGD European Fact File, 1994].

- *High speed international growth and geographic market extension* (Joint Ventures)

   Sears' joint venture with Groupe Andre was originally set up to exploit the German, Dutch, Belgian and Luxembourg markets for footwear and is now also moving in to the clothing market. Sir Alistair Grant, Chairman of Argyll, has said of the European Retail Alliance: 'Perhaps above all, the retail alliance has helped our team become serious about Europe'; and Kanter has said of the ERA: 'Externally, the ERA opens borders. Inside member companies, it opens minds' [Kanter, 1994].

- *Market entry into new product segments and trading formats* (Co-Marketing, Joint Ventures)
- *Financial investment* (Joint venture)
- *Protection from market entry* (International Alliances with Central Secretariats, Equity Participating Alliances)
- *Protection from take over* (International Alliances with Central Secretariats, Equity Participating Alliances)
- *Enhanced competitive position for subordinate players* (Buying Clubs, International Alliances with Central Secretariats, Equity Participating Alliances)

The research sets out to investigate precisely how important the above key benefits are to those alliances under study, and whether any further benefits exist.

SUMMARY AND IMPLICATIONS OF THE RESEARCH

In summary, this study has sought to explore the nature of alliance formation in international retailing. We have identified the linkages, or in other words: we know who is sleeping with whom and the nature of their relationships. What we do not know is what benefits each partner is deriving from the relationship. By investigating the nature and role of benefit accumulation within the different alliance forms, we intend to bridge this gap.

Finally, this research has raised several issues which warrant further discussion:

• Alliances are ubiquitous in Europe and are growing by the day. They represent a considerable and increasing number of retailers and collective market share. This raises the question, is retailer autonomy dead?

• Is alliance formation merely a question of retailers retaliating to the increasing power of the manufacturer? Are horizontal relationships between retailers being created to countervail the power of horizontal relationships between manufacturers, particularly in the food industry? The majority of the alliances currently in existence are grocery based.

• Is Europe becoming a single entity in that we now have greater consumer convergence, and will changes in the structure of the grocery industry result in competition between the Euro manufacturer brand and the Euro retailer brand ?

• Do retailing alliances change the way in which competitive advantage in retailing is achieved? Issues of competition, co-operation and collusion need serious analysis. Is the nature of competition going to change from 'retailer versus retailer' to one of 'alliance versus alliance' competition within a domestic market?

If these issues are broadly true, then we have to ask what impact do alliances have on the traditional way in which we view competitive advantage in retailing?

ACKNOWLEDGEMENT

The Retail Alliances project is fully funded from the University of Huddersfield Project Grants Fund.

REFERENCES

Anderson, J.C. and J.A. Narus, 1990, 'A Model of Distributor Firm and Manufacturer Firm

Working Partnerships', *Journal of Marketing*, Vol.54, Jan., pp.42–58.

Buckley, N., 1994, 'Baked Beans Across Europe', *Financial Times*, 14 April, p.19.

Bucklin, L.P. and S. Sengupta, 1993, 'Organising Successful Co-Marketing Alliances', *Journal of Marketing*, Vol.57, April, pp.32–46.

Burt, S.L., 1989, 'Trends and Management Issues in European Retailing', *International Journal of Retailing*, Vol. 4, No. 4, pp.1–97.

Burt, S.L., 1991, 'Trends in the Internationalisation of Grocery Retailing: The European Experience', *International Review of Retail, Distribution and Consumer Research*, Vol.1, No.4, pp.487–515.

Corporate Intelligence Group, 1993, *Europe's Top Retailers Vol. 1*, London: Corporate Intelligence Publications.

Corporate Intelligence Group, 1994a, *Retail Rankings*, London: Corporate Intelligence Publications.

Corporate Intelligence Group, 1994b, *Europe's Top Retailers Vol. 2*, London: Corporate Intelligence Publications.

Dawson, J. and S.A. Shaw, 1992, 'Interfirm Alliances in the Retail Sector: Evolutionary, Strategic, and Tactical Issues in their Creation and Management', *University of Edinburgh Working Paper Series*, No.92/7.

Devlin, G. and M. Bleakley, 1988, 'Strategic Alliances – Guidelines for Success', *Long Range Planning*, Vol.21, No.5, pp.18–23.

Eurostat, 1993, 'Retailing in the European Single Market', *Commission of the European Communities Statistical Office*, Brussels, p.212.

Harrigan, K.R., 1988, 'Joint Ventures and Competitive Strategy', *Strategic Management Journal*, 9, pp.141–58.

Hung, C.L., 1992–94, 'Strategic Business Alliances between Canada and the Newly Industrialised Countries of Pacific Asia', *Management International Review*, Vol.32, pp.345–61.

ICC On Line, Lotus One Source Data Base provided on subscription by Inter Company Comparison, London.

IGD European Fact File, 1994, *Retail Alliances and Buying Groups*, Section E, Institute of Grocery Distributors Business Publication, June.

James, B.G., 1985, 'Alliance: The New Strategic Focus', *Long Range Planning*, Vol.18, No.3, pp.76–81.

Kanter, R.M., 1989, 'Becoming PALS: Pooling, Allying and Linking across Companies', *Academy of Management Executive*, 3, pp.183–93.

Kanter, R.M., 1994, 'Collaborative Advantage', *Harvard Business Review*, July–Aug., pp.96–111.

Lei, D. and J.W. Slocum Jnr., 1992a, 'Global Strategy, Competence Building and Strategic Alliances', *California Management Review*, Fall, pp.81–97.

Lei, D. and J.W. Slocum, Jnr., 1992b, 'Global Strategic Alliances: Payoffs and Pitfalls', *California Management Review*, Fall, pp.81–97.

Murray, E.A. and J.F. Mahon, 1993, ' Strategic Alliances: Gateway to the New Europe?', *Long Range Planning*, Vol.26, No.4, pp.102–11.

Oxford Institute of Retail Management, 1993, Templeton College, Kennington, Oxford.

Pratley, N., 1994, 'Next Considering Natural Cosmetics Retail Venture', *Daily Telegraph*, 30 June.

Robinson, T.M. and C.M. Clarke-Hill, 1993a, 'International Alliances in European Retailing', *E.S.R.C. Seminar on International Retailing*, UMIST, Manchester, March.

Robinson, T.M. and C.M. Clarke-Hill, 1993b, 'European Retail Alliances: the ERA Retailing Experience', in M. Baker (ed.), *Perspectives in Marketing Management*, Vol.3, ch.3, pp.47–63, Chichester: J.Wiley.

Robinson, T.M. and C.M. Clarke-Hill, 1995, 'International Alliances in European Retailing', in P. McGoldrick and G. Davies (ed.), *International Retailing – Trends and Strategies*, Pitman.

Shaw, S.A., J.A. Dawson and N. Harris, 1994, 'The Characteristics and Functions of Retail Buying Groups in the United Kingdom: Results of a Survey', *International Review of Retail,*

Distribution and Consumer Research, Vol.4, No.1, Jan., pp.83–105.

Sheth, J.N. and A. Parvatiyar, 1992, 'Towards a Theory of Business Alliance Formation', *Scandinavian International Business Review*, Vol.1, No.3, pp.71–87.

Stafford, E.R., 1994, 'Using Co-operative Strategies to Make Alliances Work', *Long Range Planning*, Vol.27, No.3, pp.64–74.

The European Retail Digest, 1994, *Retailing Across Borders in Europe*, Winter Issue, pp.26–47.

The Institute of Grocery Distribution, 1992, 'International Alliances and Buying Groups', *International Key Account Profiles*, Oct..

Treadgold, A., 1988, 'Retailing Without Frontiers: the Emergence of Trans-National Retailers', *International Journal of Retail and Distribution Management*, Vol.16, No.6, pp.8–12.

Treadgold, A., 1989, '1992: The Retail Response to a Changing Europe', *Marketing Research Today*, Aug., Vol.17, No.3, pp.161–6.

Treadgold, A., 1990, 'The Developing Internationalisation of Retailing', *International Journal of Retail and Distribution Management*, Vol.18, No.2, p.411.

Woodcock, C., 1993, 'Food Stores Go Into the Mixer – Independents Have Found Alliances an Answer to to the Hypermarkets', *Guardian*, 16 Aug.

The Changing Process of Internationalisation in the European Union

HAYLEY MYERS

The accelerating nature of internationalisation in the retail sector has attracted increasing academic attention [Treadgold, 1990a; Laulajainen et al., 1993]. Despite this, a precise and comprehensive definition of the process is lacking [Alexander, 1994; Pelligrini, 1994]. The term internationalisation implies the transfer, whether it be of a company, concept or management function, across state borders, with nations being perceived as being relatively homogeneous. However, Hollander [1970] has suggested that the differences within a country may, in some instances, exceed those between them. The creation of free trade areas (FTA), such as the Single European Market (SEM), has led to the hypothesis that there may in some circumstances be greater barriers to geographical expansion at the intra-state, as opposed to international level. An empirical survey seeking the perceptions of directors of major food retail companies in six European Union (EU) countries was conducted. Overall, national borders were considered to be of diminishing importance in terms of dividing the European consumer market. The results suggest that the established perception of the process of internationalisation may be becoming increasingly irrelevant as the significance of FTAs increases. If this is so, it not only suggests a transition in the regional development of Europe, but also indicates that such issues need to be analysed from an increasingly spatial–structural perspective.

INTRODUCTION

The post-war era has witnessed a growing trend of international expansion in the retail sector [Alexander, 1993; Burt, 1989]. Academic interest in the area of retail internationalisation has developed accordingly, particularly in recent years [Bunce, 1989; Burt, 1991, 1993; Conners *et al.*, 1985; Davies and Jones, 1993; Gardner and Bennison, 1993; Goldman, 1981; Ho and Sin, 1987; Kaynak, 1985; Lord *et al.*, 1988; Martenson, 1981; Robinson and Clarke-Hill, 1990; Sternquist and Kacker, 1994; Thompson and Knox, 1991; Wrigley, 1989, 1993]. However, much of the research and literature on internationalisation addresses the issue with little regard to a precise definition of the process [Alexander, 1994; Pelligrini, 1994]. The transfer of retail operations outside the domestic market is perhaps the most literal interpretation [Dawson, 1993]. A broader approach, which includes the diffusion of particular retail concepts and formats to new markets and the internationalisation of management functions and technology, has also been taken [Baron *et al.*, 1991; Burt, 1991; Sternquist and Kacker, 1994].

As a prerequisite to the following paper, a brief definition of the way in which certain terms have been interpreted is given. The words *nation, state* and *country* have been used interchangeably to describe nation-states. *Region* has been used to define relatively large areas of a country, such as for example south-east England or north-west France. Areas on a smaller scale, for example the size of a county in the UK, are referred to as *sub-regions,* and geographical areas encompassing more than one nation, such as for instance north-west Europe, are defined as *international* or *world regions.*

The term *internationalisation* implies the movement from one *nation* to another. The national border is commonly perceived as the boundary of an homogeneous area. In terms of environmental influences, such as the factors of demographics, economics, language and even culture, this is not necessarily the case. Indeed, in some instances it may be difficult to distinguish areas of one country from another. This may be true to an even greater extent in terms of consumer characteristics, such as disposable income, household structure and lifestyle types. Furthermore, Hollander [1970] has suggested that differences within countries may, in some cases, far exceed those between them. As Alexander [1994] has expressed, once this is acknowledged, it brings into question the whole concept of internationalisation.

Following this line of argument, if the state border is not necessarily a comprehensive definition of the differences between areas, then how are regions, and the process of movement between them, to be defined? A variety of related factors shape the environment, including those of a political, legislative, economic, social, cultural and demographic nature. If quantified, each of these could be mapped and then superimposed in order to build up a more complex picture. An issue that immediately arises when carrying out cross-national research in the retail sector is the lack of directly comparative data. This problem emerges primarily from the fact that countries, and subsequently regions on a sub-national scale, use different definitions to interpret the socio-economic environment. In terms of retail internationalisation, Alexander [1994] has suggested using a proxy measure of these combined influences, namely the level of development of the retail structure. Although the problem of comparable data remains, exemplified by the differences in the various terms used to define particular formats of food retail outlets in Europe [CIG, 1991a], it is at least somewhat diminished.

RETAIL INTERNATIONALISATION IN THE POST-1992 SETTING

Undeniably, Europe has been going through major transitions in political, economic and social conditions, much of which has been brought about by the formation of the European Union (EU) and the establishment of the Single European Market (SEM) in 1992. The underlying objective is to create an area free from internal borders by harmonizing legislation and liberalising fiscal, physical and technical barriers [Heloire, 1987; I.B.I., 1989]. As Pioch and Brook [1994] have noted, by removing barriers to trade between national markets it is assumed that the SEM creates a more competitive environment and accelerates rates of growth. However, the extent to which this is impacting on the retail sector in particular has been questioned. Pioch and Brook go on to suggest that the European retail industry is not gaining the attention that its size and prominence would suggest it deserves: 'retailing, unlike manufacturing industries, operates at the interface between the "end" consumer and producer. Such a position should assign retailing to an important role in the European integration process as a whole' [Pioch and Brook, 1994: 12].

This is further evidenced by Whitehead [1992], who has assessed that retailing will benefit from the establishment of the SEM mainly through indirect gains that are filtered down. Furthermore, the complexity of the situation is intensified by the fact that the quantifiable changes in an environment, such as legislative harmonisation, do not necessarily tally with our perceptions. There is evidence to suggest that our recognition of the differences between countries, and the implied homogeneity within nations, is not keeping pace with the changing environment. Looking at the fundamental transitions that have occurred in recent years in Europe, Wijkman has suggested that our mental maps of Europe lag behind the reality of the situation: 'Concepts like "Eastern Europe" and "Western Europe", having lost their political connotations, retain only their geographic significance and refer now to different groups of countries than before' [Wijkman, 1993: 1].

In Europe, the process of retail internationalisation has accelerated particularly since the late 1980s [CIG, 1991b; Eurostat, 1993]. The creation of the SEM proved to be a catalyst for both practitioners and academics alike to assess the impact it may have on the rate and nature of internationalisation. It is perhaps most commonly perceived that whilst the SEM may be accelerating retail cross-border expansion within the EU, it is not necessarily a prerequisite or directly causal [Alexander, 1988; Burt, 1989; Hallsworth, 1992]. Salmon and Tordjman [1989] have placed greater prominence on its impact, but Treadgold emphasises the more general consensus, namely that 'The 1992 programme is facilitating the emergence of supranational retail businesses in Europe but is not, at least should not be, driving the process' [Treadgold, 1990a: 11]. Pioch and Brook [1994] conclude that there remain so many differences between nations within the EU, that the increased rates of internationalisation commonly anticipated as a result of the SEM will not occur. They perceive that consumer legislation and market conditions of member states remain very diverse, and thus national boundaries are as important as they were prior to the creation of the SEM. Additionally, they evidence the fact that the process of accelerating retail internationalisation was a growing trend before the 1992 programme was in place, and hence was not a directly causal factor. This theory is reinforced by Peschel who states that 'The completion of the Single European Market is not a revolutionary event. In general, it strengthens existing growth rates' [Peschel, 1992: 390].

The establishment of a free trade area (FTA) such as the SEM puts forward the proposition that cross-border expansion within the world region is no longer strictly a process of internationalisation. With the harmonisation of much of the legislation, is it not simply a form of regional geographical expansion? And further, are there not instances where a retailer may find it more difficult to expand in to areas within its original domestic market, than in to areas outside its national border? This concept is summarised by Alexander; 'Within a Free Trade Area, however, the term [internationalisation] becomes increasingly meaningless as integration erodes the regulatory implications of the state' [Alexander, 1994: 4]. The federal structure common to many European countries, where sub-regions within the nation have individual regulations particular to the locality, accentuates this theory. Obviously, a retailer moving from one region to another within a country is not considered to be moving internationally. However, in reality, there may actually be greater differences moving on the intra-state level, rather than at the international scale.

METHODOLOGY

Research was carried out in six EU countries: France, Germany, Italy, the Netherlands, Spain and the UK. These nations were chosen as they are home to most of the largest players in the European food retail industry, and are also the major markets. They represent a number of positions in terms of geography, political and legislative climate, socio-economic environment, and level of retail structure development. Interviews were conducted with 21 directors of large food retail companies, the results of which formed the basis of a mailed questionnaire. This was sent in spring 1994 to 700 directors of 52 companies. Ninety-two useable questionnaires were returned, a relatively low response rate of 13 per cent. However, this had been anticipated, and a census approach had originally been chosen in an attempt to gain a reasonable number of responses. A survey of this size is in line with other research that has been carried out in this field [Alexander, 1988, 1990; Williams, 1992a; 1992b]. Dutch respondents accounted for 12.0 per cent of the survey, French for 19.6 per cent, German 15.2 per cent, Italian 15.2 per cent, Spanish just 4.5 per cent, and British 33.7 per cent.

DIVISIONS IN THE EUROPEAN CONSUMER MARKET

TABLE 1

IMPORTANCE OF SPECIFIC BOUNDARIES IN DIVIDING THE EUROPEAN CONSUMER MARKET

All Respondents

Boundary Type	1	2	3	4	5	Mean	Std Dev
			percentage				
National	20.7	47.8	20.7	9.8	1.1	2.228	0.927
Cultural	15.2	39.1	40.2	5.4	0.0	2.359	0.806
Lifestyle	13.0	46.7	25.0	15.2	0.0	2.424	0.905
Socio-economic	12.0	32.6	35.9	19.6	0.0	2.630	0.934
Demographic	9.8	37.0	34.8	16.3	2.2	2.641	0.944
Regional	12.0	23.9	47.8	14.1	2.2	2.707	0.932
Urban-rural dichotomy	5.6	34.4	40.0	16.7	3.3	2.778	0.909

1 = Extremely Influential, 2 = Influential, 3 + Moderately Influential,
4 = Insignificant, 5 = Of No Significance

TABLE 2
CROSS-NATIONAL EVALUATION OF THE IMPORTANCE OF NATIONAL BOUNDARIES IN
DIVIDING THE EUROPEAN CONSUMER MARKET

	1	2	3	4	5	Mean	St Dev	n=
			percentage					
France	16.7	38.9	11.1	27.8	5.6	2.667	1.237	18
Germany	7.1	92.9	0.0	0.0	0.0	1.929	0.267	14
Italy	35.7	35.7	14.3	14.3	0.0	2.071	1.072	14
Netherlands	27.3	45.5	18.2	9.1	0.0	2.091	0.944	11
UK	22.6	41.9	35.5	0.0	0.0	2.129	0.763	31

1 = Extremely Influential, 2 = Influential, 3 = Moderately Influential,
4 = Insignificant, 5 = Of No Significance

Note: data from Spanish respondents not included for reasons of confidentiality.

It is generally agreed that the nature of the consumer market is a crucial factor for retailers considering a strategy of geographical expansion. As Hollander [1970] has suggested, even if all other considerations are favourable, the absence of a suitable consumer market would negate any possibility of a retailer entering a particular market. It was on the basis of this assumption that respondents were asked to rate the importance of factors that potentially divide the European consumer market. From the answers received, it was hoped that some tentative conclusions might be drawn as to how retailers perceive the European market, and which features they viewed as being most salient when considering expansion within it. As Table 1 illustrates, on average all the factors were rated as being more than moderately influential. National borders were rated as being the most important, with a mean score of 2.23. In fact, over two-thirds of the sample perceived national boundaries as being either *influential* or *extremely influential*. Cultural differences were viewed as being the second most important divide, with almost 80 per cent of retailers rating them as being either *moderately influential* or *influential*. Notably, regions were rated as being of little relative significance, with nearly two-thirds viewing them as being either *moderately influential* or *insignificant*.

Based on these results it is suggested that retailers still believe there are significant variations between the nature of markets within the SEM. Differences were perceived particularly on a national basis, and as a continuation of this a degree of homogeneity within national markets is implied. It is notable that whilst national boundaries were ranked as being the greatest divide within the European consumer market, regional boundaries were ranked much lower. However, these two factors may in fact be considered not as different features, but instead as being at separate points along a geographical continuum.

These findings serve to focus attention on factors of a non-spatial nature. Culture was ranked as second only to national boundaries in terms of its influence on the consumer market. Although culture is commonly perceived on a national basis, this is not necessarily the case. Depending on definition, cultures, and more notably in terms of consumer characteristics, sub-cultures, can and do cross national borders and also differ within nations [Foxall, 1980]. There is considerable debate over the extent to which culture is becoming homogenised in terms of world regions and even on a global level. Levitt's [1983] seminal paper has assessed that the global consumer market is becoming increasingly important. He does, however, stress that this is resulting in increasing segmentation rather than a mass market. It is often suggested that cultural differences prove to be the greatest problem when attempting to standardise marketing [Dunn, 1976; Green and Langeard, 1975; Urban, 1977; Ryans and Fry, 1976], and thus are a fundamental influence when expanding internationally. This has led to the assertion that businesses need to be culturally aware when considering internationalisation [Hofstede, 1989]. Indeed, Willis [1991] suggests that culture will be a fundamental factor in segmenting the pan-European market that he anticipates will develop increasingly in the post-1992 environment.

Lifestyle, socio-economic and demographic factors are all assessed by respondents in the survey as being influential. These same three factors are summarised by Burt [1989] as being not only the most fundamental influences on the European consumer market, but also major impacts on the changing nature of the European retail structure. As previously noted, there is difficulty in quantifying such characteristics on a comparative cross-national basis, and even more difficulty at the regional scale. This perhaps goes some way in explaining the emphasis placed on national boundaries in terms of respondents perceptions of divisions in the European market.

Table 2 illustrates respondents' perceptions of the importance of national boundaries broken down into sub-groups according to their country of origin. The most notable point would seem to be that whilst German, Italian, Dutch and British retailers' responses cluster around the rating of 2.0, namely that national borders are *influential* in segmenting the European consumer market, French responses were considerably distinct. The mean answer was 1.24, much closer to the *extremely influential* point on the scale. This may, to some extent, help in explaining certain phenomena arising from previous analysis of this survey, particularly that French retailers appeared to have a much more global orientation to geographical expansion strategies [Myers and Alexander, 1994]. If they do indeed see significant differences in national markets in Europe, then this may result in them having little incentive to concentrate their expansion plans on the EU, and they may feel it is just as easy to move into non-European markets that offer significant advantages.

THE CHANGING NATURE OF BOUNDARIES

TABLE 3

CHANGING IMPORTANCE OF SPECIFIC BOUNDARIES IN DIVIDING THE
EUROPEAN CONSUMER MARKET

All Respondents

Boundary Type	1	2	3	4	5	Mean	Std Dev
			percentage				
Lifestyle	7.8	36.7	36.7	16.7	2.2	2.689	0.920
Demography	10.2	21.6	53.4	13.6	1.1	2.739	0.864
Culture	11.4	23.9	40.9	22.7	1.1	2.784	0.964
Urban–rural dichotomy	4.5	21.6	55.7	18.2	0.0	2.875	0.755
Socio-economic	1.1	33.3	43.3	16.7	5.6	2.922	0.877
Regional	4.5	32.6	29.2	25.8	7.9	3.000	1.044
National	2.2	8.9	25.6	48.9	14.4	3.644	0.916

1 = Much More Important, 2 = More Important, 3 = Of the Same Importance,

4 = Less Important, 5 = Much Less Important

Respondents were subsequently asked to determine the extent to which the same seven factors were becoming more or less important, in terms of dividing the European Consumer Market. Table 3 displays their responses. Notably, national boundaries, which were rated as being the most important factor in dividing the market in the previous question, were also perceived as becoming less important the most. Regional boundaries, which had been ranked as the second least important dividing influence, were thought to remain of the same importance. The remaining factors were perceived as becoming more important than they were at present, with lifestyle, demography and culture being ranked highest. This further emphasises the perceived influence of non-spatial factors. Notably socio-economic influences were seen as increasing in importance to a lesser extent, perhaps an indication of the increasing homogeneity of such characteristics brought about by the SEM.

TABLE 4

EXTENT TO WHICH THE EUROPEAN CONSUMER MARKET IS BECOMING INCREASINGLY HOMOGENEOUS

All Respondents

Valid per cent

Much less similar	1.1	Mean	= 3.659
Less similar	1.1		
Stay the same	33.0	Std Dev	= 0.636
More similar	60.4		
Much more similar	4.4		

TABLE 5

CROSS-NATIONAL EVALUATION OF THE CHANGING IMPORTANCE OF NATIONAL BOUNDARIES IN DIVIDING THE EUROPEAN CONSUMER MARKET

	1	2	3	4	5	Mean	Std Dev	n =
				percentage				
France	5.9	11.8	23.5	35.3	23.5	3.588	1.176	17
Germany	0.0	0.0	14.3	42.9	42.9	4.286	0.726	14
Italy	7.1	21.4	14.3	57.1	0.0	3.214	1.051	14
Netherlands	0.0	0.0	27.3	63.6	9.1	3.818	0.603	11
UK	0.0	6.5	38.7	48.4	6.5	3.548	0.723	31

1 = Much More Important, 2 = More Important, 3 = Of the Same Importance,

4 = Less Important, 5 = Much Less Important

The fact that national boundaries are the only factor to be perceived as becoming less influential is significant. It implies that retailers' perceptions of the SEM environment are that it will increasingly take on a pan-European character. Taking this further, it suggests that the creation of FTAs does indeed have an impact on the expansion strategies of large scale businesses and thus may be influencing the process of internationalisation. As regions are viewed as remaining of the same degree of influence, it obviously means that they are playing a more significant role relative to national borders. This would seem to be logical as the federal structure of Europe takes on increasing prominence. It is notable that the more subjective elements of lifestyle type and culture, as well as demographic features, are seen as increasing in significance more than socio-economic influences. Again, this is perhaps due to the fact that it is believed that a process of increasing convergence is occurring in Europe, brought about by the influence of such factors as the harmonisation of legislation. By stressing factors of lifestyle, demography and culture, it implies that retailers may be specifically aiming at homogeneous target groups of consumers that are found in a large segmented market. Thus it may be considered that spatial factors retain their significance, although through association rather than direct intention. For example, marketers may analyse that a significantly large population of an appropriate consumer group is located in a particular area, and thus aim to expand there accordingly. Although they have primarily used non-spatial data in their analysis, their strategy also has an inherent spatial element. It is likely however, that this may not adhere to national, or indeed previously delineated regional boundaries, and hence may be perceived as being non-geographical.

When analysing the opinion of respondents by country of origin towards the dynamic nature of boundaries, the main feature appeared to be that the average score of French, Italian, Dutch and British retailers lay between being *of the same importance* and being *less important*, whilst the mean score given by German retailers lay further along the continuum, nearer the *of much less importance* point on the scale. In fact, all German respondents rated national boundaries as *less important* or *much less important*. This, in conjunction with previous analysis of the questionnaires which concluded that German retailers viewed Europe the most favourably [Myers and Alexander, 1994], implies that there may be a correlation between these factors. It is suggested that the fact that the German respondents perceive that national boundaries are decreasing in importance, and also see Europe as a favourable environment, provides a motive for a strategy of expanding within Europe. Further, German retailers are commonly assessed as taking a border-hopping strategy, rather than a multinational or global approach. In conclusion, that the French respondents took a more global approach and viewed national boundaries as being a very significant division in the European market, whilst German retailers took the alternative view of favouring expansion into geographically proximate markets where they view national differences are decreasing, would seem to provide evidence that there is some kind of relationship between these two factors.

HOMOGENEITY IN THE EUROPEAN CONSUMER MARKET

Respondents were requested to rate the extent to which the European consumer market was becoming more, or less, similar (see Table 3). There was a high degree of consensus among respondents. One third of the retailers questioned thought that the market was remaining the same in terms of degree of homogeneity, whilst just over 60 per cent perceived that it was becoming more similar. This might suggest that just as the manufacturing industry is increasingly competing on a pan-European scale, so too will retailers. Traditionally, there have been relatively low levels of international activity by retailers in the food sector, who have often been characterised as being predominantly reactive [McGoldrick and Fryer, 1993]. A link between the increasingly pan-European scale of manufacturers, and subsequently retailers, is provided by the numerous European alliances [Lowe, 1992]. Many of these offer advantages primarily of a buying function, although others also facilitate exchanges of know-how [Treadgold, 1990b]. It is suggested that homogenisation of significant factors of the European market is likely to result in increasing rates of standardisation [Reichel, 1990]. However, it is suggested that it is unlikely to result in a mass market, but rather that it will increasingly become further segmented [Willis, 1991].

FIGURE 1
EXPANSION IN EUROPE: THE IMPACT OF NATIONAL BORDERS

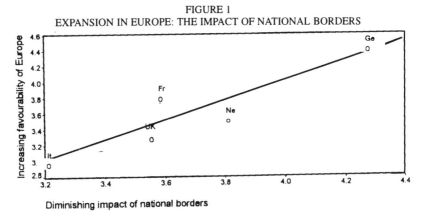

Diminishing impact of national borders

The results of the empirical research focused on the changing environment of the European food retail industry has led to the formation of an hypothesis; namely, that if retailers increasingly view that national boundaries are becoming less important in dividing the European market (see Table 5), then their perception of the desirability of Europe as a region for expansion within increases. The sample of respondents was divided by country of origin and a scatter plot constructed from the mean answers of

FIGURE 2
FAVOURABILITY OF THE SEM: THE IMPACT OF NATIONAL BORDERS

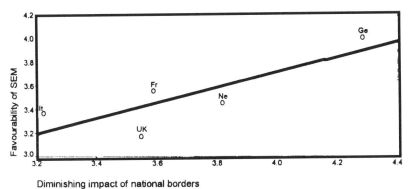

Diminishing impact of national borders

each sub-group (see Figure 1). A best fit line inferred that there did indeed seem to be a degree of correlation between retailers' perceived view of the diminishing importance of national boundaries and the increasing attractiveness of strategies of expansion within Europe. To further this theory, and also to provide a degree of internal validation within the questionnaire, the decreasing importance of national boundaries was subsequently plotted against the extent to which the SEM had made expansion within the EU more favourable (see Figure 2). A similar direct relationship between these two factors resulted; as perceptions of the degree to which the SEM had made the EU more advantageous for expansion within increased, so did the view that national boundaries were becoming less important. At one end of the spectrum Italian retailers took the view that national boundaries were remaining important and that Europe was not a particularly favourable region for expansion within. French, British and Dutch respondents fell into a mid-group, where by they perceived national boundaries were to some extent decreasing in importance and that Europe was a relatively attractive market for expansion within. The German respondents were the most positive in that they rated national boundaries within the EU as becoming significantly less influential, and also that Europe was a most favourable region for expansion within. It would appear that to some extent the retailers surveyed altered their opinion of strategies of internationalisation as their perception of the diminishing impact of national boundaries increased. If this theory is taken a step further, it would suggest that the environment of a FTA does produce an impact on internationalisation, namely, by making it a more favourable environment for geographical expansion within. As previously noted, this is exemplified by German retailers, who in the survey most strongly perceived that the importance of national boundaries is decreasing, and also that Europe is becoming a more favourable option for expansion (Figure 1).

CONCLUSION

It would appear to be conclusive that the process of internationalisation is one of a dynamic and complex nature, not helped by the lack of a comprehensive and universal definition. The creation of FTAs, such as the SEM, has further increased the complexity of the situation. It would seem likely that rates of cross-border expansion accelerate in such situations. However, whether the process may still be considered as internationalisation in such an environment has been questioned. The empirical findings suggest retailers in the survey perceive that the European consumer market is likely to become increasingly homogeneous. Although national boundaries are considered to be the greatest type of division at present, it is also thought to be likely they will play an increasingly less significant role. Prominence is given to factors of a cultural, lifestyle type and demographic nature, but targeting segments of the consumer market by such variables still implies a spatial variant, albeit of a dynamic nature that defines geographical areas not previously demarcated as specific regions. The perceived decreasing significance of national borders and increasing favourability of the EU in terms of geographical expansion would seem to suggest that the creation of the SEM is having some impact on the favourability of cross-border expansion. A furtherance of this line of argument would suggest that the establishment of FTAs does have an influence on the process of internationalisation, namely that it makes the region more appealing in terms of geographical expansion, at least for companies whose domestic market is within the FTA. It is suggested that future research may be able to provide a further insight into this hypothesis, especially by analysing data that evidence retailers actual growth strategies as well as their perceptions of likely future trends.

REFERENCES

Alexander, N., 1988, 'Marketing the UK's Retail Revolution Post 1992', *The Quarterly Review of Marketing*, Autumn, pp.1–5.
Alexander, N., 1990, 'Retailers and International Markets: Motives for Expansion', *International Marketing Review*, Vol.7, No.4, pp.75–85.
Alexander, N., 1993, 'Internationalisation: Interpreting the Motives', *ESRC Seminars: Research Themes in Retailing*, UMIST, Manchester, 15 March 1993.
Alexander, N., 1994, 'Isoagora: Retail Boundaries within Free Trade Areas', presented at *Retailing: Theories and Practices for Today and Tomorrow, The Fourth Triennial AMS/ACRA National Retailing Conferences*, Richmond, Virginia.

Baron, S., B. Davies and D. Swindley, 1991, *Dictionary of Retailing*, London: Macmillan.

Bunce, M., 1989, 'The International Approach of Laura Ashley', in *ESOMAR Proceedings, Adding Value to Retail Offerings*, Edinburgh, 24–26 April 1989, pp.101–16.

Burt, S., 1989, 'Trends in Management Issues in European Retailing', *International Journal of Retailing*, Vol.4, No.4, pp.1–97

Burt, S., 1991, 'Trends in the Internationalisation of Grocery Retailing: the European Experience', *The International Review of Retail Distribution and Consumer Research*, Vol.1, No.4, pp.487–515.

Burt, S., 1993, 'Temporal Trends in the Internationalization of British Retailing', *International Review of Retail, Distribution and Consumer Research*, Vol.3, No.4, pp.391–410.

C.I.G., 1991a, *European Retailing in the 1990s*, London: C.I.G. Research Publications Ltd.

C.I.G., 1991b, *Cross-Border Retailing in Europe*, London: C.I.G. Research Publications Ltd.

Conners, S., A. Samli and E. Kaynak, 1985, 'Transfer of Food Retail Technology into Less Developed Countries', in A. Samli (ed.), *Technology Transfer*, Westport; Quorum, pp.27–44.

Davies, B.J. and P. Jones, 1993, 'The International Activity of Japanese Department Stores', *Service Industries Journal*, Vol.13, No.1, pp.126–32.

Dawson, J., 1993, 'The Internationalisation of Retailing', *Department of Business Studies, University of Edinburgh, Working Paper*, 93/2.

Dunn, S.W., 1976, 'Effect of National Identity on Multinational Promotional Strategy in Europe', *Journal of Marketing*, Vol.39, July, pp.34–41.

Eurostat, 1993, *Retailing in the European Single Market 1993*, Luxembourg: Eurostat Publications.

Foxall, G.R., 1980, *Consumer Behaviour*, London: Croom Helm.

Gardner, H. and D. Bennison, 1993, 'The Internationalisation of Discount Grocery Operations: the Danish Experience', *ESRC Seminar on International Issues in Retailing*, UMIST, Manchester, March.

Goldman, A., 1981, 'Transfer of a Retailing Technology into Less Developed Countries: The Supermarket Case', *Journal of Retailing*, Vol.57, No.2, pp.5–29.

Green, R.T. and E. Langeard, 1975, 'A Cross-national Comparison of Consumer Habits and Innovator Characteristics', *Journal of Marketing*, Vol.39, July, pp.34–41.

Hallsworth, A.G., 1992, 'Retail Internationalisation: Contingency and Context?', *European Journal of Marketing*, Vol.26, No.8/9, pp.25–34.

Heloire, M.C., 1987, 'Community Policy toward Consumers: The Conditions for a New Impetus', *European Consumer Law Journal*, Vol.1, pp.13–17.

Ho, S., and Y. Sin, 1987, 'International Transfer of Retail Technology: The Successful Case of Convenience Stores in Hong Kong', *International Journal of Retailing*, Vol.2, No.3, pp.36–48.

Hofstede, G., 1989, 'Organising for Cultural Diversity', *European Management Journal*, Vol.7, No.4, pp.390–8.

Hollander, S., 1970, *Multinational Retailing*, East Lancing, MI: Michigan State University.

I.B.I., 1989, *1992: Planning for the Food Industry*, London: I.B.I.

Kaynak, E., 1985, 'Global Spread of Supermarkets: some experiences from Turkey', in E. Kaynak (ed.), *Global Perspectives in Marketing*, New York: Praeger.

Laulajainen, R., A. Kazutoshi and T. Laulajainen, 1993, 'The Geographical Dimension of Global Retailing', *International Review of Retail, Distribution and Consumer Research*, Vol.3, No.4, pp.367–89.

Levitt, T., 1983, 'The Globalisation of Markets', *Harvard Business Review*, May, pp.92–102.

Lord, D., W. Moran, T. Parker and L. Sparks, 1988, 'Retailing on Three Continents: The Discount Food Operations of Albert Gubay', *International Journal of Retailing*, Vol.3, No.3, pp.1–54.

Lowe, J., 1992, *European Retail Alliances: Their Impact on the Future of European Retailing*, Special Report No.2207, London: The Economist Intelligence Unit.

Martenson, R., 1981, *Innovations in Multinational Retailing: IKEA on the Swedish, Swiss, German and Austrian Furniture Markets*, Gothenburg: University of Gothenburg.

McGoldrick, P. and E. Fryer, 1993, 'Organisational Culture and the Internationalisation of Retailers', *7th International Conference on Research in the Distributive Trades*, Institute for

Retail Studies, University of Stirling, 6–8 Sept.

Myers, H. and N. Alexander, 1994, 'European Food Retailers' Direction of Growth', *Working Paper Series 6/94*, Department of Management Studies, University of Surrey.

Pellegrini, L., 1994, 'Alternatives for Growth and Internationalization in Retailing', *The International Review of Retail, Distribution and Consumer Research*, Vol.4, No.2, pp.121–48.

Peschel, K., 1992, 'European Integration and Regional Development in Northern Europe', *Regional Studies*, Vol.26, No.4, pp.387–97.

Pioch, E. and P. Brook, 1994, *Home Shopping in the Single European Market: Foundering in the Wake of Neo-Liberalism*, Working Paper, Manchester Metropolitan University.

Reichel, J., 1990, 'How Can Marketing be Successfully Standardised for the European Market', *European Business Review*, Vol.90, No.2, pp.46–51.

Robinson, T., and C. Clarke-Hill, 1990, 'Directional Growth by European Retailers', *International Journal of Retail and Distribution Management*, Vol.18, No.5, pp.3–14.

Ryans, J.K. and C. Fry, 1976, 'Some European Attitudes on the Advertising Transference Question: A Research Note', *Journal of Advertising*, Vol.5, pp.11–13.

Salmon, W.J. and A. Tordjman, 1989, 'The Internationalisation of Retailing', *International Journal of Retail and Distribution Management*, Vol.18, No.5, pp.3–14.

Sternquist, B. and M. Kacker, 1994, *European Retailing's Vanishing Borders*, Westport, Conneticut: Quorum Books.

Thompson, K. and S. Knox, 1991, 'The Single European Market', *European Management Journal*, Vol.9, No.1, pp.65–72.

Treadgold, A., 1990a, 'The Emerging Internationalisation of Retailing: Present Status and Future Challenges', *Irish Marketing Review*, Vol.5, No.2, pp.11–27.

Treadgold, A., 1990b, 'The Developing Internationalisation of Retailing', *International Journal of Retail and Distribution Management*, Vol.18, No.2, pp.8–11.

Urban, C., 1977, 'A Cross-national Comparison of Consumer Media Use Patterns', *Columbia Journal of World Business*, Vol.12, Winter, pp.53–64.

Whitehead, M., 1992, 'How Will Retailers Compete in an Integrated Market? Pan-European Retailing – Myth or Reality', presented at the *Studies in the New Europe Conference*, Nottingham.

Wijkman, P.M., 1993, 'Changing Our Mental Maps', in *EFTA Trade in 1991*, Switzerland: Economic Affairs Department, EFTA.

Williams, D., 1992a, 'Motives for Retailer Internationalization: Their Impact, Structure and Implications', *Journal of Marketing Management*, Vol.8, pp.269–85.

Williams, D., 1992b, 'Retailer Internationalization: An Empirical Inquiry', *European Journal of Marketing*, Vol.26, No.8/9, pp.269–85

Willis, G., 1991, 'The Single Market and National Marketing Thinking', *European Journal of Marketing*, Vol.25, No.4, pp.148–56.

Wrigley, N., 1989, 'The Lure of The USA: Further Reflections on the Internationalisation of British Grocery Retailing Capital', *Environment and Planning*, A21, pp.283–8.

Wrigley, N., 1993, 'The Internationalisation of British Grocery Retailing', in R. Bromley and C. Thomas (eds.), *Retail Change: Contemporary Issues*, London: UCL Press.

Reciprocal Retail Internationalisation: The Southland Corporation, Ito-Yokado and 7-Eleven Convenience Stores

LEIGH SPARKS

Retail internationalisation has become a focus of research activity in recent years. This research has become perhaps both more broad and deep than previous research, reflecting the changes in retail internationalisation itself. There remain, however, fundamental issues about the process and nature of retail internationalisation. This paper examines initially the internationalisation of a concept – the 7–Eleven convenience store – from the USA to Japan. This concept has been subsequently 'Japanized' as the convenience store sector in Japan grew rapidly and successfully. The new approach to convenience stoers has now been re-introduced into the United States through the agreed take-over of The Southland Corporation by its original Japanese franchisee, Ito-Yokado. This process of retail internationalisation is analysed and described and placed into the context of current conceptualisations on retail internationalisation.

Retail internationalisation has received increasing research attention in recent years. Dawson [1993, 1994] provides a thorough review and incisive assessment of the state of this body of knowledge. Brown and Burt [1992], in a special issue of the *European Journal of Marketing* devoted to international perspectives on retail marketing, have assembled a collection of papers which also provides an introduction to the literature, approaches and problems in this area. They conclude:

> What exactly is meant by retail internationalisation? What do retailers actually internationalize? Is it management expertise and management systems? Innovative forms of trading? Or unique retail brands? Clarification of this definitional issue will allow us to assess whether retailing faces genuinely unique problems or whether it simply faces the same problems as other industrial sectors which internationalize [Brown and Burt, 1992: 80].

There seems to be a crisis of confidence about our conceptualisations of retail internationalisation [see also Pellegrini, 1994]. This is due to a lack of understanding perhaps of the breadth of the processes undertaken, an over-concern with the monitoring of activity and simplistic conceptualisations and an unthinking borrowing of conceptions from outside retailing. It is argued here that retail internationalisation is a complex and frustrating topic that requires a deeper understanding of company operations, practices and history for our conceptualisations to be useful. It is further recognised that the variations in retail internationalisation are considerable and that at the moment we have not fully understood all the issues and aspects involved.

This belief is illustrated by the examination of the internationalisation of particular businesses. For example, the Southland Corporation developed the 7–Eleven convenience store chain in the United States in the 1940s, and became highly successful. In 1973 the company signed a franchise (area license) agreement with Ito-Yokado in Japan, which set up Seven–Eleven Japan Co. Ltd to develop a 7–Eleven convenience store chain in Japan. The development of the convenience store operations and their parent companies then began to diverge as operational practices changed. At the same time as the core convenience store market in the United States matured and then stagnated under competitive pressure, so the Japanese convenience store market expanded and boomed. After a disastrous management leveraged buy-out in 1987, The Southland Corporation emerged from a pre-arranged Chapter 11 bankruptcy with 70 per cent of the company owned by Ito-Yokado and Seven–Eleven Japan Co. Ltd. As Kaletsky [1990] notes, 'what could be more appropriate than Southland being rescued from the consequences of Wall Street's blunders by its own better-financed franchise in Japan'. From being franchisees in 1973 with no stores, the Japanese now control the entire company [Sparks, 1994]. At the same time, the Japanese, through an operational mission supported by extensive use of technology and advanced systems, have redefined the convenience store operation. This 'new model' convenience store system is now being introduced to the United States in an attempt to revitalise the performance of The Southland Corporation [e.g., Suzuki, 1991].

The brief history above raises questions about the conceptualisation of retail internationalisation, given the changes in ownership, business method and operations. Questions concern technology transfer issues, the role of franchising, knowledge transfer, business control and the direction of various flows of money, risk, knowledge, formats and information. Here, it is suggested that in addition to general assistance to deepening and broadening our conceptualisations, the case describes a process best considered as one of *reciprocal* retail internationalisation. The aim of the paper is therefore to examine the questions around retail internationalisation via a case study and to use the study to enhance our consideration of retail internationalisation. To meet this aim, the basic structure of the paper is divided into a review of retail internationalisation conceptualisation, a case on the Southland Corporation, Ito-Yokado and 7–Eleven convenience stores, and discussion and conclusions drawing out the lessons and implications of the case study for the understanding of retail internationalisation.

CONCEPTUALISING RETAIL INTERNATIONALISATION

One of the characteristics of the literature on retail internationalisation is the way in which ideas and approaches have been borrowed from other subject areas or sectors. Whilst such borrowing can be productive and highly useful, there are questions raised, as for example over whether the internationalisation of retailing is different to the internationalisation of manufacturing. It has been argued that retailing is now radically different and has therefore to develop its own approaches:

> The balance between centralized and decentralized decision-making, the relative importance of organisation and establishment scale economies, the degree of spatial dispersion in the multi-establishment enterprise, the relative size of establishment to the size of the firm, the relative exit costs if decisions are reversed, the speed with which an income stream can be generated after an investment decision has been made, different cash flow characteristics, the relative value of stock and hence importance of sourcing; all these items, and others, serve to differentiate the manufacturing firm and the retail firm not least in respect of the internationalisation process [Dawson, 1993: 28].

Despite this, however, the development of retail internationalisation concepts is heavily biased towards approaches drawn from production sectors and international business studies.

Davies and Fergusson [1994] have categorised five different conceptual strands to retail internationalisation, as identified in Table 1. It is possible to make two points from the table. First, whilst the segmented nature of the table may be considered as a categorical artifice, it is also a reflection of the approaches that have been taken in the literature. Much of the work, for example, has been in categorising various factors or in applying the value chain or the eclectic paradigm to the retail sector and/or a particular company. Whilst the broad complexity of retail internationalisation is recognised, in the main the research has been focused in discrete areas. Secondly, the derivations of the various conceptual strands are identified as

TABLE 1
APPROACHES TO INTERNATIONALISATION CONCEPTUALISATION

Approach	Meaning	Research, Critique, Extension
Push and Pull Factors	Fundamental factors stimulating expansion beyond national boundaries.	Kacker [1985], Treadgold & Davies [1988], Alexander [1990], Williams [1992].
Stages Theories	Behavioural approach where internationalisation is a gradual process, dependent upon incremental gains in international experience and increasing research commitment to foreign markets.	Aharoni [1966], Wilkins [1974], Johanson and Vahlne [1977], Cavusgil [1980], Czinkota [1982], Buckley [1983], Turnbull [1987].
Eclectic Paradigm	Advantage (ownership, internationalisation, location) based explanation of extent, form and pattern of international activities.	Dunning [1981, 1988, 1993], Pellegrini [1993], Boddewyn et al. [1986].
Value Chain Analysis	Firm-based analysis of competitive advantage through a transactionally based sequence of functions which together and individually 'add value'.	Porter [1985], Dicken and Thrift [1992], Kay [1991], Hennart [1991].
Networks and Relationships	The ability to create a net of relationships with the potential for cohesive and mutually complementary action and the ability to harness the synergistic potential of that net in pursuit of a competitive goal.	Hakansson [1982], Cunningham and Culligan [1991], Brahm [1993], Johanson and Mattsson [1988, 1991].

Source: Adapted from Davies and Fergusson [1994]

TABLE 2
UNDERSTANDING RETAIL INTERNATIONALISATION

A : Dimensions to Retail Internationalisation

    A1 : Financial Investment
    A2 : Cross-border Shopping
    A3 : Managerial Movements
    A4 : Retail Activities

B : International Sourcing

    B1 : Buyer Decisions
    B2 : International Sourcing Organisation
    B3 : Technology
    B4 : Buying Groups and Alliances
    B5 : Non-Retail-Product Sourcing

C : International Retail Operations

    C1 : Reasons
    C2 : Dimensions
    C3 : Extent and Directions

D : Internationalisation of Management Ideas

    D1 : Transferability of Retail Concepts
    D2 : Expertise Transferred
    D3 : Mechanisms of Transfer

Source: Adapted from Dawson [1993].

being manufacturing rather than service or retail based. In all cases the basic approach has been identified in other sectors before attempts have been made to apply the ideas and concepts to retail internationalisation. These in turn raise two further issues: the extent to which the direct implantation of such concepts into retailing can be sustained; and the breadth of our conceptualisation of retail internationalisation.

Several authors have made these points before, often in the context of reviewing the application of one concept into retailing. Some of these authors are indicated in Table 1. In particular, and with a more general focus, Dawson [1993, 1994] has provided a wide-ranging review of the form and extent of retail internationalisation, and has criticised the simplistic concept adoption that has characterised much of the academic literature. He identifies the key features of retail internationalisation as the need for adaption of management practices and processes in response to the cultural character of the host country, the role of individual entrepreneurs in taking an international perspective and the lack of knowledge by retailers of the impact on and value of the firm of the process of internationalisation.

The second problem noted above, of the too narrow perspective of the scope of retail internationalisation, has also been addressed by Dawson [1993]. Table 2 is adapted from the structure of his work and sets out a broad listing of possible components of retail internationalisation. If we are to understand retail internationalisation then we probably should be endeavouring to understand the activities in the table, possibly on a firm-specific basis. It is intended to use this framework in the study of Seven–Eleven Japan below.

The importance of Dawson's conceptualisation lies in its breadth. At the starting point is the idea that retail internationalisation has various dimensions. The main focus of these has been on the physical store opening activity of retailers, but, as Table 2 makes clear, there are many more dimensions and components to retail internationalisation than store openings alone. For example, Section A in Table 2 suggests that there are financial, consumer and managerial aspects to internationalisation that can operate independently of any retail store openings. These less tangible or indirect retail international dimensions form a backcloth to any decision to internationalise stores, and may be the only, or the prerequisite international activity in some cases. There may of course be barriers to such activities as there are for store openings [Davies 1993, 1995].

Arguably the most common form of retail internationalisation is the international sourcing (Section B) of products and the development of mechanisms for ensuring the supply of appropriate products. There are again a variety of approaches and companies develop networks of their own or with collaborators. Whilst products are the main preoccupation of these buying operations, services and other information based sourcing may also be undertaken.

There are then the retail operations themselves (Section C). This has been the main focus of the previous research on retail internationalisation [Burt, 1993: Pellegrini, 1994]. This research has focused on the reasons and dimensions of the store-based internationalisation as well as describing and quantifying the extent and directions of the activity. Attempts have then been made to link this description to the various theories and conceptualisations identified earlier (Table 1).

In one sense, the retail activity in terms of market entry is a realisable and tangible outcome of the retail internationalisation process. There are other outcomes as well, including measurable 'success or failure' of the

TABLE 3
ADVANTAGES AND DISADVANTAGES OF ALTRNATIVE MECHANISMS TO ESTABLISH
INTERNATIONAL OPERATIONS

Mechanisms	Advantages	Disadvantages
Internal Expansion	Can be undertaken by any size of firm. Experimental openings are possible with modest risk and often modest cost. Ability to adapt operation with each subsequent opening. Exit is easy (at least in early stages). Allows rapid prototyping.	Takes a long time to establish a substantial presence. May be seen by top management as a minor diversion. Requirement to undertake full locational assessment. More difficult if host market is distant from the home market.
Merger or Takeover	Substantial market presence quickly achieved. Management already in place. Cash flow is immediate. Possibility of technology transfer to home firm. May be used as a way to obtain locations quickly for conversion to the chosen format.	Difficult to exit if mistake is made. Evaluation of takeover target is difficult and takes time. Suitable firms may not be available. Substantial top management commitment necessary.
Franchise-type Agreements	Rapid expansion of presence possible. Low cost to franchiser. Marginal markets can be addressed. Local management may be used. Wide range of forms of agreement available. Use locally competitive marketing policy. Way of overcoming entry barriers.	Possibly complex legal requirements. Necessary to recruit suitable franchisees. Difficult to control foreign franchisees. May become locked into an unsatisfactory relationship.
Joint Venture	Possible to link with firm already in market. Help available in climbing learning curve. Possible to move later to either exit or make full entry into the market.	Necessary to share benefits. Difficulties in finding a suitable partner.
Non-controlling Interest	Find out about market with minimal risk. Allows those who know the market to manage the operation.	Passive position. Investment made over which little influence.

Source: Dawson [1993: 31].

activity internationalised. This process of transfer can include formats and ideas from all aspects of retail internationalisation as well as less visible dimensions such as management expertise (Section D).

The discussion above and Table 2 on which it is based, emphasise the very broad nature of retail internationalisation. Whilst store openings are the main focus of previous attention, it is argued here that a much broader conceptualisation of the dimensions of retail internationalisation is needed. We can highlight the important areas of non-store activity, ideas, expertise, sourcing and the learning process in terms of outcomes from retail internationalisation.

This broad view of the topic should not preclude debate on market entry and physical internationalisation, however, although the boundaries here can be blurred as well. For example there are a variety of possible entry mechanisms for a business establishing international operations. These range from the direct involvement of a business in expansion using their own operations to less direct involvement through non-controlling interests. Table 3 provides details of some of the possibilities. As the level of direct involvement declines down the table, so the level of knowledge transfer or borrowing increases. At the mid-point of the table is a franchise style agreement, which provides normally for some direct involvement (financial, managerial, product), yet also often allows local running and development of the operation. The interplay of information and business transfer is important in that the function being internationalised contains many more elements than a simple store opening.

In the context of 7–Eleven convenience stores, the franchise approach to internationalisation is the main mode of entry. There are both advantages and disadvantages to this format of business *per se* and to its use as a mode of entry to markets [Hoffman and Preble, 1991]. Table 3 argues that the advantages concern the local nature of the development that is possible and the way in which many markets, including marginal ones, can be addressed at high speed and with relatively low risk. The difficulties set out in the table concern the problems of obtaining, consolidating and managing networks of franchisees. Such concerns are not necessarily those of franchise internationalisation alone and indeed the use of format franchising in domestic markets has similar advantages and disadvantages. International activities however complicate further the situation and make the opportunities more appealing, yet the disadvantages potentially more daunting.

There are attempts to conceptualise the internationalisation process of franchise systems [Eroglu, 1992]. Eroglu's conceptualisation derives from a perceived slowness of US franchisors to internationalise despite official encouragement [Etzel and Walker, 1973]. The slowness, it is argued, is due to the perceptions of risks and benefits in internationalisation as compared to domestic expansion and these in turn derive from organisational and environmental constructs (Figure 1). This conceptualisation is based primarily on the export literature, and is really, as is obvious from the figure, supply driven. The rationale for becoming a franchisee in the international field or the reciprocal interactions and influences that such relationships achieve over time are ignored. In short, the conceptualisation provided by Eroglu is partial in its development.

FIGURE 1

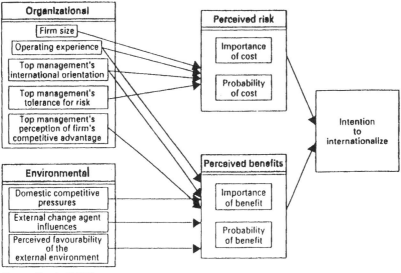

Source: Eroglu [1992].

This review of a very broad literature has thus concluded a number of points:

• there is considerable concern over the applicability of existing models of retail internationalisation due in particular to their derivation from outside the retail sphere;

• the conceptualisations of retail internationalisation that we do have are in general too restrictive in their consideration of the topic and process and possibly too dependent on physical store openings as the sole method for, and concern of, internationalisation;

• the limited work on international franchising as a method of entry is a partial conceptualisation only;

• insufficient attention has been paid to the interactions, influences and feedback from the retail internationalisation process and the mutual benefits (reciprocity) that may follow either in the short or long term.

In order to take the discussion further forward, therefore, this paper now examines a particular format of retail internationalisation, the 7–Eleven convenience store, and its transfer from the USA to Japan, and explores the issues in its internationalisation and the subsequent progress and interactions. From this case study it is intended that the need for a wide conceptualisation of the retail internationalisation process can be demonstrated.

CASE STUDY: SOUTHLAND CORPORATION, ITO-YOKADO AND 7–ELEVEN CONVENIENCE STORES

This section of the paper provides a case study of the growth and development of the 7–Eleven convenience store chain, initially in the United States and then internationally. The focus of the international expansion has numerically (to date) been Japan and in 1991 the Japanese rescued the 7–Eleven parent company from bankruptcy. In eighteen years a licensee had developed to control the worldwide operating rights. The case study is divided into sections on the development of 7–Eleven stores in the United States, international franchising of the concept, 7–Eleven store development in Japan, the decline and fall of the Southland Corporation, the take-over and rescue by the Japanese and finally some brief explanations for the events outlined. The material for this case study has been obtained from written sources (see references), annual reports, case studies [Lewison and Hawes, 1989; Sparks, 1994; Bernstein, 1994] and from store and site visits and interviews with experts and senior personnel. Given the space constraints, the description is somewhat limited to facilitate explanation.

The Development of 7–Eleven Stores in the United States

7–Eleven convenience stores came into existence in 1946 as the umbrella title for the convenience store operations of The Southland Corporation which was based in Dallas, Texas. The Southland Corporation itself had been in operation since 1927, when Claude S. Dawley bought eight ice-manufacturing plants and twenty-one retail ice stores and incorporated them as The Southland Ice Company, a name that remained in use until 1945 [Liles, 1977]. One of the initial investors and board members was Joe C. Thompson, Jr., who bought out the company from bankruptcy (due to the parent company performance) in 1932 and whose family remained at the helm of the company until the late 1980s, retaining an involvement even now. In essence, the company had been in the convenience store business since 1927 as, early on, requests from customers had led to sales of bread, milk and eggs, as well as the core product, ice (for home refrigeration), from the ice dock. The number of such outlets grew steadily, mainly under the Tote'm name, but with acquisitions, increasingly in a variety of formats and trading fascias. By the end of 1947, Southland operations consisted of 74 convenience stores located mainly in Dallas, a number of ice production companies and Oak Farm Dairies producing produce for sale in the stores. These operations were all combined as The Southland Corporation in 1948.

In 1947 the convenience store operations shared some common characteristics, if not trading names and formats. They were open-front, drive-in stores, open from early in the morning until late at night, seven days a week, selling ice, cold drinks, groceries and drug sundries.
As Liles [1977: 67] comments

> The Tracy-Locke Company (ad agency) deliberated, brainstormed and then came up with an idea. If all of the store operators involved in the co-op program would agree to stay open from 7am to 11pm seven days a week, the stores could be called '7–Eleven' stores.

FIGURE 2
7–ELEVEN STORES IN THE UNITED STATES
Number of Stores

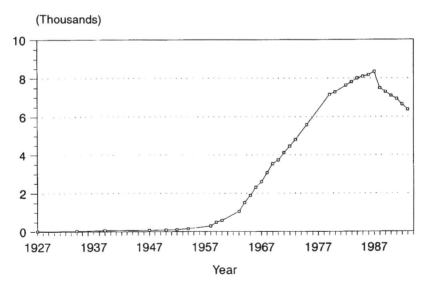

Note: Figures include Southland operated stores in Canada.

With a new name for the convenience store chain, and an updated retail format as new stores were built, together with centralised advertising, promotion and so on, the company began to expand its operations. Initially based in North Texas, 7–Eleven stores began to populate first Texas and then the reminder of North America. Laulajainen [1987] illustrates how the expansion was initially in the home state followed by 'external' growth initiated in the 1950s. Florida was the first destination for the company, being away from Texas thus allowing both trialing and regional autonomy, yet sharing the same climate and expanding quickly in population size. In 1957, however, a new region of Washington, DC was entered. The success of this venture north and east told the management that the stores could be successful across the country, in all climates, although there were occasional setbacks and market retrenchment in certain areas [Laulajainen, 1987].

An important market was California, but this had proved difficult to enter through management concern over high wages and the widespread use of franchising. In 1963 a major take-over (Speedee-Mart) followed a series of small expansions and a management used to operating a franchised system was effectively purchased. Expansion could then continue apace across the United States.

As Figure 2 shows, the first 20 years of the company saw 74 stores being built. Expansion in the 1950s was more rapid, but with hindsight was still relatively slow. By the end of the decade there were about 500 stores in the United States. Many of the new stores had been gained by take-over of existing companies and operations, but at the same time internal expansion was important. The pace of this expansion accelerated enormously in the 1960s as new markets were entered and as franchising was embraced (rather than regional autonomous companies). The net increase in stores between 1960 and 1970 was over 3,100 and by the end of the decade approximately 40 per cent of stores were franchised (a process aided by the introduction of area franchises). This sevenfold increase in the 1960s was followed by a further doubling of store numbers in the 1970s, from a much higher base. The vision and drive to mount this expansion had been enormous. By the end of the 1970s the United States was extensively covered and major growth for The Southland Corporation was overseas and in other retail and production sectors.

Whilst this expansion was occurring, the products in the stores and the stores themselves were being developed. From being open front stores, the now familiar 7–Eleven look was introduced. The other activities of The Southland Corporation were also expanding, particularly on the dairy side, allowing new products to be provided for the convenience stores, often on a regional market basis. One particular product, the Slurpee frozen carbonated drink became wildly successful. Other extensions included a wide range of support services, which varied depending on the customer needs and as the technology changed (e.g., television valve testers!). The major operating change occurred in 1963 when 24-hour opening was introduced. Liles [1977] records at least two experiments of 24-hour opening, one in Las Vegas where 24-hour activity was common, and one in Austin, Texas when the staff were unable to close the store due to customer volume associated with a football game. Whichever is the true origin, from 1963 the stores began to open for 24 hours on a consistent basis.

By the early 1970s The Southland Corporation was a very successful company with important operating arms including the 7–Eleven convenience store chain. Retail experience overseas had been gained by the expansion of company operated convenience stores into (contiguous) Canada (75 stores) and Mexico (4) and take-overs of other operations including some in the United Kingdom. The first true expansion of convenience stores internationally came in 1973 with the licensing of the 7–Eleven name and concept to Japan. This demonstrates the increasing confidence of the company.

International Franchising of the Concept

The rapid extension of store numbers allowed by the franchising concept and in particular by area franchising encouraged and facilitated growth in the United States. Area franchising gave a licence to a company to develop the 7–Eleven format over a spatially discrete area, subject to the terms and conditions of the franchise agreement and the provision for royalty payments. The area franchise effectively gave control of the expansion of the stores to other companies. Within the USA this allowed the rapid numerical expansion of the 1960s and 1970s. Extending this process into an international market was not a particularly major step.

The international expansion chosen however was dramatic. Liles [1977: 221] reports the announcement of December 1973:

> We are extremely pleased that Southland will be participating in the modernization of Japan's retail food distribution system. Agreements were finalised in December for the introduction of the 7–Eleven concept into Japan through an area license granted to Ito-Yokado Co Ltd., one of that nation's largest and most successful retailers. We are extremely optimistic about the future of this venture.

The expansion to Japan can be seen in a variety of ways. The account provided by Liles [1977] is clearly couched in the framework of the United States helping to modernise a weak country's infrastructure. The scope for convenience stores given the nature of Japanese society and the physical landscape was considered to be great. The involvement of a leading retailer in the franchise operation was also a bonus. On the reverse side, however, the distance between the two countries is such that the risk of failure was arguably (for the Americans) not too important. The Japanese view is of interest. Liles [1977] indicates how the Americans visited Japan to vet Ito-Yokado and to ascertain the scope for convenience stores. Dawson [1993: 16] points to visits to the United States by Masatoshi Ito which encouraged him to pursue the possibility of transferring the concept to Japan through Ito-Yokado. Certainly Mr Ito has been a visitor to the United States since the early 1960s and has unashamedly borrowed concepts for implantation into Japan. Tanzer [1986] claims Mr Ito saw early the potential of 7–Eleven stores and, although rebuffed initially, continued to pursue the possibility of taking the concept and name to Japan. This account is challenged by Bernstein [1994] and Iwabuchi [1993] who indicate Toshifumi Suzuki, another Ito-Yokado director, as being responsible for introducing 7–Eleven into Japan. They also point out that there was considerable opposition within Ito-Yokado to the agreement with The Southland Corporation and that The Southland Corporation was initially uninterested in the proposal. There is confusion over the origins of the idea, as Bernstein [1994] also reports that Professor Yoshihiro Tajima may have originated the idea of a link-up.

The success of the Japanese venture and the interest in and from overseas prompted The Southland Corporation to pursue internationalisation as a growth strategy. The next area licence was to Australia in 1976 and subsequently such agreements have seen 7–Eleven stores open in various foreign countries and three United States territories, with The Southland Corporation having an equity stake in a number of the foreign licensees (Table 4). As Figure 2 and in particular Figure 3 show, the primary expansion of 7–Eleven stores in the 1980s has been through international expansion, and of these the Japanese venture has been the most dynamic, although rapid growth has occurred in Taiwan and Hong Kong [Ho and Sin, 1987] and much is expected of China, where to date two licenses have been agreed.

The selection of franchisees and the ability to set up and enforce the franchise agreement are vital critical success factors. In Japan, the partner, Ito-Yokado, is a major successful retailer with a high reputation [Larke, 1994]. Such partners have not always been used and development in some countries has either been very slow or even failed (Table 4). The 'vetting' procedure for franchisees in the past may not have been sufficiently strong. Secondly, the agreements with franchisees or area licensees also vary. In the United States, for legal reasons the franchise agreement is relatively loose:

franchisees are required only to carry merchandise of a type, quality, quantity and variety consistent with the 7–Eleven image. Except for consigned merchandise, franchisees are not required to purchase

TABLE 4
INTERNATIONALISATION OF 7-ELEVEN STORES

Date	Location	No of Stores Dec 1993
1968	Canada	471
1971	Mexico[b]	201
1973	Japan	5401
1976	Australia	162
1977	United Kingdom[ce]	50
1979	Taiwan	809
1980	Sweden[b]	31
1981	Hong Kong	296
1983	Singapore	75
	Philippines	46
1984	Malaysia	85
1986	Panama	5
	Norway[ad]	35
	Guam/Micronesia	7
	Ireland[ai]	-
1987	Puerto Rico[a]	13
	Spain[ac]	69
	Indonesia[f]	-
1988	South Korea	73
	Thailand	271
1989	Turkey[a]	12
	US Virgin Islands[h]	-
1990	Brazil[a]	14
1992	China[j]	10
1993	Denmark	2

Notes: [a] - equity stake in area license
          [b] - subsidiary/affiliate
          [c] - subsidiary initially then area licence (1983)
          [d] - now area license includes Denmark, Finland and Sweden
          [e] - equity stake sold 1993
          [f] - license granted 1987, store numbers reached 6 in 1990, declining thereafter
                 and license terminated in 1992
          [g] - equity stake sold 1990
          [h] - area license terminated end 1992, 3 stores open 1989-1992
          [i] - store numbers reached 19 in 1990, before franchise ran into difficulties in
                 1991
          [j] - licenses only granted to date to Guangdong and Shenzhen

Sources: Developed from Southland Corporation annual reports and 10-K forms and
Liles [1977].

merchandise from the Company or vendors it recommends, or to sell their merchandise at prices suggested by the company [Securities and Exchange Commission, 1994: 6].

Whilst in practice there may be only limited disagreements, this franchise agreement is looser than in other countries and does open up the possibilities for franchisees to operate semi-autonomously and not to follow the 'corporate' line. Consistency of approach is a problem and much effort has to be spent in convincing franchisees of the merits of certain activities. Many retail franchisors have had 'problems' with their franchisees in this way (e.g., Body Shop, Benetton).

7–Eleven Convenience Store Development in Japan

There are particular reasons why convenience stores are successful in Japan and there can be little questioning of their relative efficiency and scope for modernising Japanese retailing and distribution [Goldman, 1991, 1992; Czinkota and Kotabe, 1993; Larke, 1994]. Convenience stores in Japan account for approximately 2 per cent of the retail sector sales. Major chains dominate the market. The top three (Seven–Eleven, Daiei Convenience Systems and Family Mart [Seiyu]) account for over half the market, with Seven–Eleven itself being the market leader with approximately a one-third share. Currently there are over 50,000 convenience store outlets in Japan with the potential possibly for the same number again [Convenience Store Report, 1994].

FIGURE 3
7–ELEVEN STORES WORLDWIDE 1973–1993

1973 (Total 4801)   1980 (Total 8380)   1993 (Total 14156)

Seven–Eleven Japan Co. Ltd, set up to operate the 7–Eleven name in Japan, is a subsidiary of Ito-Yokado Co. Ltd. Ito-Yokado themselves run a large variety of successful retail chains, including superstores and supermarkets, department, discount and speciality stores and restaurants and is amongst the most profitable and effective Japanese retail business [see Larke, 1994: 207–9]. In market capitalisation terms Seven–Eleven Japan Co. Ltd is now Japan's leading food retailer. By the end of financial year 1994 (Feb.) there were 5,523 stores in the chain, sales had reached 1,282 billion Yen and the company was recognised as a pioneer and master in convenience store operations – one of the most dynamic areas of Japanese retailing. The comparative development of the Japanese chain has already been seen from Figure 3. Whilst store numbers are not vastly more than its main competitors, the sales and especially the profit that Seven–Eleven generates dominates the returns by the competition. This has been the subject of much popular writing in Japan [e.g., Kunitomo, 1987, 1993; Ogata, 1991; Iwabuchi, 1993].

The common explanation for the success of Seven–Eleven Japan is that it is an exceptionally efficient retailer which harnesses technology, systems and relationships with manufacturers and franchisees constantly to reinforce its knowledge of, and success in meeting changing consumer demands. Customer focus is its primary mission, managed on a store-by-store and item-by-item basis. In delivering this focus, Seven–Eleven (and Ito-Yokado) have had to redefine convenience store systems and operations and also effectively transform components of the Japanese distribution system. The ways in which these aims were achieved are detailed below [see also Sparks, 1994], given the subsequent aim of revitalising the American operation.

Unlike The Southland Cooperation, Seven–Eleven Japan is based almost entirely (95 per cent) on independent franchises. These are direct franchises rather than area-based franchises and operate very differently to The Southland Corporation system. Southland are much more involved in store/land purchase and construction whereas Seven–Eleven Japan recruit store owners and convert their stores using a long-term strict contract [Bernstein, 1994]. Seven–Eleven Japan 'supports' the franchisee by providing management advice, PoS systems, utility cost sharing, a minimum guaranteed annual gross profit, and strives to raise the productivity and profits of franchised stores. Franchise commission is calculated on the basis of an individual store's gross margin. In practice, however, franchisees in convenience stores in Japan, and particularly in Seven–Eleven Japan, have very limited freedom of action, and certainly nothing like that of the United States. To ensure efficiency and stability, the store expansion policy is based upon a market dominance strategy which is built around clusters of 50 or 60 stores. By such local saturation and clustering, Seven–Eleven Japan gains a high-density market presence and thus raises distribution and advertising efficiency, improves brand awareness, raises system efficiency and the efficiency of franchisee support and prevents competitor entrance into the local areas. Thus despite such a large number of stores, Seven–Eleven Japan is still present in only 21 of Japan's 47 prefectures. Figure 4 presents details of the recent growth of stores and sales.

FIGURE 4
SEVEN-ELEVEN JAPAN CO. LTD - NUMBER OF STORES AND SALES

(a) Number of Stores

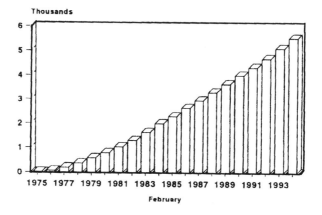

(b) Net Sales

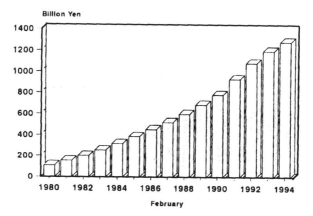

Over 1.8 billion customer visits occurred in fiscal year 1994. From these visits some 7.0 billion items of PoS data were collected on customer's age and sex, sales volume of all products, what products sold out and how product sales patterns are changing. The level of data collected allows item-by-item inventory control and patterns of sales by parts of the day, and other

time periods. The basic components of Seven–Eleven Japan's information system have been developed in-house and in association with dedicated Nomura Research staff. PoS cash registers speed up the checkout operation and record data such as time of purchase and type of customer. Such information is processed by Seven–Eleven Japan's host computer and returned to the store computer, where it can be accessed and used. The store computer can be used to place orders, display sales and store information, evaluate store product assortment and function generally as a management information system. The Graphics Order Terminal (GOT) is a notebook-sized portable computer that provides product sales information and advice to store employees as they check shelves for items that need to be ordered. These components within the company and its suppliers are linked and integrated via an Integrated Services Digital Network (ISDN) which Seven–Eleven Japan claim is the largest of its kind in the world. The system outlined above and shown in Figure 5 has been developed over time as the company and its needs have grown [see Sparks, 1994 for fuller details].

FIGURE 5
SEVEN–ELEVEN JAPAN CO. LTD – INFORMATION SYSTEMS

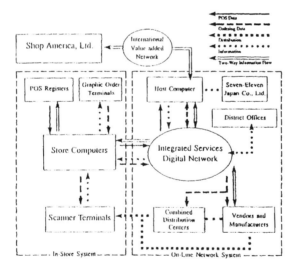

The use of information technology in the company has had a number of performance effects (Figure 6). Fundamentally, there has been a large reduction in inventory and an increase in gross profit margins. Not related solely to information technology but clearly linked to the way in which the stores meet customer needs, the average per store daily sales have risen dramatically. Seven–Eleven Japan is a very profitable and efficient company.

FIGURE 6
SEVEN–ELEVEN JAPAN CO. LTD: BUSINESS PERFORMANCE

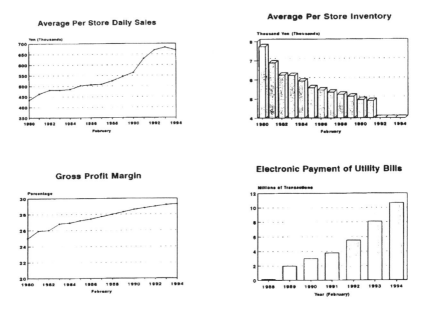

The item-by-item data capture provides the basis for a sophisticated merchandising system. The merchandising innovations began with inventory paring and item-by-item control. Fine-tuning product line-ups involves the replacement of slow-moving products with fast-moving ones in demand. The result is a reduction of opportunity loss owing to sold-out products and an increase in customer loyalty. Replenishment of product lines can be made to maximise the sales of certain products at certain times of the day and night. For example, prepared dishes might have three purchase peaks in a 24-hour period, e.g., at 07.00–09.00, 13.00–15.00 and 17.00–23.00 and deliveries are timed to ensure an appropriate product mix and amount at these times and to ensure freshness and quality eg at 03.00, 11.00 and 19.00. The merchandise mix can thereby be adjusted by the dimensions of breadth, location and time.

The information usage is aimed at keeping product line-ups current by putting the customer at the centre of all the operations. The data analysis enables slow-selling products to be eliminated and replaced by faster selling lines. In any one year it is estimated that approximately 50–65 per cent of the lines are replaced. In the soft drinks market, for example, there has been little price differentiation among the 4,000 lines on the market. Seven–Eleven Japan have identified the most important 70–80 of these, i.e.,

2 per cent of those available, and stores stock from these using a process they term product consolidation. Product consolidation is based on item-by-item control using information from head office and ordering advice from field consultants. Purchasers (i.e., stores) make hypotheses about what will sell and confirm their accuracy through analyses of these items' sales results. Hypothesising, ordering, verifying and repetition of this process focuses the store on successful products. This lower range and choice and reduced inventory are constantly refocused on the 'best' products to meet consumer demands and increase sales, and refreshed through new product offerings to the store.

The provision of information also involves manufacturers. The benefit of the supply of information electronically to manufacturers is an increase in co-operation and a reduction in total system costs. The rapid provision of accurate, detailed data allows informed production decisions to be made. For some products, Seven–Eleven Japan has entered dedicated production agreements involving new site developments for production. Particularly in the field of delicatessen, prepared dishes and filled rice balls, such developments allow the product range to be tailored to the market and also to be dedicated and differentiated from the competition. The unique nature of the products again enhances the store operation. The system is such that filled rice balls for example have the time of production and the maximum time for sale (hours of the day) on the label, allowing the customer to be satisfied over freshness and quality. Only with a sophisticated and accurate item-by-item merchandising and distribution operation can such guarantees be given at reasonable cost. At the same time Seven–Eleven Japan have gone further with some suppliers and taken on the risk themselves by agreeing not to return unsold items. This reliance on the information breeds confidence in the system within the company and manufacturers.

With an information network already in place, Seven–Eleven Japan Co. looked for ways to exploit their investment, particularly if such exploitation could involve the idea of improved convenience. In 1987, Seven–Eleven Japan pioneered the electronic payment of electricity and gas bills through the stores and the computer network. This had the merit of providing an enhanced service to existing customers and also attracting to the stores potential new customers. The company made no payment for such a service, instead holding on to the money for a number of days and placing it on deposit. Subsequently the service has been expanded to allow payment of for example life assurance premiums, television fees and telephone bills as well as adding further utilities. In fiscal year 1994, over 10 million such electronic payments were made using the system (Figure 6). This service is a major differentiator for Seven–Eleven Japan and is accepted by consumers as providing a better and more convenient service than that of the banks.

In addition to electronic payments, other service provisions have been expanded in the search to meet consumer needs. Services such as photocopying and fast photo processing enhance the physical service provision as does the provision of vending machines for telephone cards and the acceptance of prepaid cards for payments at the stores. It is also possible to use the electronic network to ensure the delivery of gift packaged fresh flowers and made to order lunch boxes. Such product personalisation is a reflection of a commitment to meet changing customer needs.

The final (to date) expansion of the use of the network is the provision of a service called Shop America. This catalogue service provides products from overseas to the Japanese market and uses the stores and network for customers to place orders for these. Such merchandise can only be ordered at 7–Eleven stores. The service had 300,000 subscribers by February 1992. This service has been at the centre of considerable discussion between the original American operators and Ito-Yokado [Khalili, 1991]. The breadth originally envisaged for the concept has been abandoned, perhaps at the initiation of Japanese manufacturers, concerned about the pricing.

Electronic data dissemination enables the faster understanding of activities across a more widespread spatial area. The corollary of this however is that the provision of 'better' data places a sterner requirement on physical movement. The Seven–Eleven Japan distribution system has therefore had to alter as the information and technology revolution was introduced. Seven–Eleven Japan have had to grapple with the existing distribution system in Japan which focused on many vehicle journeys and links in the distribution channel. In the conventional system only one supplier's goods are carried at a time on delivery vehicles and there are many layers in the channel [e.g., Goldman, 1991, 1992]. To change this a combined small-lot delivery system, incorporating different suppliers' products, delivered on the same delivery vehicle was developed. From 1976, the company began to develop the combined delivery system allowing consolidation of products before delivery to stores. From the mid-1980s this has involved temperature-controlled combined delivery and subsequently the strategic development of a dedicated distribution operation. To improve the freshness of perishable foods, as well as to improve efficiency, deliveries now combine products from different suppliers in a system which separates products by temperature rather than by producer or wholesaler. In such a way, product freshness is enhanced and the store location pattern around centres ensures prompt yet frequent delivery if required. Deliveries per store per day are claimed to have fallen from 70 in 1974 to 11 in 1992. The aim, however, is to minimise deliveries by maximising the content of the deliveries through the merchandising system. Producers are forced to co-operate if they wish to have access to

Seven–Eleven Japan's business.

The operations outlined above have been presented at some length to emphasise the focus that Seven–Eleven Japan place on meeting customer needs rapidly and effectively at a local level. This detailed concern has enabled the company to out-perform its rivals historically and to be successful even in the current Japanese economic downturn. This success it is argued [e.g., Bernstein, 1994; Sparks, 1994] is based on the triumvirate of the franchise approach, the technology and data use and the reconstructed distribution system. The focus at all times is finding the best way to meet changing consumer demands.

FIGURE 7
7–ELEVEN STORES IN THE USA – PRODUCT CATEGORIES

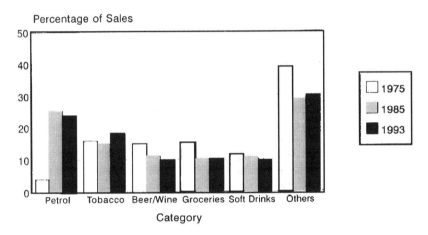

The Decline and Fall of The Southland Corporation

The growth of 7–Eleven stores in the United States in the 1960s and 1970s has already been noted. During this time of net addition to the store base, considerable upgrading of the format and movement of locations was occurring [Lewison and Hawes, 1989]. A modern 7–Eleven store includes fast foods and petrol retailing as well as the 'basic' convenience items and the product mix has changed (Figure 7). Petrol retailing proved to be a major attraction for The Southland Corporation. As this expanded its role within the company, so The Southland Corporation moved to diversify its operations further and to secure its supply of petrol, by purchasing Citgo Petroleum Corporation in 1983. This diversification was symptomatic of a growing movement away from the core convenience store business, and was a move that The Southland Corporation saw as helping them vertically integrate. Other purchases in the 1970s and 1980s included safe control systems, snack foods and auto parts as well as real estate.

TABLE 5
DIVESTITURES BY SOUTHLAND AFTER THE LBO

Effective Date	Divestiture	Acquirer	Price ($ mil)
1/2/88	270 convenience stores	National Convenience Stores	67
3/7/88	MovieQuik System (video rental)	Cevaxs Corp	52
4/4/88	Tidel Systems Division	David H Monnich (Houston)	16
4/5/88	Dairy Group	Morning Star Foods, Inc	247
4/5/88	473 7-Eleven Stores	Circle K Corp	148
4/26/88	21 7-Eleven stores	FFP Partners	8
5/3/88	Chief Auto Parts	Management Acquisitions Group	135
5/26/88	Reddy Ice	Management Acquisitions Group	23
6/20/88	Arthur C Trask Division (chemicals)	Climax Performance Material	2
8/16/88	Snack Foods Division: El Ge Potato Chip Company Keystone Pretzel Bakery Pate Foods	Vesper Corp	15
4/21/89	79 7-Eleven Stores	National Convenience Stores	25
7/27/89	66 7-Eleven Stores	Super America Group, Inc	27
12/26/89	58 7-Eleven Stores	Seven-Eleven Japan Co, ltd	75
1/31/90	Citgo Petroleum Corp	Petroleos de Venezuela	662

Source: Bernstein [1994: 21].

Problems in the mid-1980s in the general United States economy, together with a lesser performance in the business itself due to enhanced competition, led The Southland Corporation to review its business operations. At the same time there was considerable concern over possible attempts to take over the company, as part of the general corporate raiding of this time [Hallsworth, 1991, 1992; Magowan, 1989]. In 1987, a Canadian, Samuel Belzberg announced his plans to take control via a

Leveraged Buy Out (LBO). This was a particular concern to the Thompson family as original founders of the business and their view of the business as a family concern despite their (by then) small shareholding. They had to therefore respond.

In July 1987 it was announced that there was to be a LBO of The Southland Corporation by the Thompson family at a far higher price than that proposed by Belzberg [Bernstein, 1994]. This duly went ahead during 1987, followed by a re-focusing by the family on the core convenience store business. The buyout was financed by the sale of some assets combined with high-risk investment mechanisms such as 'junk bonds'. The Southland Corporation that emerged was focused on the convenience stores, the distribution and food centres supplying the stores and a 50 per cent stake in Citgo. The plans put forward however were very ambitious. With the stock market crash of October 1987, the problems for the LBO began immediately. With high levels of debt ($3.6bn in 1990), stock market problems, and a weaker performance than anticipated in the convenience store businesses due to the competition and in particular 'g-stores', i.e., petrol (gasoline) station shops, the company was in trouble. Servicing of the debt became the key issue and a moratorium on capital spending and advertising was introduced. A number of sales of non-core businesses followed, including the sell-off of the convenience store operations in Hawaii to Seven–Eleven Japan Co. Ltd in December 1989 (Table 5). It is arguable whether these occurred in sufficient number or at sufficient speed.

Throughout this period store openings were comparatively few due to the capital spending moratorium and some stores were also sold. In essence the store base was deteriorating in both quantity and quality. Business performance could not meet the very ambitious targets of the LBO and the problems in the core business continued to mount. Figure 8 illustrates the problems of stagnating revenues, mounting interest payments and staggering financial operating losses ($1.3bn in 1989).

One aspect of solving these problems was the execution of a favourable finance deal arranged via Ito-Yokado, with a syndicate of Japanese institutions for 41 billion yen ($325m), in exchange for the annual Japanese royalty stream, with the brand name for collateral. This agreement reflected the strength of Seven–Eleven Japan and Ito-Yokado and their convenience store performance and systems at this time. It also illustrates their concern over the future of Southland and the 7–Eleven name. Ohmae [1990: 132] indicates that as part of the deal, the 7–Eleven name in Japan would effectively be of no consequence to The Southland Corporation, as it was to revert to the Japanese. Despite this finance raising, other commercial deals and some cost-cutting exercises, the problems continued and in March 1990 an agreement in principle for a take-over by Ito-Yokado was announced.

This was eventually realised via a pre-arranged Chapter 11 bankruptcy entered in October 1990, from which the new Southland Corporation, owned by the Japanese, emerged in March 1991.

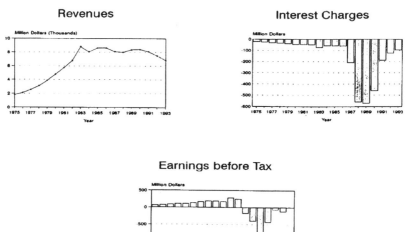

FIGURE 8
THE SOUTHLAND CORPORATION

In retrospect, the seeds for the decline of The Southland Corporation had been sown some time before. The move away from the core business took the emphasis away from the stores. Whilst international store expansion had continued, the United States operation was stagnant, despite its seeming potential. In 1987, 7–Eleven stores were open in 42 states, yet in only 18 of these were there more than 100 stores and in 19 states there were less than 50 stores. The store base itself was deteriorating in location and quality (no maintenance) terms. At the same time the competition was increasing massively, particularly from the so-called 'g-stores' (petrol station shops). For the first time, The Southland Corporation could not rely on convenience store expansion for growth, as there were fundamental operating problems to be solved. Operational practices had been allowed which gradually positioned 7–Eleven stores as high-price ('insult' pricing), dirty and inconvenient with poor product ranges and in-stock positions. Discounting on certain lines to meet the competition only further confused and alienated the customer base. The LBO and subsequent debt crisis simply reinforced and exacerbated these issues.

The Take-over and Rescue by the Japanese

The vehicle for the take-over by the Japanese was the specially created Ito-Yokado Group Holding Company, which was 51 per cent owned by Ito-Yokado and 49 per cent by Seven–Eleven Japan Co Ltd. After the take-over this controlled 70 per cent of The Southland Corporation, a stake that has reduced to 64 per cent as share options have been taken up. Since the take-over the Japanese have been using their knowledge and expertise to attempt to revitalise The Southland Corporation through its convenience store operations. The financial outcomes of this are seen in Figure 8 which shows the decline in revenues (but see also the massive decline in stores in Figure 2), but the rather better interest and pre-tax earnings performance. In essence the Japanese are introducing their knowledge of convenience store approaches, systems and operations to the Americans, and encouraging the Americans to rethink their methods of operation.

This process of revitalising the performance of the Southland Corporation has a number of components all of which are geared to improving the performance in meeting Southland's revised Business Concept:

> To service the customer through 7–Eleven stores that achieve a sustainable competitive advantage through superior merchandising ... a proprietary process that gives us item-by-item control at each store, providing convenience-oriented customers with what they want ...
>
> SPEED .... a fast transaction
> QUALITY .... on those fresh, high-quality products
> SELECTION .... that they want and need
> PRICE .... at a fair price
> ENVIRONMENT .... in a clean, safe, friendly store.
>
> This can only be accomplished through a productive, motivated and efficient organisation of franchisees, licensees and employees and with the support of our suppliers and manufacturers [The Southland Corporation Annual Report, 1992: 9].

These five items, which deliver value to the customer, are the key tests against which all activities are judged. Changes have to lead to improvements in performance on these elements. The changes focus on a continuous improvement policy (situation, hypothesis, execution, results, situation, hypothesis, etc.) which seeks to improve operations through a consistent and iterative decision-making process adopted at all levels of the company. The process it is hoped increases sales, reduces lost opportunities, focuses on the best lines and improves the quality of decision-making.

The revitalisation can be categorised into seven components:

Merchandising. An Accelerated Inventory Management (AIM) system has been introduced to the stores, initially paper driven, but increasingly computer-based (eventually store 'automation' as in Japan will be used). This system is not focused on inventory reduction *per se*, although this occurs, but rather is aimed at enabling stores to remove rapidly products that do not sell, maximise the space allocated to the best selling products, and provide space for new products appropriate to the store's target population. In short, better decisions are made more rapidly at store level, focusing on customer demands. On the basis of AIM and the development with field consultants of Individual Store Development Plans, stores gain a more appropriate merchandise mix and a more rapid response to changing consumer demands and changing product performance. This is delivered at the *individual* store level. More generally, The Southland Corporation has introduced more food products to the stores, added services such as ATMs, and begun to change the product mix (Figure 7).

Pricing. The pricing policy of The Southland Corporation in the 1980s had seen 7–Eleven stores compete sharply on price through deep discounting in certain lines combined with 'insult' pricing on others. The new pricing policy of 'everyday fair pricing' has sought to remove the discounting emphasis and replace it with an overall reasonable price position offered consistently. Ito-Yokado would argue that convenience stores must compete on convenience not price, but must not get too out-of-line on price in any direction. Discounting is a price-based, not a convenience-based strategy. The approach taken has been to be more realistic on pricing, focusing on the market place rather than internal business inefficiencies and encouraging premium pricing only where it reflects core competencies or a particular opportunity in a product life cycle. The value concept is being used more, reflecting a better focus on customer needs, not the business operations.

Delayering. Thirdly, the company has seen some central employment losses through reorganisation and consolidation. This has been both to reduce the overhead costs of the company and also to focus more on the business process. Delayering has improved communications and at the same time decision-making has been devolved to as close to the customer as possible. This has speeded the business information transfer in both directions, and improved communications both to the shop level and from the store staff level to the board.

Store Base. There are three components to the changes with respect to the store base. First, the base itself has been shrinking, as has been shown in

Figure 2 before. Unprofitable stores have been closed and some replacement stores opened in areas with previously poor locations. This base will continue shrinking in the short-term. Secondly a new model store format has been developed and tested (initially in Austin, Texas and Reno, Nevada). The success of the stores in these tests in improving sales and profit performance has seen a massive store re-modelling process introduced (c.1300 stores a year), covering the entire North American operation by 1996. This store re-modelling has also taken care of the massive amount of deferred maintenance built up during the problems of the 1980s. Thirdly, this remodelling has involved improving the lighting inside and outside to make the stores brighter, widening of aisles for a less cluttered look allied to lower maximum shelf height to improve visibility, upgrading of equipment to improve speed of operation, opening up of the store through more open cases and less posters on the windows allowing clear sight lines and a new external facade in three colours.

Business Concentration. In order to concentrate on the 7–Eleven convenience store business, the distribution and food processing operations have been disposed of. The petrol business was sold off in the late 1980s. Essentially, the company is now a convenience store operator.

Outsourcing. In connection with the sale of the distribution business, an agreement has been developed with McLane Company Ltd to handle much of the distribution to the convenience stores. Such outsourcing is common elsewhere to reduce direct costs and to improve the service through the use of specialist expertise. This use of dedicated operations should also enable 7–Eleven stores to get better quality merchandise at better times. In the past, individual stores have been a relatively unimportant customer of many suppliers, particularly in products delivered direct to store. By agreements such as those with McLane and the other changes outlined below, the distribution chain is operated by more specialist businesses and should deliver a better service to the stores. The fact that McLane is a Wal-Mart subsidiary may also be of importance to Ito-Yokado (see later).

A second distribution change is the development of combined distribution centres. At the moment these are limited, but over 30 will eventually be developed for operation by dedicated distribution companies. These centres provide a more appropriate delivery mechanism than direct to store delivery by vendors and at a better price. This is an illustration of the retailer gaining control of the operation from the manufacturer/vendor and of the benefits of spatially concentrating or clustering stores. One unanticipated consequence of centralisation is that store managers have become more positive about trialling new products in stores rather than being risk-averse with vendors products.

In addition to these distribution operations, Southland are now working with partners to develop dedicated production facilities (commissaries) for food products to supply the 7–Eleven stores. The commissaries require centralised distribution systems to be in place, but basically allow the production of dedicated merchandise for the company, from which stores can order according to customer demands. The store gains specialised merchandise that is freshly prepared (e.g., salads, fruit salads, sandwiches, etc.) to rigorous standards and schedules. Different stores can therefore have different ranges depending on their customer demands.

Debt Restructuring. Finally, the financial problems of the company have been addressed further through more debt restructuring backed by the Ito-Yokado parent company. This has helped the financial situation and has encouraged an up-rating of Southland's debt/credit rating.

The list of changes above is extensive and fundamental, a fact recognised by the series of 7–Eleven television commercials on the theme of 'So Many Changes, It's Not Even Funny' utilising famous comedians. The changes also have a basic similarity with the operational practices of Seven–Eleven Japan described earlier. The rationale behind the changes is encapsulated in the Japanese view of American 7–Eleven stores: 'convenience stores in the United States should be where customers want to shop and buy what they want .... Past practices (have) turned c-stores into soft drink, beer and cigarette shacks. That is not a c-store. People have illusions that these are c-stores' [Chain Store Age Executive, 1992: 38].

The fundamental point is that the Japanese believe that the focus of The Southland Corporation has not been closely enough on the customers and stores. Whilst the practices imported are to some extent copies of the Japanese convenience store operation, the outcomes may well be different. A direct transplant from Japan would be a dangerous step as cultural specificity could cause problems. Instead, the systems and approaches being introduced allow the store managers to decide what best suits their customers and gives them the tools to achieve this closer matching. In essence, the Japanese are importing their conceptualisation of a convenience store and asking the Americans to implement the approach. They are also moving somewhat slowly on the technology and systems side recognising the gradual and incremental development required to be fully successful in such areas (as was the case in Japan). The outcome in financial terms to the end of financial year 1993 of the programme of changes can be seen in Figure 8.

Explanations?
The history and development that has been presented above has shown divergent paths for Seven–Eleven Japan and The Southland Corporation

since the license agreement in 1973. Both companies continued to expand in the 1970s by focusing on their convenience store base. In the 1980s however, whilst the Japanese expanded, The Southland Corporation convenience stores began to stagnate. Arguably the company focused too much on other components of the business. Whilst the LBO can undoubtedly be seen to exacerbate the issues, there were underlying problems for 7–Eleven stores in the United States that pre-date this.

In Japan, the focus in the 1980s in particular has been on the incremental changes to the business that have enabled the company to focus on customers and their needs. The process has been long term and has involved a considerable set of changes both within the company and to traditional business practices in Japan. The emphasis has been on rapid and flexible communications and decision-making which focuses on customer needs. The take-over by the Japanese of the Hawaiian 7–Eleven stores in 1989 confirmed their view that the stores had too much inventory and too few lines compared to Japan. By introducing the Japanese approach, the business performance and profitability of these stores was improved. This gave Seven–Eleven Japan confidence about the potential for the approach to work in the United States.

By contrast, the United States has seen a changing situation for the company as a whole, within which the convenience stores received declining emphasis. The stores themselves did not receive the investment or changes that were necessary and the focus was more on the corporate rather than the customer dimensions. By introducing the Japanese approach to convenience stores, it is anticipated that business performance will be enhanced. The detailed outcomes may differ, but the underlying approach is the same.

UNDERSTANDING RETAIL INTERNATIONALISATION: SOUTHLAND AND ITO-YOKADO

The case provided in the previous section of this paper details a considerable number of aspects of a retail internationalisation process spanning over two decades and operating in numerous directions. In order to synthesise the aspects contained in the case, the framework developed from Dawson [1993] and outlined in Table 2 is used. Table 6 therefore provides a summary of the internationalisation dimensions and attributes as suggested by the case. Clearly there are influences of the timing and method of internationalisation that condition the findings in the table, but at the same time we need to seek a deeper understanding of why these activities occur in the ways that they do.

The initial process of internationalisation by The Southland Corporation

TABLE 6
RETAIL INTERNATIONALISATION DIMENSIONS AND ATTITUDES: SOUTHLAND AND ITO-YOKADO

Internationalisation	Southland to Ito-Yokado (1973)	Ito-Yokado to Southland (1991 -)
A : Dimensions to Retail Internationalisation		
A1 : Financial Investment	None	Massive, Multi-Layered
A2 : Cross-border Shopping	None	Shop America?
A3 : Managerial Movements	None	Board of Directors
A4 : Retail Activities	Franchise	Heavy Involvement
B : International Sourcing		
B1 : Buyer Decisions	None	Yes-Retailer Brand
B2 : International Sourcing Organisation	None	Yes-Product Exchange
B3 : Technology	None	Yes
B4 : Buying Groups and Alliances	None	Potentially
B5 : Non-Retail-Product Sourcing	None	Yes-Service Operations
C : International Retail Operations		
C1 : Reasons	Modernisation/Expansion	Protection of Name
C2 : Dimensions	Franchise	Equity Stake
C3 : Extent and Directions	Agreement Only	Takeover and Full Involvement
D : Internationalisation of Management Ideas		
D1 : Transferability of Retail Concepts	High	High but Unproven
D2 : Expertise Transferred	Practical and Name	Operations and Personnel
D3 : Mechanisms of Transfer	Franchise	Equity Stake Plus Personnel

took place against a background of massive expansion in the United States and predicted further massive growth. The agreement that was signed was a license agreement that broadly accorded with the area licenses used by The Southland Corporation at this time. In terms of dimensions to the process therefore, for Southland it is straightforward – a franchise agreement involving the transfer of the name to the Japanese market.

The Southland Corporation has been criticised for this approach by Morgan and Morgan [1991] who accuse them of sacrificing global expansion opportunities for 'easy-money and short-term gains', and as a consequence of 'missing out on the opportunity to build relationships with important suppliers, real estate companies and distributors' [Morgan and Morgan, 1991: 169]. Given the timing, potential risks and the unwillingness of Ito-Yokado to enter a joint venture, this criticism may be too harsh. The consequence of a franchise agreement does not have to be independent operation, however, and in this regard The Southland Corporation could have benefited rather more from Japan.

As a straightforward franchise agreement and with the loose terms adopted in such agreements by The Southland Corporation effectively allowing franchisees to operate as they wish, then there is little mutuality or exchange in terms of international sourcing. Whilst The Southland Corporation may well have had some international sourcing activity in place, the agreement with Ito-Yokado did not extend this.

The third area of the framework – the operations themselves – reveal a variety of issues. The motivation and reasons for The Southland Corporation's internationalisation seem to be a mixture of expansionary motives and the opportunity to modernise the retail sector of a 'disadvantaged' country. There is thus a financial motive through the income and expansion and a more altruistic motive in terms of 'technology' transfer. It is clear that restrictions on expansion at home were not a factor in this; indeed the opportunities in the United States may well have encouraged the use of a franchise/license agreement rather than setting up themselves or entering a joint venture, although franchises and licenses were by 1973 very much the core of Southland's internal expansion policy. The extent and direction of the move was limited in Japan to the agreement itself, although it is true to note that the success of the franchise in Japan probably encouraged the extensive franchising internationally seen in Table 4 and also accounted for its focus on the Asia–Pacific region, a somewhat unusual focus for American companies during this period.

Finally, there is the issue of the transferability of management ideas. In the case of The Southland Corporation, the concept has a high degree of transferability although the expertise transferred in essence is the name and some operating practices and practicalities. There is little contact or involvement beyond this and the mechanism of transfer is a financial payment on the success of the transferred operation (the royalty). Eventually of course the management links to Japan did provide an opportunity to save the business!

The review of the initial process of internationalisation (i.e., Southland to Ito-Yokado) illustrates the basically limited nature of the approach at the time and the relatively narrow concerns of this franchise arrangement. The focus is on the transfer of the name and of the basic practice in return for an ongoing financial consideration. As far as this goes therefore, this franchise seems to fit the simple conceptualisations that have characterised much of the approaches to understanding retail internationalisation.

If we use the same framework for the second retail internationalisation, (i.e., of Ito-Yokado to Southland), then the conclusions are somewhat different (Table 6). As has been noted earlier, there are basic differences in involvement between the franchise mechanism and majority equity participation and we might expect the framework to highlight these. At the same time, there are other fundamental differences in approach, as illustrated by the case.

In terms of the dimensions of retail internationalisation, Ito-Yokado have massive and multi-layered financial involvement in the United States through their ownership. This financial involvement in The Southland Corporation pre-dates the take-over, albeit on a smaller scale, but can be seen as a direct consequence of the earlier franchise agreement. Ito-Yokado also acted as the facilitator in placing other financial deals with Japanese banks for The Southland Corporation. It is the case that Ito-Yokado have been somewhat untypically international in their finance arrangements since their inception, reflecting perhaps their lack of networks in Japan initially and their often-illustrated willingness to operate outside conventional Japanese business practices [Crum and Meerschwam, 1986: 291–3; Uno *et al.*, 1988]. Secondly, Ito-Yokado have had for a few years a cross-border shopping operation (Shop America), which whilst the total amount of imported product carried and sold is in dispute [Khalili, 1991], provided Seven–Eleven Japan customers with an opportunity to purchase imported products. The third dimension, that of managerial movements has also been expanded dramatically by the take-over. Whilst there was some clear discussion between Japan and America at the senior management level prior to the take-over, the take-over has enabled the Japanese to replace the Board of Directors of The Southland Corporation with Japanese executives. This financial and managerial involvement is conducive to a total re-direction of The Southland Corporation by the Japanese. Whilst many Americans may not meet the Japanese in the business operations, there is a tremendous influence being exerted through the approaches and systems being put into place. There is an undoubted 'Japanization' of The Southland Corporation underway, but one typically that is not based on occupying offices or direct edicts but rather on underlying processes and influences. As the case shows, the involvement of the Japanese in *directing* the changes and overseeing their implementation is considerable.

The second area of the framework is that of international sourcing. Here, the involvement of Ito-Yokado is in stark contrast to the involvement indicated earlier for The Southland Corporation. Ito-Yokado have for a number of years been sourcing products on an international basis, particularly in the retailer brand sphere. The expansion into the United States has furthered this operation, in particular through tie-ups with Philip Morris and Wal-Mart (and retailer brand suppliers such as The Cott Corporation to Wal-Mart and The Southland Corporation). As these suppliers are important to 7–Eleven stores and as the distribution operations were out-sourced, so the opportunities to collaborate in product exchange into Japan became clearer. There is potential here for Ito-Yokado to forge further alliances with strategic partners. Finally within this section, it is clear that the technology base of the Japanese is being used to drive and change the American operation. Whilst not a direct copy from the Japanese stores in equipment and software terms, the basic approach is identical and the technology platform in the United States should increasingly resemble that of Japan.

The operations themselves are being transformed by the Japanese. The reasons for the take-over, however, are not totally clear. On the one hand, there was obvious concern in Japan at the financial predicament of The Southland Corporation and the danger this might represent to Seven–Eleven Japan Co. Ltd and Ito-Yokado. A take-over of, or bankruptcy for The Southland Corporation could have been a threat to the continuance of the 7–Eleven name in Japan, although steps had been taken to protect this. At one level therefore the take-over is a defensive reaction. On the other hand, the Japanese have been so successful with the format that there must also be some attraction to the opportunity that 7–Eleven in the United States represents. With limited (but essential) experience via the Hawaii 7–Eleven store purchase, Ito-Yokado must have felt that the potential financial benefits were immense. Again, competition in the home market seems a subsidiary factor. There may also have been a residual feeling of repaying the Americans for their 'modernisation' campaign. The thought of baling out the original franchisors and helping to modernise American retailing may have been too strong to resist - a colloquial 'one over' or reciprocal move!

The final component of the framework is that of the internationalisation of management ideas. The basic convenience store concept has high transferability, but the new Japanese approach remains unproven in the United States, although the initial results are highly encouraging. The expertise transferred has been both operational and personnel, with the personnel transfer being bi-directional and involving visits to Japan by key managers and personnel as well as Japanese management of The Southland Corporation. This is a fundamental component of the transfer together with the obvious financial element via the equity stake.

This review of the case utilising this internationalisation framework demonstrates a much more complex and broad pattern in the second component under study ie the Japanese take-over of The Southland Corporation. It appears to contain more elements, operates at a greater variety of spatial scales and is a more fundamental process than the initial franchising. The take-over does not fit easily with the more simplistic of the conceptualisations of retail internationalisation outlined at the start of the paper. Some of the reasons behind this complexity can now be explored.

First, the different modes of entry may have some effect on the depth of the internationalisation. Franchise agreements are a method of rapid entry at relatively low risk because the majority of the effort is with the franchisee. Whilst the franchise relationship can vary in its depth, as can equity involvement, it is probably true that the equity stake, particularly in the circumstances outlined here, condition a rather more extensive involvement in many aspects of the internationalisation process. To some extent therefore the differences identified are due to the method of entry adopted.

Secondly, there is a question over the timing. The early 1970s were a period of considerable international expansion in retailing, but with hindsight, the level, type and direction of this activity are somewhat less than the current internationalisation [e.g., Burt, 1993; Davies, 1993]. As the world has become more integrated and information driven, so linkages have increased in quantity and quality, building on the initial steps. Whilst not an inevitable outcome, we should not be surprised if the later steps in internationalisation, by companies already involved in the process, are somewhat broader than previous steps. To some extent this is also true of The Southland Corporation, who use equity involvement as well as franchise agreements in their later area licenses (Table 4). However, the deeper nature of the Japanese involvement is not replicated by The Southland Corporation.

This then raises the question as to whether the differences are inherent to the country of origin. It could be argued for example that the more 'hands off' business format franchising is classically American in its operation whereas the deep involvement is characteristic of the relationship-development societal approach of the Japanese. In other words, are there business and cultural specificities to retail internationalisation? Certainly

Davies [1995] has argued extensively and persuasively that our conceptualisations of retail internationalisation have to be adapted for the cultural and societal (governmental) situations in the Asia–Pacific region. It has to be true that the business situation in Japan has conditioned the focus of market entry, whereas the American market is rather more open to external equity investment and operations.

Finally, there is the associated question of the cultural situation within the company. The approaches by The Southland Corporation and Ito-Yokado (and Seven–Eleven Japan) can be seen to be fundamentally different. Whilst both use franchises in their operations, the level of advice (control) exercised through the franchise agreement are vastly divergent. The central advice and control culture in Ito-Yokado allied to the relationship ethos is unlike the hands-off approach by The Southland Corporation. Again, it could be argued that these company cultures condition the depth of involvement in internationalisation in its broadest sense.

CONCLUSIONS

The review of the case presented here has attempted to outline the various degrees of retail internationalisation that need to be considered. We can now review these ideas in the light of the earlier questioning of our conceptualisations.

A number of commentators have questioned the way in which retail internationalisation has been studied and understood. In general they point to conceptualisations that misunderstand the nature and breadth of retail internationalisation. This study has attempted to investigate this topic via a case study of the internationalisation process between two companies, The Southland Corporation and Ito-Yokado. From the details of the case we can make perhaps three main conclusions about the nature of retail internationalisation.

First, the case study has emphasised the potential of the topic. The breadth of involvement in the internationalisation by Ito-Yokado reflects their business style and concerns. Commentators have to take cognisance of these detailed company-based issues. Retail internationalisation is not simply a matter of store openings, but is far deeper and more broad than this. In committed operators, internationalisation opens up a very wide set of business possibilities. Secondly, these possibilities can only be realised through a long-term involvement in the market. Internationalisation, to be successful, is a long-run operation. This does mean however that the study of retail internationalisation has also to be long-term and has to involve the study of all the aspects of the topic. Thirdly, the long-term nature of the process is an encouragement to inter-dependencies amongst those involved. The implantation of a retail format or company into a country as a form of colonial occupation without building long-term relationships or 'grounding' the operation, is likely to have only limited or short-term success. The most successful form of retail internationalisation, it could be argued, is that which builds broader relationships and attempts to provide a deepening of the aspects of internationalisation. In such cases there are mutual benefits that can be derived and indeed the process of retail internationalisation may be more to do with reciprocity than market entry. Long-term this reciprocity is the 'glue' for global linkages, networks and relationships.

In terms of our understanding of retail internationalisation, therefore, it is hoped that this case has shown the potential for further work in enhancing and extending our understanding. It is argued that the best way to achieve this understanding is through long-term and detailed work in, and with, companies inherently involved in the processes.

ACKNOWLEDGEMENTS

The author acknowledges gratefully the patience, courtesy and helpfulness of Mr Sekine of Ito-Yokado and Seven–Eleven Japan and Mr Keyes of The Southland Corporation and the assistance of and discussions with various of their colleagues, during visits to Tokyo and Dallas. Comments on an earlier draft of this paper by Drs Burt, Davies and Larke were particularly useful. Dr Roy Larke provided hospitality, photocopies and interpretation during visits and interviews in Japan and subsequently, without which this work would have been immeasurably more difficult to complete. Ms Seiko Sakata has provided valuable translations and summaries of much Japanese literature. All this assistance has been much appreciated. As ever the resultant paper reflects the author's views alone.

REFERENCES

Aharoni, Y., 1966, *The Foreign Investment Decision Process*, Boston: Harvard University Press.
Alexander, N., 1990, 'Retailers and International Markets: motives for expansion', *International Marketing Review*, Vol.7, No.4, pp.75–85.
Bernstein, J., 1994, Convenience Store Retailing in Two Countries: Southland and Seven–Eleven Japan, *Harvard Business School Case N9–794–121*. Boston: Harvard Business School Publishing.
Boddewyn, J.J., M.B. Habrich, and A.C. Perry, 1986, 'Service Multinationals: Conceptualisation, Measures and Theory', *Journal of International Business Studies*, Vol.17, pp.41–58.
Brahm, R., 1993, 'Globalisation and Strategy Content Research: Critical Reflections and New Directions', in Shrivastava, P., Huff, A. and J. Dutton (eds.), *Advances in Strategic Management*, London: JAI Press, pp.3–21.
Brown, S., and S.L. Burt (eds.), 1992, Special Issue on Retail Marketing: International Perspectives, *European Journal of Marketing*, Vol.26, No.8/9, pp.1–84.
Buckley, P.J., 1983, 'New Theories of International Business', in M. Casson (ed.), *The Growth of International Business*, London: Allen and Unwin.
Burt, S.L., 1993, 'Temporal Trends in the Internationalisation of British Retailing', *International Review of Retail, Distribution and Consumer Research*, Vol.3, pp.391–410.
Cavusgil, S.T., 1980, 'On the Internationalisation Process of Firms', *European Research*,

November, pp.273–81.

Chain Store Age Executive, 1992, 'Ito-Yokado Rolls a 7–Eleven', *Chain Store Age Executive*, January, pp.33–48.

Convenience Stores Report, 1994, *Annual Survey* (in Japanese).

Crum, M.C. and D.M. Meerschwam, 1986, 'From Relationship to Price Banking: The Loss of Regulatory Control', Ch.8 in T.K. McCraw (ed.), *America Versus Japan*, Boston: Harvard Business School Press.

Cunningham, M.T., and K. Culligan, 1991, 'Competitiveness through Networks of Relationships in Information Technology Markets', in S.J. Paliwoda (ed.), *New Perspectives on International Marketing*, London: Routledge.

Czinkota, M.R., 1982, *Export Development Strategies: US Promotion Policies*, New York: Praeger.

Czinkota, M.R. and M. Kotabe (eds.), 1993, *The Japanese Distribution System*, Chicago: Probus.

Davies, B.K., 1993, 'Trade Barriers in East and South East Asia: The Implications for Retailers', *International Review of Retail, Distribution and Consumer Research*, Vol.3, pp.345–65.

Davies, B.K., 1995, 'The Regulation of Retail Internationalisation: Examples from the Pacific–Asia Region', in P. McGoldrick and G. Davies (eds.), *International Retailing:Trends and Strategies*, London: Pitman.

Davies, B.K. and F. Fergusson, 1994, 'Networks, Value Chains and Retailer Internationalisation in Pacific–Asia', Paper prepared for AMA/KMA Conference, Seoul, Korea, May 1995.

Dawson, J.A., 1993, 'The Internationalisation of Retailing', in R.D.F. Bromley and C.J. Thomas (eds.), *Retail Change: Contemporary Issues*, London: UCL Press.

Dawson, J.A., 1994, 'Internationalisation of Retailing Operations', *Journal of Marketing Management*, Vol.10, pp.267–82.

Dicken, P. and N. Thrift, 1992, 'The Organisation of Production and the Production of Organisation: why business enterprises matter in the study of geographical industrialisation', *Transactions of the Institute of British Geographers*, Vol.17, pp.279–91.

Dunning, J.H., 1981, *International Production and Multinational Enterprise*, London: Allen and Unwin.

Dunning, J.H., 1988, 'The Eclectic Paradigm of International Production: a restatement and some possible extensions', *Journal of International Business Studies*, Vol.19, pp.1–31.

Dunning, J.H., 1993, *The Globalisation of Business*. Routledge: London.

Eroglu, S., 1992, 'The Internationalisation Process of Franchise Systems: A Conceptual Model', *International Marketing Review*, Vol.9, No.5, pp.19–30.

Etzel, M.J. and B.J., Walker, 1973, 'The Internationalisation of US Franchise Systems', *Journal of Marketing*, April, pp.38–46.

Goldman, A., 1991, 'Japan's Distribution System: institutional structure, internal political economy and modernisation', *Journal of Retailing*, Vol.67, pp.154–83.

Goldman, A., 1992, 'Evaluating the Performance of the Japanese Distribution System', *Journal of Retailing*, Vol.68, pp.11–39.

Hakansson, H. (ed.), 1982, *International Marketing and Purchasing of Industrial Goods, An Interaction Approach*, Chichester: John Wiley.

Hallsworth, A.G., 1991, 'The Campeau take-overs: the arbitrage economy in action', *Environment and Planning A*, Vol.23, pp.1217–24.

Hallsworth, A.G., 1992, *The New Geography of Consumer Spending*, London: Belhaven.

Hennart, J.F., 1991, 'The Transaction Cost Theory of the Multinational Enterprise', in C.N. Pitelis and R. Sugden (eds.), *The Nature of the Transnational Firm*, London: Routledge.

Ho, S-C. and Y-M. Sin, 1987, 'International Transfer of Retail Technology: the successful case of convenience stores in Hong Kong', *International Journal of Retailing*, Vol.2, No.3, pp.36–48.

Hoffman, R.C. and J.F. Preble, 1991, 'Franchising: selecting a strategy for rapid growth, *Long Range Planning*, Vol.24, No.4, pp.74–85.

Ito-Yokado, 1980–1994, *Annual Reports*, Tokyo: Ito-Yokado.

Iwabuchi, A., 1993, *Seven–Eleven: towards the next generation*, Tokyo: OS Inc (in Japanese).

Johanson, J. and L.G. Mattson, 1987, 'Internationalisation in Industrial Systems – a network approach', in N. Hood and J.E. Vahlne (eds.), *Strategies in Global Competition*, London: Routledge.

Johanson, J. and L.G. Mattson, 1991, 'Strategic Adaptation of Firms to the European Single Market', in L.G. Mattson and B. Stymme (eds.), *Corporate and Industry Strategies for Europe*, Amsterdam: North Holland.

Johanson, J. and J.E. Vahlne, 1977, 'The Internationalisation Process of the Firm: a model of knowledge development and increasing foreign market commitments', *Journal of International Business Studies.*, Vol.8, No.1, pp.23–32.

Kacker, M., 1985, *Transatlantic Trends in Retailing: Take-overs and Flow of Know-How*, London: Quorum.

Kaletsky, A., 1990, 'Japan Devours an American Totem', *Financial Times*, 27 March .

Kay, N.M., 1991, 'Multinational Enterprise as Strategic Choice: Some Transaction Cost Perspectives', in C.N. Pitelis and R. Sugden, *The Nature of Transnational Firm*, London: Routledge.

Khalili, S., 1991, 'Shop America Feud: Mail-Order Bust', *International Business*, Vol.4, No.5, pp.46–9.

Kunitomo, R., 1987, *Seven–Eleven: Surprising Profit System*, Tokyo: Paru (in Japanese).

Kunitomo, R., 1993, *The Information Reform of Seven–Eleven*, Tokyo: Paru (in Japanese).

Larke, R., 1994, *Japanese Retailing*, London: Routledge.

Laulajainen, R., 1987, *Spatial Strategies in Retailing*, Dordrecht: D Reidel.

Lewison, D.M. and J.M. Hawes, 1989, 'Southland Corporation – 7–Eleven Stores', Case 29, pp.229–244 of D.M. Lewison and J.M. Hawes (eds.), *Cases in Retail Management*, Columbus: Merrill.

Liles, A., 1977, *Oh Thank Heaven! The Story of The Southland Corporation*, Dallas: The Southland Corporation.

Magowan, P.A., 1989, 'The Case for LBOs: The Safeway Experience', *California Management Review*, Vol.32, pp.9–18.

Morgan, J.C. and J.T. Morgan, 1991, *Cracking The Japanese Market*, New York: Free Press.

Ogata, T., 1991, *Seven–Eleven/Ito-Yokado: the revolution of distribution information*, Tokyo: TBS Bulitanica (in Japanese).

Ohmae, K., 1990, *The Borderless World*, London: Collins.

Pellegrini, L., 1994, 'Alternatives for Growth and Internationalisation in Retailing', *International Review of Retail, Distribution and Consumer Research*, Vol.4, pp.121–48.

Porter, M.E., 1985, *Competitive Advantage*, New York: The Free Press.

Securities and Exchange Commission, 1994, *The Southland Corporation: Form 10–K*, Washington: SEC.

Southland Corporation, 1979–1993, *Annual Reports* (including Form 10–K), Dallas: The Southland Corporation.

Sparks, L., 1994, 'Seven–Eleven Japan Co. Ltd: from licensee to owner in eighteen years', Case 29, pp.336–52 of P. McGoldrick (ed.), *Cases in Retail Management*, London: Pitman.

Suzuki, T., 1991, 'The Quest to Rebuild Seven–Eleven Founder Southland', *Tokyo Business Today*, September, pp.44–5.

Tanzer, A., 1986, 'A Form of Flattery', *Forbes*, 2 June, pp.110–16.

Treadgold, A. and R.L. Davies, 1988, *The Internationalisation of Retailing*, Harlow: Longman.

Turnbull, P.W. 1987, 'A Challenge to the Stages Theory of the Internationalisation Process', in P.J. Rosson and S.D. Reid (eds.), *Managing Export Entry and Expansion: Concepts and Practice*, London: Praeger.

Uno, M.S., S. Ichikawa and M. Katayama, 1988, *The Distribution Business Sector*, Japan: Kyoikusha Shinkon (in Japanese).

Wilkins, M., 1974, *The Maturing of Multinational Enterprise*, Boston: Harvard University Press.

Williams, D.E., 1992, 'Retailer Internationalisation: An Empirical Enquiry', *European Journal of Marketing*, Vol.26, No.8/9, pp.8–24.

The International Activities of Japanese Retailers

KERI DAVIES and FERGUS FERGUSSON

Despite the upsurge of academic and commercial interest in the changes taking place in the retail sector within Japan, little has been published on the international activities of Japanese retailers. This paper illustrates the range and scale of activities which have been undertaken by such companies. While Europe and America were favourite destinations up until the mid-1980s, most Japanese retailers have now refocused their expansion plans on Asia as the level of consumers' disposable income has risen and trade barriers have been lowered. At the same time, the early entrants into international markets, the development stores, have been joined by companies operating supermarkets, convenience stores, clothing stores, electrical outlets and so on. The paper considers the nature of these changes and the factors which have driven them.

INTRODUCTION

There is now a very large literature on the Japanese distribution system [see, for example, Flath, 1989; Czinkota and Woronoff, 1991; Dodwell, 1991; Goldman, 1991 and 1992; Czinkota and Kotabe, 1993; Nishimura, 1993; Anwar and Taku, 1993; and Larke, 1994]. Some of this literature has looked at the problems facing foreign retailers and marketers hoping to gain access to the Japanese market [Batzer and Laumer, 1989; Itoh, 1991 and Miyagiwa, 1993] and at the changing levels of efficiency in Japanese distribution.

There has been much less interest in the expansion of Japanese retailers overseas, however. Malayang [1988] provides a brief overview of the presence of Japanese retailers in the countries of Pacific Asia. Johansson [1990] looked at the overseas potential of the Japanese service industries in total and Davies and Jones [1993] noted the activities of the Japanese department store groups. Apart from these, the literature is restricted to asides during country profiles [for example, Davies, 1994a] or the reporting of individual activities in the trade and business press [for example, Anon,

1991; Dobrzynski, 1993]. Such reports tend to focus on the larger companies, particularly the department store groups, and far less is known about the growth in the number of Japanese convenience store, supermarket, clothing and electrical goods chains overseas or in the non–store activities of Japanese retailers.

This paper will look, first, at the context of the existing literature on retail internationalisation. Secondly, a database of the activities undertaken by Japanese retailers will be presented and then, finally, the underlying motives for the trends shown will be analysed.

EXISTING FRAMEWORKS FOR TESTING RETAIL INTERNATIONALISATION

Most of the theoretical issues relating to retail internationalisation have emerged after renewed interest in recent years in the international activities of European and American retailers. There are several competing models that have been put forward as explaining retail expansion beyond national boundaries, most of which have emerged from the literature on international business. We will now look at each of these proposed frameworks in turn.

'Push' and 'Pull' Factors

'Push' and 'pull' factors refer to those fundamental factors stimulating retail expansion beyond national boundaries. Notable research includes that of Kacker [1985], Treadgold and Davies [1988], Alexander [1990], Laulajainen [1991], and Williams [1992]. Factors range from being 'reactive' to 'proactive' depending upon the internal and external factors influencing given retail organizations.

'Stages' Theories

Expansion across national boundaries is an inherently risky business and companies can be expected to attempt to reduce or control the degree of risk to which they are exposed. From a review of the literature, Burt [1993] identified a number of factors which might be expected to affect the type and rate of international activity undertaken by retailers. Geographical and cultural (psychic) distance were believed to be closely related to perceptions of risk, as well as the effect of the nature of the business on the strategy adopted.

Any temporal trends in international activity should then find some consideration in factors relating to changing environmental conditions, which would influence motives and patterns of investment; the choice of geographical markets and entry mechanism which will affect risk perceptions; and the nature of the business which will itself influence the strategic approach to market choice and entry. The pattern to be expected would initially be tentative (risk reducing) steps in terms of entry mechanisms and choice of markets for certain companies, whilst for others the characteristics of the retail business may allow a more risky approach to markets even in the early stages. For both types of company as the experience curve is climbed 'riskier' choices (in terms of geographical and psychic distance and entry mechanism) will be made.[Burt, 1993]

'Stages' theories, most notably characterized by the Uppsala Model [Johanson and Wiedersheim-Paul, 1975; Johanson and Vahlne, 1977; 1990], and the Innovation-Related Models theorists [Bilkey and Tesar, 1978; Cavusgil, 1980] have characterized the internationalization process by a behavioural approach, where internationalisation is a gradual process, dependent upon incremental gains in international experience and increasing resource commitment to foreign markets, not deliberate strategic choices. The stages theories have been criticized over their applicability to retailing, not least because they are based largely on the findings of two empirical studies [Turnbull, 1987]. In particular, Dawson [1993: 28] believes their direct application to retailing is fraught with problems:

The balance between centralized and decentralized decision-making, the relative importance of organization and establishment scale economies, the degree of spatial dispersion in the multi-establishment enterprise, the relative size of establishment to the size of the firm, the relative exit costs if decisions are reversed, the speed with which an income stream can be generated after an investment decision has been made, different cash flow characteristics, the relative value of stock and hence importance of sourcing; all these items, and others, serve to differentiate the manufacturing firm and the retail firm not least in respect of the internationalization process.

In other words, where a manufacturing company may proceed cautiously through stages to test the market, many services require foreign direct investment or alternative non-equity forms of participation from the very beginning, when part of the production–delivery–use chain must be performed abroad [Boddewyn et al., 1986: 43]. Indeed, a retailer may have to open stores immediately, although in the knowledge that withdrawal from the market is relatively risk free.

The Eclectic Paradigm

More recent attention has been concentrated on the eclectic paradigm of internationalization [Dunning, 1993]. The paradigm endeavours to explain the extent, form, and pattern of international production relying on three distinct sets of advantages, namely Ownership specific (or competitive advantage) factors, Internalization advantages, and Location bound and market advantages (OLI advantages). Whilst Boddewyn *et al.* [1986] and Segal Horn [1993], amongst others, argue that service industries have reached a stage where the eclectic paradigm and manufacturing based theories can be applied to their internationalization with little amendment, this is not generally accepted as yet.

One of the main difficulties in the application of the paradigm has been its focus on industry or sector advantage, rather than on the individual firm. In an effort to fill this gap, both Porter [1990] and Dunning [1993] have tried to link the national factors, which provide the context and help to determine which firms will move, with the value chain which helps to determine the form which those moves will take for an individual organization.

The Value Chain

The value chain is probably best described as a means of achieving competitive advantage via a strategy of 'differentiation', where differentiation is likely to be associated with strong marketing abilities, creative flair and a good reputation for quality and/or innovation [McGoldrick, 1990: 98]. The core of the chain is a transactionally linked sequence of functions, each stage of which is presumed to 'add value', hence the notion of the value chain [Porter, 1985]. By examining each of the stages in the chain and their interrelationships, companies may be able to find ways to cut costs or to exploit existing comparative and competitive advantages. A number of authors have applied the concept to retailing, rather than allowing it to be confined to manufacturing [see, for example, McGee, 1987]. Dawson [1993] has stressed the importance of sourcing and buying networks in an international context, both as a means of controlling the cost structure within the value chain and as a means of differentiating the output from the chain.

Dicken and Thrift [1992], drawing on the work of authors such as Johanson and Mattsson [1987], have argued that studies should consider more than just the regulation of the value chain through the transactional costs of exchange between each element. In addition, recognition must be accorded to the complex and dynamic sets of networks of interrelationships between firms which have differing degrees of power and influence. For example, Davies [1993] stressed the influence of supranational organisations such as GATT or the SII negotiations on retail internationalization in Pacific Asia.

Networking

This leads us to the work of Hakansson and the IMP group [1982] which stressed the role of networks of relationships in business. In the retail field this is seen in the increasing importance attached to the development of international buying networks and international sourcing [Burt, 1993]. Thus we can see that the ability to create and maintain networks of business relationships can significantly enhance the competitive ability of the organization. Cunningham and Culligan [1991: 252] state that:
Networking is taken to be the composite of two abilities:

(1) the ability to create a net of relationships with the potential or cohesive and mutually complementary action;
(2) the ability to harness the synergistic potential of that net in pursuit of a competitive goal.

However, Brahm [1993] considers that traditional strategy content theories do not adequately explain contemporary global competition, primarily because of their parochial origins. He argued that it is necessary to go beyond analysis of network operating flexibility and develop theories that account for how differences between national institutional environments affect firms operating within global markets, regardless of how fully developed those firms are as multinational enterprises [Brahm, 1993:10]. According to Brahm the development of strategic networks is not only proceeding apace but so is the complexity of the links within those networks.

> The use of interorganizational collaboration, or strategic alliances, as a means of competition has become ubiquitous within industries, across vertical and complementary industry segments, and across national boundaries. Cross-licensing, joint marketing agreements, joint ventures, R&D consortia, minority equity networks, value-added partnerships, and so forth are all collaborative mechanisms that are widely employed in today's global industries. Moreover, firms frequently use many of these mechanisms simultaneously. [Brahm, 1993:12]

Efforts to draw together these varying frameworks to create a polyparadigmatic model of retail internationalisation are described elsewhere [Davies and Fergusson, 1994]. The aim of this brief summary of some of the approaches suggested has been to show the variety of factors which are now believed to be important in internationalisation. We will now turn to look at the type of activities with which Japanese retailers have been involved. In order to gain further insight into these activities, we will then break these down to look at both store and non-store activities, the changing nature of their value chains, and the networking activities which have been undertaken by Japanese retailers.

A DATABASE OF INTERNATIONAL ACTIVITIES BY JAPANESE RETAILERS

As a first stage in this study, a database of international activities by Japanese retailers has been produced. The database has been constructed from a range of sources including company reports, academic articles, reports published by market research companies and other commercial organisations, and continual monitoring of the retail trade press and composite newsletters. (The material is taken almost wholly from English–language sources; efforts are in hand to tap into the Japanese language literature.) Items involving internationalisation were recorded providing the following details:

* date of activity;
* company and product sector involved;
* country of origin and country of destination;
* the nature of the activity designated as one of the following categories:
  · acquisition;
  · internal growth (store openings and concessions);
  · joint ventures;
  · franchises;
  · representative offices;
  · management agreements.

On this basis over 1,000 actions by retailers have been identified involving either origins or destinations within the Asian region in the period 1958–95.[1] Given the focus of this study, only the entry points and methods of Japanese retailers moving into overseas markets have been extracted for examination here. Also, the database has been culled for only the first entry into a market by those retailers; no account has been taken of the relative sizes of any of those actions, nor of the subsequent scale of the overseas operations, nor, finally, of the subsequent fate of an operation. (See Burt [1993] for further discussion of the advantages and drawbacks of this approach.) The net outcome is that 271 activities involving Japanese retailers could be identified; overseas activities in distribution channels by Japanese manufacturers, such as Sony and Hitachi, have not been included, nor have the numerous joint ventures which Japanese retailers have entered into with overseas companies but which are targeted at the Japanese market itself.

Within this sample of 271 activities, 180 could be dated to a particular year, whilst the remaining 91 could be dated by decade only. Of these, 140 related to store-based openings, 27 to Representative Offices or sourcing arrangements, and 13 to flows of expertise and management agreements. When plotted by year over the period 1958–95, the annually dated records reveal a small peak in the early 1970s, followed by a lull in activity (excepting 1979) and then a resurgence from the mid-1980s (Figure 1). Some caution must be exercised when looking at this pattern because of the underlying nature of the database sources. This remains a sample of all the activities undertaken and, as such, is reliant on the accuracy of the sources used. The use of primarily English language sources was noted above. The general coverage of the Japanese retail scene in both European and American journals increased markedly from the mid-1980s, providing more opportunities for the reporting of international activities. Also, a number of regional information sources, such as Asian Retailer and Retail Asia, did not start publication until the early 1990s. So, we would expect a slight bias towards the reporting of store–based activities and towards the 1980s and 1990s.

FIGURE 1

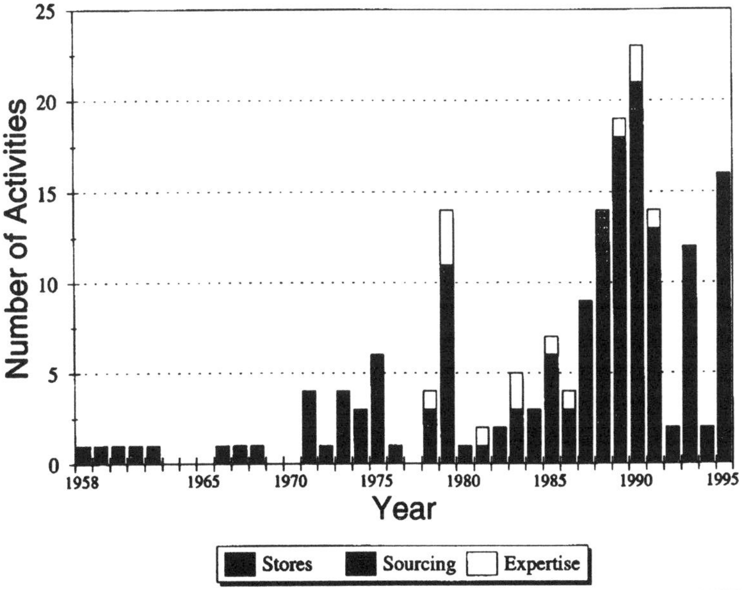

Part of this problem can be overcome by including those activities which could only be dated by decade. Table 1 suggests that there were considerably more non–store activities in the fields of sourcing and flows of expertise than are shown in Figure 1. The forms of these activities and the reasons behind them will be discussed below. Whilst much of the early activity was directed at Europe and the United States (Table 2), Asia became far more important in the 1980s and this trend has continued into the 1990s. Indeed, some companies such as Mitsukoshi began to close down some of their more peripheral trading operations in the United States and in countries such as Austria in the early 1990s. Finally, department stores dominate the activity to date (Table 3) but increasingly other sectors such as general merchandisers (GMS), supermarkets, convenience stores (CVS) and clothing companies are going overseas. As we shall see, the scale of these operations and the markets at which they are aimed mean that the influence of these chains is likely to be much greater in their host markets than that which has been exerted by the department stores in the past [Davies, 1994a].

In terms of entry mechanisms, acquisitions have been almost non-existent (in terms of numbers, although they are fairly important in terms of scale or monetary value) and, true to their methods of operating at home, Japanese retailers have made great use of joint ventures. franchises, representative offices and management agreements.

Acquisitions

Acquisitions took place in two markets only: the United States of America and the United Kingdom. This would appear to relate to the prevailing investment culture and the state of the capital markets in those two countries. Acquisition was founded on the purchase of retail property, in a few cases only, and, more importantly, on the purchase of retail brands which could be exploited in Japan initially and then, if successful, throughout Asia. Foremost amongst these in the United States were Ito-Yokado's acquisition of 7–Eleven (Hawaii) (followed by its take-over of The Southland Corporation) and the acquisition of Gump's by Tobu, whilst in the United Kingdom we saw the take-overs of Aquascutum by Renown, Daks Simpson by Sanyo Seiko and the stake which Aeon-Jusco took in Laura Ashley. The pattern is very different, therefore, to the use of acquisitions by British retailers to gain a foothold in an overseas market [Burt, 1993].

Joint Ventures

Joint ventures have been the most popular means of establishing stores in

TABLE 1
INTERNATIONAL ACTIVITY BY ENTRY MECHANISM, 1958–95

Decade	Stores	Sourcing	Management Agreements	Total
1950s	2			2
1960s	4	3		7
1970s	23	19	5	47
1980s	70	57	17	144
1990s	64	4	3	71
Total	163	83	25	271

TABLE 2
DESTINATION OF INVESTMENT BY DECADE, 1958–95

Decade	Australia	East Asia	South-East Asia	Americas	Europe	Total
1950s				2		2
1960s		2	3	1	1	7
1970s		11	5	14	17	47
1980s	2	58	40	19	25	144
1990s	3	24	18	8	18	71
Total	5	95	66	44	61	271

KEY
East Asia: People's Republic of China, Republic of China, Republic of Korea, USSR and Vietnam
South-East Asia: Brunei, Hong Kong, Indonesia, Macau, Malaysia, Philippines, Singapore and Thailand
Americas: USA, Brazil, Canada, Costa Rica, Dominican Republic and Puerto Rico
Europe: Austria, France, Germany, Italy, Spain and UK.

international markets. Some of these have been joint ventures with other retailers who can provide market knowledge and distribution networks. The establishment of the joint venture between the Saison Group and Liberty's to bring Muji to the United Kingdom market is a case in point here. Joint ventures between retailers and landowners or property developers have been as common. Many of the department store operations in Hong Kong and Singapore were developed in this manner [Davies, 1994a]. However, these sorts of joint venture are ones which have, in large part, been entered

TABLE 3
PRODUCT SECTOR ACTIVITY BY DECADE, 1958–1995

Decade	Department Stores	GMS/ Supermarkets	CVS	Clothing	Electrical	Books	Other	Total
1950s	2							2
1960s	7							7
1970s	31	14					2	47
1980s	52	51	6	18	6	6	5	144
1990s	25	15	3	21	2	1	4	71
Total	117	80	9	39	8	7	11	271

into freely. The popularity of joint ventures can also be explained by the barriers to trade put up by many governments, forcing minority equity participation for foreign companies or joint control over an enterprise, as in Malaysia, the Republic of Korea and the People's Republic of China [Davies, 1993; 1994c].

Franchising and Licensing

Franchising has not been a popular mechanism. Instead of using franchises to circumvent the rules on foreign investment, some companies have become involved in licensing agreements, such as the ventures by Sogo and Yaohan in Indonesia. Here, the retail name and concept have been licensed to a local company and the Japanese retailer is supposed to provide technical advice only to a local manager. If the Indonesian market is deregulated, then it is likely that these stores will be bought back by the Japanese companies involved [Mulchand, 1992].

One area which has been picked up only haphazardly in the search of the English language literature is the number of specialist Japanese retailers which have gone overseas in tandem with larger retailers. Companies such as Taka-Q, Suzuya and Best Denki often operate shops-within-shops and these have been fairly common because of the Japanese department stores' habit of renting out some of their floorspace to such concessions. The size of this group and its effect on the perceived risk of both the host retail group and the concession holder to international activity is difficult to judge.

Representative Offices

Representative offices (ROs) are purchasing offices established by Japanese retailers as a means of sourcing products and learning more about foreign markets. They are most common among the department store and general merchandise store groups. In most instances, an RO is followed by store development, although the time lag can be considerable, varying from just six months to over a decade. Davies and Jones [1993] note that, whilst ROs appear first in many of the markets targeted by retailers, they are more widespread than most store networks. For example, many department store groups established ROs in China immediately following the announcement of *The Four Modernisations* Programme in 1978, but stores only began to be opened in the early 1990s in line with further opening up of the market [Davies, 1994c].

Management Agreements

These are trading agreements between companies in which, in these instances, Japanese retailers are transferring their expertise abroad. They may range from efforts to organise international buying groups, as with the establishment of the Asian Retailers Affiliation Network (ARAN) by the Saison Group, through to loose affiliations between two large groups, such as that between Daiei and some of the large department stores in the People's Republic of China. In some instances the Japanese retailer is helping its partners to develop and modernise; in others, the foreign partners have helped to source products for the Japanese market.

This, then, is a brief overview of the patterns revealed by the analysis of the database of activities. In order to be able to probe more deeply into the motives behind some of the moves which have taken place, further analysis has been based around the frameworks outlined above. It is broken down therefore between what we have called store-based moves (active retail involvement in a foreign market), sourcing agreement and the reorientation of retailer value chains, and the transfer of expertise to foreign retailers.

STORE-BASED ACTIVITY

Push–pull factors

There have been a number of push–pull factors which have affected where Japanese retailers have chosen to open stores, namely, economic trends, legislation affecting the retail sector at home and abroad, and the presence of large numbers of Japanese tourists or ethnic Japanese within host markets.

Economic Trends. The trends in store-based investment (see Figure 1) can be related in part to the general level of confidence in the Japanese and international economies. The pattern is similar to that shown by British companies in Burt's study, although the levels of activity are much lower for the Japanese companies [Burt, 1993]. The decline in investment in the mid-1970s in both cases is probably related to the after-effects of the 1973 oil crisis and the subsequent world recession. The 1980s saw a substantial growth in investment, fuelled by general economic confidence and a booming global economy, linked in Japan with the general strength of the yen (the period of *endaka*). Many Japanese retailers were awash with funds. At the same time, the emergence of significant consumer markets in many Asian countries presented opportunities for re-investing this cash and a means of tapping into new growth.

The slowdown in investment in some sectors in the early 1990s, on the other hand, reflects the general malaise of the Japanese retail sector at home. Retail sales slumped, particularly for the department store sector, and companies had to fight the growing number of discount chains. Sogo, for example, was badly affected by the property crash because its store expansion programme in the late 1980s and early 1990s was based on the sale and leaseback of its stores once the buildings had been completed [Friedland, 1993].

Economic slowdown in the target markets of Europe and in the United States has not helped either, and the effect has reached even well-established companies. For example, Takashimaya's new store in New York, opened in April 1993, has an art gallery on the first two floors to attract customers who may then buy expensive Japanese art and craft products on the other three floors. Since the building was first planned in 1988 the art market has crashed; it now seems unlikely that Takashimaya will meet their profit forecasts in their first few years of operation [Dobrzynski, 1993].

However, whilst falling sales at home have affected the department store sector in particular, the effect on the general merchandisers, supermarkets and convenience stores has been less marked. The Japanese Large Store Law restricted the development of the former at home [Larke, 1994] and they have also been keen to be first movers into many of the Asian markets. For example, whilst the department stores have continued with their plans for a small number of stores in China, concentrating on Beijing and Shanghai, the supermarket chains have very ambitious plans for that country. Between them, Daiei, Yaohan, Nichii and Jusco have announced plans for the development of close on two thousand stores by the early years of the next century [Davies, 1994c]. Whereas the department stores generally have a limited effect on the overall retail sectors of the markets they enter, these plans, if fulfilled, are likely to revolutionise the distribution systems in countries such as the People's Republic of China. It is also likely that with such significant proportions of their operations overseas, they will have a large effect on the ways in which these retailers do business at home too.

Legislation. Legislation has been a major issue affecting the location decisions of Japanese retailers. Davies [1995] distinguishes between state–state interactions and firm–state interactions in this context [see also, Dicken, 1994]. State–state interactions have included the multilateral GATT negotiations and the bilateral Structural Impediments Initiative involving Japan and the United States [Brooks, 1993]. These have set a general tone aimed at the liberalisation of regimes and the opening up of markets, including retailing, to foreign investment.

Firm–state interactions include measures designed to prevent foreign retailers from controlling domestic markets [Davies, 1993] and those aimed primarily at the domestic market, but which will apply also to foreign firms. Trade barriers of the former type have affected the means of entry used by

Japanese retailers and they have also controlled the time of entry into some markets. The lifting or partial removal of barriers in some countries was also responsible for some of the more notable peaks in the trend shown in Figure 1. The relaxation of controls in the People's Republic of China (1979 and 1991), the Republic of China (1985) and the Republic of Korea (1990) produced sudden increases in the number of activities in those years. Legislation of the latter type includes the Large Store Law in Japan. The application of such laws may vary through space due to the involvement of local bodies with their own aims and interpretations of national policies [Blomley, 1989; Christopherson, 1993]. Thus, the Large Store Law helped to focus the attention of many Japanese companies on foreign expansion in the late 1980s and early 1990s; the relaxation of the law due to the pressures exerted in the state–state interactions of the Structural Impediments Initiative is now likely to affect future decisions over the scale and speed of internationalisation.

Tourists and ethnic enclaves. A further factor affecting the markets entered has been that many Japanese retailers have made their first forays overseas into markets which have either an established enclave of overseas Japanese or a large number of Japanese tourists. Many of the overseas outlets of the department store groups are better described as 'boutiques' or 'gift shops' than department stores. They cater to those Japanese tourists who want to be able to buy local products for gifts quickly, in familiar surroundings, with Japanese speaking assistants and even using the Japanese yen in payment. In addition, during the era of *endaka*, with the high distribution costs of Japanese stores and the high level of government taxes, it often made sense to purchase abroad high-priced merchandise for personal consumption, particularly clothing and luggage [Davies, 1994a]. Almost all of the Japanese department store outlets in London fall into this category. A number of the outlets in Hong Kong and Singapore have been associated with hotel developments which have catered particularly to the Japanese market. Similarly, a substantial proportion of the store openings in Europe during the early 1990s were actually linked to the Barcelona Olympic Games, showing both an increased awareness about Europe in Japan and a reaction to the expected increase in Japanese tourists visiting southern Europe.

A further element is added by the existence of Japanese or East Asian enclaves in a host country. Yaohan, for example, has targeted stores at Japanese and Korean communities in the United States, Brazil, the UK and Canada, as well as the smaller number of expatriate managers in Hong Kong, Singapore, Thailand and Malaysia [Tanzer, 1988; Wada, 1992]. These groups can provide an easy base from which to build demand from the host population. Finally, attitudes towards the Japanese following their expansionist military policies in the first half of the century may also help to explain their slow progress in some Asian countries.

Sourcing and the Value Chain

Initial expansion outside Japan has come, for most companies, in the shape of ROs and buying networks. In both the United States and Europe these have been important for the sourcing of branded products back to Japan. In some instances these offices have then been linked to 'gift shops' which sell the same products to tourists who are actually visiting the source countries. The increase in ROs in the 1970s and 1980s was concentrated in Paris and Milan for the sourcing of high fashion items, whilst British and American companies were purchased for their brand names and products. Representative or liaison offices are now to be found throughout the world, including London, New York, Singapore, Shanghai and Beijing, They also act as sources of information about local markets and to act as buying points for local products [Davies, 1993].

As a second stage, efforts to control sourcing and to tailor products to home markets have led to the promotion of licensing deals, franchises and other more formal links between Asian retailers and manufacturers (and, in some sectors, other retailers). For example, Dodwell Marketing Consultants [1991] listed 112 licensing deals undertaken by major Japanese retailers, mainly for clothes (77 per cent) and all but 5 per cent of the licensers came from just four Western countries (France, United States, Italy and the UK). These deals have provided an exclusive right to the merchandise for the firms involved and the retailers have further added value through deals which allow for manufacturing to be undertaken in Asia using materials and sizing developed specifically for the Japanese market.

Finally, a third stage which has become more important during the early 1990s has been what the Japanese term *kaihatsu yunyu* or 'develop and import' [Onoki, 1992]. The most recent survey of the distribution industry by the *Nikkei Ryutsu Shinbun* (summer 1994) showed that this practice is increasing phenomenally. Basically, it involves the manufacture of products in low-cost operations (mainly in Asia) to the retailer's specifications and it is often linked to the establishment of a retailer's 'private national brand' or 'own brand'. For example, the Aeon Group used its liaison offices to develop its 'Visage' brand in electrical home appliances; the Daiei 'Savings' brand is another leading example. The main countries for this sort of sourcing have been South Korea, China, Taiwan, Hong Kong and Thailand. Because of the importance of costs in such operations, some retailers are already talking of moving their manufacturing from Taiwan or

China to Myanmar or Sri Lanka. Another way of keeping costs down has been explored by Seiyu which has established a buying network called the Asian Retail Affiliate Network (ARAN) amongst affiliates in a number of countries; Seiyu provides its expertise in setting specifications and an entry into the Japanese market, whilst the affiliates bring their knowledge and contacts in their markets.

In recent years the functions of the buying offices and retail stores have been growing closer together. Jusco's stores in Thailand and Hong Kong are explicitly involved in developing sources of supply both for their own operations and for the Japanese stores and Isetan is using its Singapore base to co-ordinate the development of goods and product exchanges throughout the Asian region.

Transfers of Expertise and Networking

Strategic networks and inter-firm ties have been a long–recognised and often studied aspect of Japanese industry. Tyrni [1994], Czinkota and Kotabe [1993] and Tselichtchev [1994] have examined their role in retailing within Japan. The establishment of 'kone' or connections in Japanese business life has always been a way for Japanese businesses to create and sustain beneficial links with business partners on both the domestic and international levels. Brahm [1993: 10], citing Japan as a developmental state considers that we have to consider three issues in the realm of international competition:

1. how does a firm's embeddedness within a societal system affect its behaviour in domestic markets?
2. how does a firms' national institutional environment affect its competitive conduct in international markets?
3. what is the relationship between corporate strategy and the evolution of the world trading system?

There is an increasing development of and growing dependence on strategic competitive networks by Japanese retailers (see also Davies [1994b] and the thesis extended by Bartu [1993]). This is shown by the establishment and increasing importance attached to the development of retail stores in East and South-East Asia and China, and the establishment of international sourcing networks and *kaihatsu yunyu* systems. Because networking is such an integral function of Japanese business operations (on an industry-wide basis), it should be considered a corporate function in the Japanese context. It could even be added to the value chain as a means of explaining the creation and sustaining of competitive advantage for Japanese retail companies.

Evidence of the growing importance Japanese retailers attach to the establishment of strategic networks can be presented by looking at their most recent efforts to achieve as much in China. Since opening its first store with a Chinese partner in Sha Tau Kok in September 1991, Yaohan International Holdings (YIH) has announced:

- A joint venture between itself, Yaohan Japan and the Shanghai No.1 Department Store to construct the first foreign run large department store to be given approval by the Chinese government since the investment rules were changed in early 1992.
- A joint venture agreement with China Venturetech International, a wholly-owned subsidiary of the Beijing-based China Venturetech Investment Corporation and the Japanese Nippon Investment and Finance Co. Ltd (the venture capital arm of Daiwa Securities Group and Niten Enterprises Ltd). The joint venture CC&Y will invest in consumer products, distribution and retail companies. The company has announced plans to open 1,000 stores in the Shanghai–Nanjing region by the year 2010.
- In March 1994 YIH entered into an agreement with Wal-Mart to participate in a broad range of operations, including retailing, wholesaling and product development. Initially, the agreement will allow Yaohan's stores to sell the products and Yaohan can also wholesale products supplied by Wal-Mart in Singapore, Hong Kong, Malaysia, Thailand, Indonesia and the Philippines via its own sales network.
- In May 1994 YIH signed a further deal with the Shanghainese municipal government to redevelop a train station into a shopping centre containing retail shops, restaurants and souvenir shops. The company also plans to put retail and food shops into seven hundred train stations in the region.
- YIH will open a large-scale computerised international distribution centre in Shanghai in 1994 (a joint venture with the Minhang Municipal Government in Shanghai) and a similar centre in Beijing in 1995.
- In addition to these retail activities, YIH has entered into joint ventures with Chinese and Japanese companies to produce paper products, shoes and clothing for sale in its stores, food processing, and an employment agency.

Similarly, Daiei is working with Japanese companies, such as Kanebo, Marubeni, Toshiba and Matsushita, in order to utilise their overseas production and purchasing facilities to enhance the products on sale in Daiei's stores in Japan. Daiei has also capitalised on its links in China, where its Chairman, Isao Nakauchi, is an economic adviser to the city of Tianjin, as it has announced plans to open over 5,000 stores in China by the end of the century. Finally, Nichii has used contacts with a former mayor of Dalian, now a vice president of CITIC, and the current mayor of Dalian, the son of a former Chinese vice premier, as a means of easing their entry into China. The announcement of their intentions to set up a wholly-owned subsidiary, rather than a joint venture, was felt to be greatly influenced by their ties with Chinese officials.

Networks and connections are not confined to developments in China however. Seiyu's expansion into Vietnam comes as part of a joint venture with Mitsubishi Corporation – a company which has considerable experience of trading there already. Equally, Seiyu has used its links with Wing On, the Hong Kong based department store company, to involve Wing On in a variety of overseas projects, including the Bugis Junction development in Singapore and the redevelopment of a department store in Tianjin, China. 7–Eleven, the Ito-Yokado subsidiary, has struck an agreement with Philip Morris, the American foods and tobacco group, to develop jointly processed foods and canned beers to be sold in its stores in both Japan and the United States. Finally, Sazanami [1993] shows that a number of Japanese wholesalers set up operations in Taiwan in the 1980s at the request of Japanese retailers, such as Family Mart, who were already operating in the country, even though many of the products which they supplied to those retailers actually originated in Taiwan. The retailers felt happiest dealing with companies with which they already had relationships.

CONCLUSION

This paper has sought to show the pattern of international activity among Japanese retailers. A database of 271 activities has been analysed and the patterns found have been looked at further in terms of a variety of the frameworks for retail internationalisation proposed in the literature. What is clear is the sheer diversity of motives for international activity and, also, the need to increase our understanding of the role of non-store activities retail internationalisation.

This has been a preliminary investigation. Further work is needed to allow us to include the scale and duration of the involvement of retailers in international markets. Whilst the current analysis has thrown up some interesting patterns, it is clear that weighting needs to be given to these factors, particularly when looking at the risks involved in such moves [Burt, 1993]. Further work is also needed to look at the patterns of internationalisation in Pacific Asia among non-Japanese retailers. This will help to determine how far some of the features of store-based activity, sourcing and networking are unique to the Japanese companies and how far they are trends common among similar companies throughout the world.

NOTE

1. Two points need to be made about these dates. First, there was a small amount of international activity by Japanese retailers in the first half of this century. For example, Yamanaka operated in New York and London in the 1930s and Matsuzakaya had a store in Shanghai between 1941 and 1945 [Hollander, 1970]. These activities were brought to an end by 1945 at the latest and are not included here. Secondly, only firm plans for 1995 have been included in the sample examined here.

REFERENCES

Alexander, N., 1990, 'Retailers and International Markets: Motives for Expansion', *International Marketing Review*, Vol.7, No.4, pp.75–85.

Anon, 1991, 'Japanese Distribution Business Advancing into Korea', *Korea Trade and Business*, July, p.38.

Anwar, S.T. and M.A. Taku, 1993, 'Productivity and Efficiency in the Japanese Distribution System', *Journal of World Trade*, Vol.25, October, pp.83–110.

Bartu, F., 1993, *The Ugly Japanese. Nippon's Economic Empire in Asia*, Tokyo: Yenbooks.

Batzer, E. and H. Laumer, 1989, *Marketing Strategies and Distribution Channels for Foreign Companies in Japan*, Boulder, CO: Westview Press.

Bilkey, W.J. and G. Tesar, 1978, 'The Export Behavior of Smaller-sized Wisconsin Manufacturing Firms', *Journal of International Business Studies*, 2nd quarter, pp.209–31.

Blomley, N.K., 1989, 'Text and Context: Rethinking the Law–Space Nexus', *Progress in Human Geography*, Vol.13, No.4, pp.512–34.

Boddewyn, J.J., M.B. Halbrich and A.C. Perry, 1986, 'Service Multinationals: Conceptualization, Measurement and Theory', *Journal of International Business Studies*, Vol.17, Fall, pp.41–58.

Brahm, R., 1993, 'Globalization and Strategy Content Research: Critical Reflections and New Directions', in P. Shrivastava, A. Huff and J. Dutton (eds.), *Advances in Strategic Management*, London: JAI Press, pp.3–21.

Brooks, W. L., 1993, 'MITI's Distribution Policy and US–Japan Structural Talks', in M.R. Czinkota and M. Kotabe (eds.), *The Japanese Distribution System. Opportunities and Obstacles. Structures and Practices*, Chicago: Probus, Ch. 16.

Burt, S., 1993, 'Temporal Trends in the Internationalization of British Retailing', *International Review of Retail, Distribution and Consumer Research*, Vol.3, No.4, pp.391–410.

Cavusgil, S.T., 1980, 'On the Internationalisation Process of Firms', *European Research*, November, pp.273–81.

Christopherson, S., 1993, 'Market Rules and Territorial Outcomes: The Case of the United States', *International Journal of Urban and Regional Research*, Vol.17, pp.274–88.

Cunningham, M.T. and K. Culligan, 1991, 'Competitiveness through Networks of Relationships in Information Technology Markets', in S.J. Paliwoda (ed.), *New Perspectives on International Marketing*, London.

Czinkota, M.R. and M. Kotabe (eds.), 1993, *The Japanese Distribution System. Opportunities and Obstacles. Structures and Practices*, Chicago: Probus Publishing.

Czinkota, M.R. and J. Woronoff, 1991, *Unlocking Japan's Markets. Seizing Marketing and Distribution Opportunities in Today's Japan*, London: Pitman.

Davies, B.J. and P. Jones, 1993, 'International Activity of Japanese Department Stores', *Service Industries Journal*, Vol.13, No.1, pp.126–32.

Davies, K., 1993, 'Trade Barriers in East and South-East Asia: The Implications for Retailers', *International Review of Retail, Distribution and Consumer Research*, Vol.3, No.4, pp.345–65.

Davies, K., 1994a, 'The Implications of Foreign Investment in the Retail Sector: The Example of

Singapore', *The Developing Economies*, Vol.22, No.3, pp.299–330.

Davies, K., 1994b, 'The Expansion of Japanese Retailers in Asia: Economic Hegemony or Cultural Confusion?' Paper presented to the Annual Conference of the Institute of British Geographers, University of Nottingham, 4–7 January.

Davies, K., 1994c, 'Foreign Investment in the Retail Sector of the People's Republic of China', *Columbia Journal of World Business*, Fall, Vol.29, No.3, pp.56–69.

Davies, K., 1995, 'The Regulation of Retail Internationalization: Examples from the Pacific Asia Region', in P. McGoldrick and G. Davies (eds.), *International Retailing: Trends and Strategies*, London: Pitman.

Davies, K. and F. Fergusson, 1994, 'Networks, Value Chains and Retail Internationalisation in Pacific Asia', Working Paper, Institute for Retail Studies, University of Stirling.

Dawson, J.A., 1993, 'The Internationalization of Retailing', in R.D.F. Bromley and C.J. Thomas (eds.), *Retail Change. Contemporary Issues*, London: UCL Press.

Dicken, P., 1994, 'Global–Local Tensions: Firms and States in the Global Space-Economy', *Economic Geography*, Vol.70, pp.101–28.

Dicken, P. and N. Thrift, 1992, 'The Organization of Production and the Production of Organization: why business enterprises matter in the study of geographical industrialization', *Transactions of the Institute of British Geographers*, N.S. Vol.17, No.3, pp.279–91.

Dobrzynski, J.H., 1993, 'Takashimaya bets on art for mart's sake', *Business Week*, No. 3316, 26 April, p.38.

Dodwell Marketing Consultants, 1991, *Retail Distribution in Japan*, Authors, Tokyo.

Dunning, J., 1993, *The Globalization of Business*, London: Routledge.

Flath, D., 1989, 'Why are there so many retail stores in Japan?', *Japan and the World Economy*, Vol.2, pp.365–86.

Friedland, J., 1993, 'Sogo's woes. Japanese retailer pays price of rapid expansion', *Far Eastern Economic Review*, 15 April, p.64.

Goldman, A., 1991, 'Japan's Distribution System: Institutional Structure, Internal Political Economy, and Modernization', *Journal of Retailing*, Vol.67, No.2, Summer, pp.154–83.

Goldman, A., 1992, 'Evaluating the Performance of the Japanese Distribution System', *Journal of Retailing*, Vol.68, No.1, Spring, pp.11–39.

Hakansson, H. (ed.), 1982, *International Marketing and Purchasing of Industrial Goods. An Interaction Approach*, London : John Wiley.

Hollander, S. C., 1970, *Multinational Retailing*, Michigan State University, East Lansing: MSU International Business and Economic Studies,.

Itoh, M., 1991, 'The Japanese Distribution System and Access to the Japanese Market', in P. Krugman (ed.), *Trade with Japan. Has the Door Opened Wider?*, Chicago: University of Chicago Press.

Johanson, J. and Paul F Wiedersheim, 1975, 'The Internationalization of the Firm – Four Swedish Cases', *Journal of Management Studies*, Vol.12, No.3, pp.305–22.

Johanson, J. and Mattsson, L.G., 1987, 'Internationalisation in industrial systems – a network approach', in N. Hood and J.E. Vahlne (eds.), *Strategies in Global Competition*, London, Routledge.

Johanson, J. and J.E. Vahlne, 1977, 'The internationalization process of the firm: a model of knowledge development and increasing foreign market commitments', *Journal of International Business Studies*, Vol.8, No.1, pp.23–32.

Johanson, J. and J.E. Vahlne, 1990, 'The Mechanism of Internationalization', *International Marketing Review*, Vol.7, No.4, pp.11–24.

Johansson, J.K., 1990, 'Japanese Service Industries and their Overseas Potential', *Service Industries Journal*, Vol.10, No.1, pp.85–109.

Kacker, M., 1985, *Transatlantic Trends in Retailing: Takeovers and Flows of Know-How*, London: Quorum.

Larke, R., 1994, *Japanese Retailing*, London: Routledge.

Laulajainen, R., 1991, 'Two Retailers Go Global – The Geographical Dimension', *International Review of Retail, Distribution and Consumer Research*, Vol.1, No.5, pp.607–26.

Malayang, R.V., 1988, 'The Distribution Industry in Asian NIES and ASEAN Countries and the

Effects of the Entry of Japanese Retailers', *Management Japan*, Vol.21, No.2, pp.15–28.

McGee, J., 1987, 'Retailer Strategies in the UK', in G. Johnson (ed.), *Business Strategy and Retailing*, London: John Wiley.

McGoldrick, P., 1990, *Retail Marketing*, London: McGraw Hill.

Miyagiwa, K., 1993, 'Reforming the Japanese distribution system: will it boost exports to Japan?', *Journal of the World Economy*, Vol.5, No.4, pp.321–36.

Mulchand, S., 1992, 'Setting up shop in Indonesia', *Singapore Business*, November, pp.32–8.

Nishimura, K.G., 1993, 'The distribution system of Japan and the US: a comparative study from the viewpoint of final-goods buyers', *Japan and the World Economy*, Vol.5, No.3, pp.265–88.

Onoki, S., 1992, 'The Japanese Distribution Industry's Development-and-Import Scheme and the Emerging International Division of Labour in the Western Pacific Region', *Regional Development Dialogue*, Vol. 13, No.2, pp.123–31.

Porter, M.E., 1985, *Competitive Advantage. Creating and Sustaining Superior Performance*, New York: The Free Press.

Porter, M. E., 1990, *The Competitive Advantage of Nations*, London: Macmillan.

Sazanami, Y., 1993, 'Japanese Service Enterprises in the Pacific', in G. Sletmo and G. Boyd (eds.), *Pacific Service Enterprises and Pacific Cooperation*, Boulder: Westview Press.

Segal Horn, S., 1993, 'The Internationalization of Service Firms', in P. Shrivastava *et al.* (eds), *Advances in Strategic Management*, London: JAI Press, pp.31–53.

Tanzer, A., 1988, 'Southeast Asia's Missionary Retailer', *Forbes*, 21 March, pp.120,122.

Treadgold, A. and R.L. Davies, 1988, *The Internationalization of Retailing*, OXIRM Paper.

Tselichtchev, I.S., 1994, 'Rethinking Inter-firm Ties in Japan as a Factor of Competitiveness', in H. Schütte (ed.), *The Global Competitiveness of the Asian Firm*, London: St Martin's Press.

Turnbull, P.W., 1987, 'A Challenge to the Stages Theory of the Internationalization Process', in P.J. Rosson and S.D. Reid (eds.), *Managing Export Entry and Expansion. Concepts and Practice*, London: Praeger.

Tymi, I., 1994, 'The Japanese Management Structure as a Competitive Strategy: The Importance of a Nexus of Long-Term Treaties, Common Knowledge and Firm-Specific Learning', in H. Schütte (ed.), *The Global Competitiveness of the Asian Firm*, London: St Martin's Press.

Wada, K., 1992, *Yaohan's Global Strategy. The 21st Century is the Era of Asia*, Hong Kong: Capital Communications.

Williams, D.E., 1992, 'Retailer Internationalization: An Empirical Enquiry', *European Journal of Marketing*, Vol.26, Nos 8/9.

Differences between International and Domestic Japanese Retailers

YUNG-FANG CHEN and BRENDA STERNQUIST

The first part of this study uses a descriptive analysis of Japanese retail stores' overseas involvement. Japanese retailers have used joint ventures, representative offices and management agreements and to a lesser degree, acquisitions. International markets are attractive to Japanese retailers because of the strong yen, government's restrictions on domestic expansions, high costs of land and labor, and increased competition at home. Discriminant analysis was used to profile Japanese retailers with and without international involvement. The results indicate that those retail companies who expanded overseas have higher sales volumes, longer histories of establishment, larger sales floor spaces at domestic stores, possess more assets, liabilities and have more employees as well as have higher bank loans. In addition, no significant differences are found in sales productivity, profitability and growth ratios between those Japanese stores who expanded overseas and those who did not. Managerial implications are discussed.

INTRODUCTION

As the concept of a global market has gradually evolved, retailers' interest in crossing borders has been greatly enhanced. However, international operations are not new to many Japanese retailers. Their first move to overseas markets began in the latter half of the 1950s, and they now seem to be successfully transplanted in various regions of the Far East. This study has two major purposes. One is to explore the present conditions of Japanese retailers' operations in the international markets, the other is to identify differences between the Japanese retailers who seek international expansions and those who do not, with an emphasis on their financial performance. The first part of this paper, therefore, will use a descriptive analysis coupled with supportive literature to examine the methods of operation used by the Japanese retail companies that expanded internationally as well as their reasons for expansion. The second part will use an empirical application technique to discover the determinants that can be used to discriminate among Japanese retailers' international expansions.

REVIEW OF LITERATURE

The internationalisation of retailers' activities has attracted considerable attention for researchers. Dunning's eclectic theory [1988] provides general motives for internationalising; these are categorised as ownership advantages, internalisation advantages and location advantages. Ownership advantages are related to innovative or unique products or processes that a retail company can use to obtain market power. Internalisation advantages determine whether it is in the company's interest to sell or lease its 'secrets' to other firms, or to make use of the secrets itself. At times, a retail company may need to internalise its innovations or secrets to maintain a competitive advantage. Location advantages refer to the suitability of host country to the company's strategies. Geographical as well as cultural proximity, market size and the competitors' moves are four relevant issues.

Motives for internationalisation can also be classified as 'push', 'pull' and 'facilitating' factors [McGoldrick and Fryer, 1993]. Push factors include saturated domestic markets, trading restrictions, rising costs and unfavourable economic conditions. Corporate philosophy, perceived growth opportunities, undeveloped markets and niche opportunities are included among pull factors. Facilitating factors are identified as an accumulation of in-company expertise, lowering of barriers and the vision of senior management. Two types of companies, global and multinational, are profiled [Salmon and Tordjman, 1989]. Global companies generally transport a standardised retail format throughout the world, focus on niche markets and use highly centralised management. On the other hand, the multinationals adapt their retail formulas to fit local markets and use more decentralised management. Treadgold [1990] believes that the majority of retailers considering operations abroad are inclined to use the multinational approach, adapting their formats to serve local markets. Department stores, because they are mature businesses, are more likely either to diversify at home, moving into more promising areas of specialised retailing, or to export their original formula into less developed markets [Pellegrini, 1993]. Hollander [1970] also indicates that the flow of investments will go mainly from more to less developed countries in order to exploit relative innovation advantages.

Geographical and cultural proximity have been found to influence the entry modes used by British retailers [Burt, 1993]. This result conforms to Dunning's theory. Although Japanese department stores have more distinctive business packages than their Western counterparts, it remains unknown if the unique Japanese style is transportable and profitable [Johansson, 1990]. Davies [1993] observes that the Japanese department store groups have been the most active in establishing outlets overseas, but this development is more closely related to their desire to establish buying networks and to serve existing customers who happen to be overseas than to the saturation of the Japanese market. McGoldrick and Ho [1992] use the Hong Kong department store market as an example of considerable success in repositioning by international retailers, most notably the Japanese.

INTERNATIONALISATION OF JAPANESE RETAILERS

Department stores have a long history in Japan, dating back to the seventeenth century [Davies and Jones, 1993]. Rather than focusing only on merchandising and salesmanship, Japanese department stores have developed superior personal services through extensive staff-training programmes. Moreover, many big department stores, especially those located in Tokyo or Osaka, often add grand facilities such as art museums, multipurpose halls for concerts, drama and film as well as sports clubs as part of the store's expansion. In addition to being shopping malls, Japanese department stores function as community centres to provide services, cultural events and entertainment [Gill, 1992].

Japanese retailers also have a long history in foreign countries. Their first move to overseas markets was in the latter half of the 1950s. At that time, most of the companies heading overseas were department stores focusing on European countries; they established specialty stores selling souvenirs, clothing and accessories. While most of the companies went to Europe, some expanded their operations to Southeast Asia. Daimaru Department Store went to Hong Kong in 1960 and Yaohan to Singapore in 1974 [Goldstein, 1988]. As trade barriers eased, cross-border investments by Japanese retail companies increased . The numbers of Japanese retail stores in overseas locations increased to two hundred at the end of 1990, with the sales floor space of all the outlets totalling about one million square meters [Maruki, 1991]. In Singapore and Hong Kong, the Japanese department stores hold even larger shares of the large-sized stores sales market than their native counterparts [Maruki, 1991]. Currently there are 17 major Japanese companies with overseas outlets and/or offices [Davies and Jones, 1993]. Twenty-three Japanese stores are located in the Americas, 52 in Asia and 18 in Europe [Davies and Jones, 1993]. In South-East Asia, Hong Kong, Singapore and Bangkok account for over 40 per cent of Japanese foreign outlets [Davies and Jones, 1993]. While increasing their penetration of established markets such as Hong Kong and Singapore,

Japanese retailers are expanding to other Asian countries, including Taiwan, Thailand, Malaysia and Mainland China.

ENTRY MODES FOR INTERNATIONALISATION

Japanese retailers have made use of joint ventures, representative offices (ROs) and management agreements, while using acquisitions to a lesser extent [Davies, 1993]. However, it remains to be seen if these alternatives are intended as short-term strategies. They may be designed to generate needed experience in foreign markets and will perhaps be replaced by wholly owned subsidiaries [Johansson, 1990].

Joint Ventures

Joint ventures are used most extensively by Japanese retailers [Davies, 1993]. For those who are involved internationally, the establishment of a joint venture with local firms is a means of achieving cost-effectiveness and risk-reduction. Such co-operation not only supplies the Japanese with sufficient market knowledge and distribution networks but also prevents their heavy investment in fixed assets in a foreign country that is perceived as politically unstable (e.g., Hong Kong). In addition, 'the popularity of joint ventures can also be explained by the barriers to trade put up by many governments, forcing minority equity participation for foreign companies or joint control over an enterprise, as in Malaysia, the Republic of Korea and the People's Republic of China' [Davies, 1993].

Representative Offices

Another common entry mode among department stores and general merchandise stores is the establishment of ROs. According to Maruki [1991], there were more than 160 Japanese retail ROs overseas at the end of 1990, and now local offices are being opened on a regular basis by Japanese retailers. The purpose of setting up ROs is to lay the groundwork for product development, merchandise sourcing and the establishment of full-fledged stores outlets. As a result, ROs are more widespread than most store networks, and sometimes the pattern of the offices' location is different from that of the stores [Davies, 1993].

Management Contracts

Management agreement is also a popular mode for international entry. For example, several department stores in Taiwan, including Today, Evergreen, Hsin-Hsin and Hsin-Kuang, have signed management contracts with

Japanese department stores such as Seibu, Tokyu, Matsuya and Mitsukoshi [Chang and Sternquist, 1993]. Japanese partners transfer their expertise to help Taiwan companies develop and modernise, and in return they can help the Japanese to source products for the Japanese market [Anon., 1988b].

Acquisition

Acquisitions by Japanese are found more frequently in the US and the United Kingdom than in other countries. Examples include the Ito-Yokado Group's acquisition of Seven–Eleven [Davies, 1993] and the purchase of the Criterion site by Sogo Co. Ltd. from the Mountleigh Group in Great Britain [Anon., 1991]. Davies [1993] speculates that the prominence of acquisition in the US and United Kingdom may result from the prevailing investment culture and the stability of the capital markets in these two countries. Moreover, according to Davies, the ultimate goal of Japanese retailers is not the purchase of retail property but the purchase of retail brands, which can be exploited later in domestic as well as international markets.

Franchising and Licensing

Franchising is rarely used. However, Sogo did make a licensing agreement with its Indonesian partner through which it provided technical assistance, supervised management and technical services and rented its name to the local company [Davies, 1993]. Mulchand [1992] speculates that the Indonesian store will be bought back by the Japanese company if deregulation occurs in Indonesia.

REASONS FOR INTERNATIONAL EXPANSION

Several internal factors may have made international markets especially attractive to Japanese retailers.

Internal Factors

Strong yen – pull factor. During the past few years, the strengthening of the yen has stimulated Japanese tourists to spend more abroad. The effect of the strong yen became apparent when Japanese consumers rapidly lost their resistance to foreign goods, and Japanese tourists noticed great price differentials between products purchased domestically and abroad [Kikuchi, 1992; Muramatsu, 1994; Sterngold, 1994]. This contributed to the speed with which Japanese companies began to streamline operations internationally [do Rosario, 1991].

Government restrictions on expansion – push factor. One major push factor is directly tied to Japan's Large-Scale Retail Store Law, enacted in 1973. Intended to protect the interests of mom-and-pop stores, the law not only limits the opening of new stores by the major retailers, but also restricts the hours and days they may operate [Goldstein, 1988]. Because of the legal restriction on the expansion of large retailers, the decline in the number of retail stores since 1985 has spread across all sectors of the retail industry. To be able to open a store, the retailers require 73 applications for 26 separate approvals under 12 different laws [Wagstyl, 1989]. Moreover, the approval of an application may take seven or eight years, or even 15 years in some cases. Although the law has recently been amended to reduce the waiting time to one year and to increase the law's transparency [Sternquist and Ogawa, 1993], it still serves as a major impetus for retailers' expansion overseas.

High cost of land and labour – push factor. Another internal factor resulting in overseas expansion is the astronomical price of Japan's real estate. The price of land and cost of construction in Japan are the highest in the world [Sternquist and Ogawa, 1993]. In addition, over-built cities make site selection difficult and sometimes impossible. In contrast, the cost of building or leasing overseas seems very attractive because the retail space is not only available but cheap. Moreover, lower construction costs can be achieved by means of joint ventures with local partners. For instance, Sogo Department Store's Taipei partner, the Pacific Construction Co., provided the land and 51 per cent of the building costs as well as start-up costs [Goldstein, 1988]. Labour costs outside Japan are also much cheaper. For example, labour costs are 5 per cent of sales in Singapore whereas in Japan they are 10 per cent [Sternquist and Ogawa, 1993]. Furthermore, with the introduction of the land price tax in 1992, many department stores have complained that their earnings in Japan have been depressed [Ikeya, 1993].

Increased competition at home – push factor. Japanese retailers' international expansion can also be attributed to intense competition in domestic markets. The rapid growth of general merchandisers seems to be at the expense of Japanese department stores' market shares and profits, which declined as much as 25 per cent in 1991 and have continued to drop each year since [Sternquist and Ogawa, 1993]. In addition, as Japanese consumers become more and more frugal, department stores are under great pressure from tough discounters who feature prices 30 to 40 per cent lower than those of traditional department stores [do Rosario, 1993; Sterngold, 1994]. Encountering increased competition at home, many Japanese retailers, especially department stores, consider expansion in the international markets to be an appropriate opportunity for growth.

Comparative advantages – pull factor. Since many Japanese retail companies seem to have powerful ownership advantages over their counterparts in other countries, making international moves appears to be promising. Kajima [1978] believes that the weaker firms are more likely to relocate in less developed countries in order to exploit their comparative advantages. For example, Sogo, which is not so successful in the home market, now has the largest volume of any Japanese department store chain, and it is the largest Japanese retailer in South-East Asia [Friedland, 1993].

External Factors for Increasing Involvement in Asia
The location advantages that Dunning identifies such as cultural proximity and geographical proximity, prove to be critical in influencing Japanese retailers' internationalisation. Davies [1993] finds that the majority of the international activities of Japanese retailers are concentrated in Asia. Davies [1993] also points out that in Hong Kong, Singapore and Taiwan store-based activities are the prime entry mechanisms, whereas ROs are more popular in Mainland China, and management agreements are used more in Thailand, Korea and Indonesia [Davies, 1993]. He further concludes that the increasingly eminent presence of Japanese retailers in Asian countries derives from the following three factors:

1. Market potential: Japanese retailers increasingly enter Asia because countries in that region such as Taiwan, Hong Kong, and Singapore, have high levels of market growth and market potential as well as high levels of disposable income that can offer a reasonable return on investment.
2. Legislation: Previous restrictive regulations in countries such as Korea and Taiwan have been eased, so it makes more sense for Japanese retailers to expand to geographically close countries than to limit their internationalisation to the more open markets of Hong Kong and Singapore.
3. Tourists and ethnic enclaves: A substantial proportion of overseas outlets opening in this region cater to Japanese tourists. Therefore, establishment of familiar surroundings and stores seems practical, and it is easy for Japanese retailers to target their countrymen.

OPERATIONS OF JAPANESE DEPARTMENT STORES OVERSEAS

To determine whether or not the Japanese department store concept can be exported in its original format, the following section will examine the ways in which operations of retail stores outside Japan are adapted to local demands.

Store Format and Target Audience

In areas outside Asia, Japanese department stores have limited their store establishments to major cities and have primarily appealed to Japanese tourists or expatriates [Johansson, 1990]. This may perhaps be attributed to the Western customer's belief that a Japanese department store is more like an exotic land than a serious shopping environment [Johansson, 1990]. Moreover, Japanese department store operators offer mostly limited-line gift shops or fashion boutiques rather than full-scale department stores in areas outside Asia. Takashimaya's and Mitsukoshi's overseas outlets are examples of this [Davies and Jones, 1993]. In contrast, stores developed within South-East Asia are larger in scale, perhaps because this area is known as a popular destination for tourists and a shopping paradise, because the costs of land, construction and personnel in the South-East Asian nations are relatively cheap, and because historical connections with this region are deep. Though the target consumer for many Japanese department stores in Asia is the Japanese tourist, Japanese department stores like Daimaru largely ignore the tourist trade, aiming at local shoppers [Anon., 1988a].

Merchandise, Sourcing and Positioning

Merchandise selection is directly related to the target market and audience. Matsuzakaya and Mitsukoshi in Hong Kong, for example, draw about 20 per cent of their revenues from Japanese tourists. Therefore, they orient their merchandising strategies around their countrymen's tastes and cater to European's taste to a lesser degree. The popularity of luxury American or European brands is clearly reflected in their stores. US-made goods constitute about 60 per cent of the merchandise, while Japanese products make up another 20 per cent [Anon., 1988a]. On the other hand, Daimaru which draws less than 5 per cent of its revenues from tourists, stocks a substantially higher per centage of Japanese-made goods (about 60 per cent of the total) in order to attract local customers [Anon., 1988a]. In addition, the Japanese stores make more extensive use of concessions than do stores in the Western retail system. Concessions with well-known luxury brands, such as Chanel, Gucci, Dior, and Hermes have become the Japanese department store's mainstays as well as their best selling tools. In Thailand, this strategy cannot be used because of high import tariffs, up to 100 per cent on many of the products in a standard merchandise mix. As a result, locally made goods are sold almost exclusively in Thailand's stores [Anon., 1988b]. The positioning strategy of many Japanese department stores overseas is clearly to promote their 'country of origin' [McGoldrick and Ho, 1992]. On the one hand, promotion of 'Japanese' may ensure that the store's name is associated with Japan's latest technology, affluence, modernity and efficiency; on the other hand, the same or similar business logo may easily draw Japanese tourists [McGoldrick and Ho, 1992].

METHODOLOGY

Discriminant analysis was used to profile characteristics of Japanese companies with international involvement and those without international involvement. Secondary data was acquired primarily from three sources: the *Japan Company Handbook* 1993; company reports in the Investext Database distributed by Information Access Co.; and the *Company Distribution Yearbook* 1991. Fifty-three Japanese companies under the 'Retail' category were selected in the *Japan Company Handbook* 1993, which served as the major source for financial information. Meanwhile, additional information, such as financial growth ratios and number of stores overseas was supplied by two other sources. The sample included several retail categories: 17 department stores, 20 supermarket chains and 16 general merchandisers. Among the 53 selected companies, 8 were excluded because of missing data. Twenty-two of the 45 companies were found to have no international involvement, while the remaining 23 were involved in international markets. The following hypotheses were tested to investigate whether or not there are distinctive differences between these two groups of Japanese retailers. Multiple Analysis of Variance (MANOVA) was used to determine if any of the following financial variables were viable discriminants of Japanese retailers who moved toward internationalisation. The independent variable was the establishment of categorised international stores versus the absence of international stores, and the dependent variables were selected financial characteristics.

H1: There is no significant difference between Japanese retailers who went international and those who did not in their a) sales productivity per employee and b) sales productivity per square meter.

H2: There is no significant difference between Japanese retailers who went international and those who did not in their a) return on assets, b) return on equity, c) profit margin, and d) asset turnover.

H3: There is no significant difference between Japanese retailers who went international and those who did not in their growth ratios associated with a) net sales, b) operating income, c) equity , d) employees, and e) book value per share.

H4: There is no significant difference between Japanese retailers who went international and those who did not in their a) assets, b) liability, c) amount of working capital, d) bank borrowings, e) capital surplus, and f) shareholders' equity.

H5: There is no significant difference between Japanese retailers who went international and those who did not in their a) sales, b) total number of domestic stores , c) total sales floor spaces at domestic stores, d) number of employees, e) years in operation, f) the facility investment expenditures, and g) research and development (R & D) expenditures.

RESULTS

The first three hypotheses were not significant. No significant differences were found in sales productivity, profitability ratios, or growth ratios between Japanese retail companies who expanded overseas and those who did not. However, the fourth and fifth hypotheses were significant. The fourth hypothesis was significant (Hotellings' T=.67; Significance of F=.01).(See Table 1.) Significant differences were identified in variables such as the possession of assets, liabilities and amount of bank loans. The results showed that liabilities ($234,706 million yen) as well as assets ($324,718 million yen) possessed by Japanese companies who went international were both approximately three times greater than those who did not. The amount of bank loans for the Japanese retailers who set up stores overseas ($185,527 million yen) was four times as high as those who did not ($49,516 million yen). The fifth hypothesis was significant (Hotellings' T= .37; Significance of F=.10). (See Table 2.) Differences were identified in sales, total sales floor spaces of domestic stores, number of employees hired, and length of operation between Japanese retail stores who went international and those who did not. Sales of retailers who went overseas ($566,210 million yen) were twice those of retailers who did not ($249,202 million yen). The international retailers had larger sales floor space in the home market (358,681 m² versus 165,911 m²). Retailers with stores operating overseas had more employees (6,792 versus 3,055). Retailers who sought international expansion also appeared to have been established longer in the retailing industry (Average date of establishment was 1930 versus 1944 for stores that did not internationalise.) Though research and development expenditures (685 million yen) were higher for companies who expanded internationally than for those who did not (1 million yen), no significant difference was found. This is not consistent with the study of Sternquist and Ogawa [1993], who found that R&D funds were significantly different in the two groups. Sternquist and Ogawa also found a significant difference in the amount of facility investment of retailers with and without international expansion at P< .05 level. To further explore the relationship between length of operation in retailing and relevant variables, correlation analyses were run, and significant correlations were found between year of establishment and sales as well as between year of establishment and the number of international offices at P<.01 level (See Table 3.) Additionally, among the 45 selected retail companies, Japanese department stores were found to have significantly more offices overseas than supermarket chains and general merchandisers (Hotellings' T= .29; Significance of F= .03). (See Table 4.) The average numbers of international offices controlled by department stores, supermarket chains and mass merchandisers are 4.2, 1.4 and 0.5, respectively. However, no significant differences were found in the number of stores operated overseas by department stores (4.6), supermarket chains (12.7) and general merchandisers (0.2).

TABLE 1

MULTIPLE ANALYSIS OF VARIANCE: FINANCIAL VARIABLES BY INTERNATIONALISATION OF JAPANESE RETAIL COMPANIES

Test	Value	Approximate F	Significance
Hotellings' T	.666891	3.15342	.01***

Group Means

Retail Classification

Statement (million yen)	No International Stores	International Stores	F-Ratio	Sig. Of F
Fixed Assets	119,494.0	324,718.0	9.19	.00
Current Assets	81,897.3	197,201.0	4.31	.05
Liabilities	78,475.0	234,706.6	8.23	.01
Working Capital	3,425.2	-32,742.5	1.91	.18
Bank Borrowings	49,515.6	185,527.0	4.89	.03
Capital Surplus	22,159.6	32,207.4	1.50	.23
Shareholders' equity	67,180.8	100,806.7	2.30	.14

*** Significance at P<.01 level

TABLE 2
MULTIPLE ANALYSIS OF VARIANCE: FINANCIAL VARIABLES BY INTERNATIONALISATION OF
JAPANESE RETAIL COMPANIES

Test	Value	Approximate F	Significance
Hotellings' T	.36704	1.88764	.10*

Group Means

Retail Classification

Statement	No International Stores	International Stores	F-Ratio	Sig. Of F
Sales (million yen)	249,201.9	566,209.1	7.48	.01
Domestic Sales Spaces (square metres)	165,910.6	358,681.4	4.53	.04
# of Stores at Home	57.4	68.4	.34	.57
# of Employees	3,054.9	6,791.8	10.26	.00
Year of Establishment	1944.6	1930.1	5.84	.02
Amount of Facility Invesmtne (million yen)	12,078.8	23,387.5	3.26	.08
R&D Expenses (million yen)	0.7	684.8	1.51	.23

* Significant at $p < .10$ level

TABLE 3
CORRELATION: SALES AND OFFICES BY YEAR OF ESTABLISHMENT

Variable:

Year of Establishment

	Number	Mean Std.	Deviation	Coef.
Sales (million yen)	41	770,233.6	775,092.8	-.56***
# of Offices Overseas	41	2.4	3.7	-.42***

*** Significant at $P < .01$ level

TABLE 4
MULTIPLE ANALYSIS OF VARIANCE: RETAIL COMPANIES' INTERNATIONALISATION BY
RETAIL CATEGORIES

Test	Value	Approximate F	Significance
Hotellings' T	.29041	2.90	.03*

Group Means

Retail Categories

	Department Stores	Supermarket Chains	General Merchandisers	F-Ratio	Sig. Of F
# of Stores Overseas	4.59	12.72	.20	.656	.52
# of Offices Overseas	4.24	1.39	.50	5.371	.01

** Significance at P<.05 level

DISCUSSION

The results showed that retailers with business involvement abroad tended to possess more assets, more liabilities and larger sales floor spaces than retailers who have not internationalised. Significantly higher amounts of bank loans and a larger number of employees imply that international expansion requires a great many financial as well as managerial resources to support or back up retailers' investments in foreign countries. Retailers seeking international expansion employ more people because retailing is a labour-intensive industry. Again, this explanation underscores the indispensability of financial and managerial investments. It also reinforces the need for retailers to search for locations that offer low costs for land, construction and labour, so that retailers can reduce their liabilities and lighten their interest burdens from bank loans. The results also showed that the longer the retailer's history of operation, the more likely it was to expand overseas. The interrelation between history of operation and international moves can be confirmed by the previous analysis. The average year of establishment for department stores, supermarkets and mass merchandisers is 1929, 1943, 1955, respectively; and Japanese department stores, which were established long before the supermarkets and mass merchandisers, were found to be setting up more offices overseas than the other two types of retailers. In addition, after examining the correlation between the year of establishment and relevant variables, we found significantly negative relationships between the year of establishment and sales in dollars as well as between the year of establishment and the number of international offices. That is to say, the older the retail company was (in terms of years in operation), the better its sales performance was and the more international offices it had. Based on Dunning's [1988] theory, we postulate that older, established retail stores have superior ownership advantages. This is because the older companies, with longer histories in the industry, are more experienced and skilful in managing, operating and controlling their businesses. As a result, the established older retail companies have a great impetus to spread their specialties and/or strengths beyond their national borders and to search for growth opportunities outside the domestic market. Their superior ownership advantages can also be tied to Japanese culture, where established ranking order is based on duration of service within a group and on age rather than on individual ability. Similarly, companies with long histories in the industry are respected and viewed as being superior. Consumers perceive a company with a long history as having 'seniority', and this contributes to the firm's sales performance and impetus for further expansion. However, the relationships between the types of retailers and their international involvement were not clearly identified. The results of this study did not confirm that those retailers with international involvement have significantly higher sales productivity and profitability ratios than those who did not. Moreover, no differences were found between retailers with and without internationalisation in the number of domestic stores they possessed. In other words, the results showed that going for international expansion is not necessarily the privilege of the stronger, older or larger retailers (e.g., Mitsukoshi, Takashimaya). On the contrary, the weaker, younger or smaller stores (e.g., Matsuzakaya, Sogo) whose sales performances were lower and less efficient are also likely to expand in order to avoid fierce competition at home and to search for comparative and/or first-mover advantages. This result is consistent with Sternquist and Ogawa's propositions [1993]. Moreover, significantly greater increases in sales indicate a promising future for those retailers expanding overseas, and this reinforces the possibility of their further international involvement.

CONCLUSION

In this study, we found that possession of assets, amount of bank loans, liabilities, sales, sales floor space, number of employees and length of operation can be used to discriminate between those Japanese retailers who have moved towards internationalisation and those who have not. Further explorations are needed to discover determinants that may help predict Japanese retailers' internationalisation and to examine the feasibility of transporting the Japanese store package overseas. It is hoped that this study will assist the readers in understanding Japanese retailers' international activities, characteristics, underlying motives, and methods.

REFERENCES

Anon., 1988a, 'Free-Spending Japanese Boast Superstore Sales', *Far Eastern Economic Review*, 26 May, Vol.140, No.21, pp.84–5.

Anon., 1988b, 'Locals Under Pressure to Upgrade Outlets', *Far Eastern Economic Review*, 26 May, Vol.140, No.21, p.84.

Anon., 1991, 'Criterion Project', *Financial Times* (London), 11 January, p.8.

Burt, S., 1993, 'Temporal Trends in the Internationalisation of British Retailing', *International Review of Retail, Distribution and Consumer Research*, Vol.1, No.4.

Chang, L., and B. Sternquist, 1993, 'Product Procurement: A Comparison of Taiwanese and U.S. Retail Companies', *International Review of Retail, Distribution and Consumer Research*, Vol.4, No.1, pp.239–57.

Company Distribution Yearbook, 1991. Japan Economic News Company, 5141.

Davies, K., 1993, 'The International Activities of Japanese Retailers', presented in the 7th International Conference on Research in the Distributive Trades, Vol.8, September, pp.534–43.

Davies, B.J., and P. Jones, 1993, International Activity of Japanese Department Stores', *Service Industries Journal*, Vol.13, No.1, January, pp.127–32.

do Rosario, L., 1991, 'Japan's Aging Population Catches Out Marui: Middle-Age Spread', *Far Eastern Economic Review*, 9 May, Vol.151, No.19, p.44.

do Rosario, L., 1993, 'Nihonmart: Discount Houses Now Compete With Japan's Leading Retailers', *Far Eastern Economic Review*, 16 September, Vol.156, No.37, pp.62–4.

Dunning, J. H., 1988, 'The Eclectic Paradigm of International Production: A Restatement and Some Possible Extension', *Journal of International Business*, Vol.19, No.1, pp.1–31.

Friedland, J., 1993, 'Sogo's Woes: Japanese Retailers Pay Price of Rapid Expansion', *Far Eastern Economic Review*, 15 April, Vol.156, No.15, p.64.

Gill, P., 1992, 'Japan's Tobu: A Rising Star', *Stores*, June, Vol. 74, No.6, pp.26–30.

Goldman, A., 1992, 'Evaluating the Performance of the Japanese Distribution System', *Journal of Retailing*, Vol.68, No.1, pp.11–39.

Goldstein, C., 1988, 'The Bargain Hunters', *Far Eastern Economic Review*, 26 May, pp.82–5.

Hollander, S. C., 1970, 'Multinational Retailing', East Lansing, Michigan: Michigan State University.

Ikeya, A., 1993, 'Department Stores See Another Rough Year', Nikkei Weekly, 26 April, pp.16.

Japan Company Handbook, 1993, Tokyo: Yoyo Keizai Inc.

Johansson, J.K., 1990, 'Japanese Service Industries and Their Overseas Potential', *Service Industries Journal*, Vol.10, No.1, pp.85–119.

Kajima, K., 1978, *Direct Foreign Investment: A Japanese Model of Multinational Business Operations*, London: Croom Helm.

Kikuchi, T., 1992, 'Changing Trend of Consumer Behavior and Distribution Practice in Japan', *Journal of International Consumer Marketing*, Vol.4, No.3, pp.109–20.

Maruki, T., 1991, 'Overseas Expansion by Japanese Retailers Picks Up Momentum', *Tokyo Business Today*, May, p.41.

McGoldrick, P.J., and S.L.Ho, 1992, 'International Position: Japanese Department Stores in Hong Kong', *European Journal of Marketing*, Vol.26, No.8/9, pp.61–73.

McGoldrick, P.J., and E. Fryer, E., 1993, 'Organizational Culture and the Internationalisation of Retailers', presented in the 7th International Conference on Research in the Distributive Trades. University of Stirling: Institute For Retail Studies.

Mulchand, S., 1992, 'Setting up shop in Indonesia', *Singapore Business*, November, pp.32–8.

Muramatsu, S., 1994, 'Falling prices captivate wine lovers', *Nikkei Weekly*, 12 Dec., p.10.

Pellegrini, L., 1993, 'Alternatives For Growth and Internationalisation in Retailing', presented to Montreal International Symposium on Retailing, Montreal, Canada.

Salmon, W.K. and A. Tordjman, 1989, 'The Internationalisation of Retailing', *International Journal of Retailing*, Vol.4, No.2, pp.3–16.

Sterngold, J., 1994, 'Is Japan's Sam Walton Up to the Job?', *The New York Times*, 4 Dec., Sec. 3, p.1.

Sternquist. B., and T. Ogawa, 1993, 'Internationalisation of Japanese Department Stores', East Lansing, Michigan: Michigan State University Working Paper #9204.

Treadgold, A. 1990, 'The Emerging Internationalisation of Retailing: Present Status And Future Challenges', *Irish Marketing Review*, Vol.5, No.2, pp.11–27.

Wagstyl, S., 1989, 'Japan's Master of Retailing', *World Press Review*, Vol.36, No.1, p.52.

International Comparisons of Supply Chain Management in Grocery Retailing

This paper discusses a neglected area of international retailing research, namely an international comparison of supply chain management practices. The focus of this research is on the grocery industry sector and the comparative analysis is between US retailers and their counterparts in parts of Europe. The research shows that the logistical environment differs markedly between and even within countries. The amount of stock held in the grocery supply chain varies from over 100 days in the US to 29 days in the UK. The main reasons for these differences can be attributed to the intensity of price competition, conflict rather than collaboration between suppliers and retailers, commodity purchasing and holding of promotional stock and the varying rates of adoption of information technology, especially EDI usage. No two countries are the same, however, and range of factors such as geography and distribution 'culture' will require the international marketeer to assess all these factors in developing a logistics strategy for different country markets.

INTRODUCTION

The internationalisation of retailing has attracted a burgeoning literature and a conference circuit replete with international retailing themes [see Alexander, 1994, for a review of recent work]. Most research activity has focused upon retail operations and has drawn heavily from the international business and international marketing literature on the motives for international expansion and market entry strategies. With a few exceptions [Dawson, 1993; Fernie, 1992,1994; Peck and Christopher, 1994], the international logistical environment within which companies operate largely has been ignored by researchers. This paper attempts to go some way towards redressing the imbalance in international retailing research. The grocery industry is the sector chosen for investigation and a comparative analysis will be undertaken between practices carried out by

US retailers and their counterparts in parts of Europe. The reasons for differences in logistical networks will be highlighted and areas for further research will be proposed.

SUPPLY CHAIN MANAGEMENT IN THE US GROCERY SECTOR

The catalyst for much of the interest in supply chain management on an international, comparative basis was the programme of 'efficient consumer response' initiated in the United States in the wake of an influential report of the same name by Kurt Salmon consultants [Kurt Salmon, 1993]. Kurt Salmon was commissioned to carry out this research because of the US grocery industry's declining profitability in the face of intense competition from discount mass merchandisers such as Wal-Mart and warehouse clubs.

The report stresses the inefficiencies of the grocery supply chain in the early 1990s. As can be seen from Figure 1, it takes 104 days on average for dry grocery products to pass through the supply chain from the supplier's packing line to the consumer at the checkout. This figure reduces to 75–80 days if perishable products are included in the overall grocery chain. The main reason for such a large volume of stock being held is the fragmentation of the chain. Stock is pulled through the supply chain by replenishment orders for stores but inventory tends to be pushed through the warehouse network because of trade promotions and forward buying.

The move to forward buying began in the 1970s when heavy discounting by manufacturers was used to circumvent price controls introduced by the Nixon administration. Instead of being phased out in the 1980s, forward buying became more important; indeed, grocery manufacturers' promotional spend between 1981 and 1991 focused more and more on trade promotions (increasing from 34 to 50 per cent) at the expense of other elements of the promotion mix, for example, advertising spend fell from 43 to 25 per cent. In addition to the financing and management of this excessive inventory, the complexity of deals incurs considerable administrative costs. Kurt Salmon [1993] maintains that some retailers have 7,000 to 8,000 deals on file at any one time with buyers and sales representatives spending 10–15 per cent of their time resolving price discrepancies. Further administrative costs are encountered with consumer promotions, especially coupon redemption, in the processing of the 3 per cent of 280 billion coupons which are redeemed each year.

At the store level, the utilisation of category management and improvements in back room efficiency were proposed to achieve further savings. For example, Table 1 shows the saving which could be achieved through the releasing of in store warehouse space for selling space as lead times are reduced and replenishment to stores increases.

FIGURE 1
COMPARISON OF AVERAGE THROUGHPUT TIME OF DRY GROCERY CHAIN BEFORE AND AFTER ECR IMPLEMENTATION

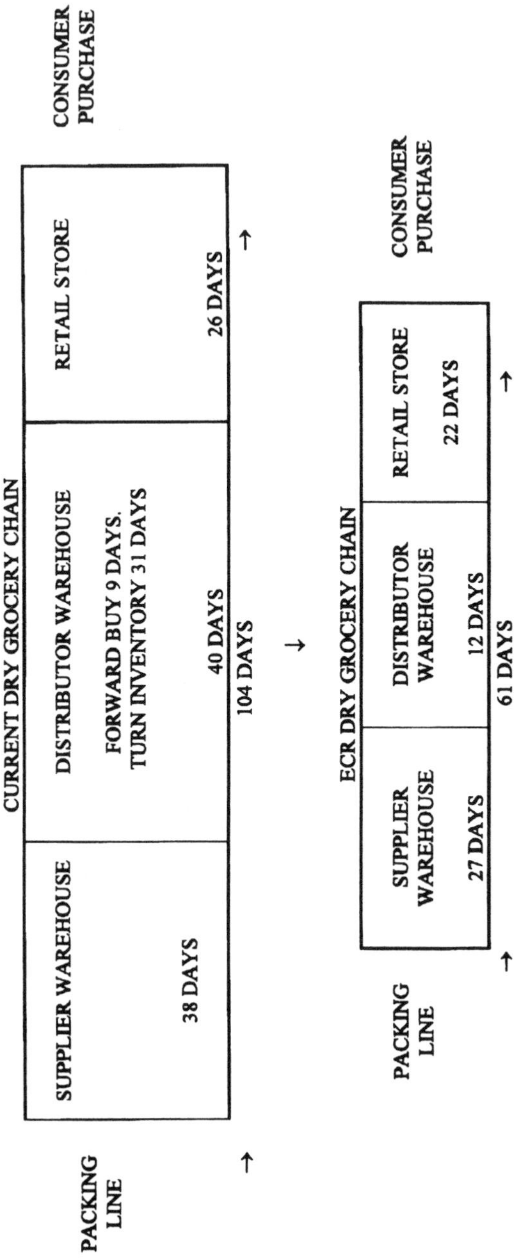

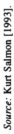

CURRENT DRY GROCERY CHAIN

PACKING LINE	SUPPLIER WAREHOUSE	DISTRIBUTOR WAREHOUSE	RETAIL STORE	CONSUMER PURCHASE
	38 DAYS	FORWARD BUY 9 DAYS. TURN INVENTORY 31 DAYS 40 DAYS	26 DAYS	

104 DAYS

ECR DRY GROCERY CHAIN

PACKING LINE	SUPPLIER WAREHOUSE	DISTRIBUTOR WAREHOUSE	RETAIL STORE	CONSUMER PURCHASE
	27 DAYS	12 DAYS	22 DAYS	

61 DAYS

Source: Kurt Salmon [1993].

The bottom line as far as Kurt Salmon was concerned is that around $10 billion – representing 10.8 per cent of sales turnover – could be saved in the dry grocery chain with the implementation of an efficient consumer response programme. Clearly, much remains to be achieved in the US grocery sector and the implementation of such a programme will depend on collaboration between all parties involved throughout the supply chain.

SUPPLY CHAIN MANAGEMENT IN EUROPEAN GROCERY DISTRIBUTION

A few months after the publication of the Kurt Salmon report, the Coca-Cola Retailing Research Group, Europe (CCRRG,E) commissioned research into the European grocery supply chain by GEA Consulentia Associata. At the onset of the project, GEA decided to use the same terminology as the Kurt Salmon report in order that meaningful comparisons could be made of cross-cultural experiences.

The research was carried out between March 1993 and January 1994 involving the participation of 175 companies whose turnover exceeded 300 billion ECUs. The final report, published in May 1994, demonstrates that there is no clear programme which can apply to *all* European countries in the same way as efficient consumer response is being applied in the United States. This can be attributed to the varying stages in the development of grocery markets in Europe and the consequent supply chain experience curve which also varies from country to country. Nevertheless, the benefits of efficient consumer response programmes in Europe will yield significantly less benefits than in the US. GEA [1994] estimate that savings of 2.3 to 3.4 per cent of sales turnover can be achieved compared with the 10.8 per cent quoted in the Kurt Salmon report. These figures imply that European retailers are much further down the road to logistical excellence than their counterparts in the United States. Such a conclusion must be treated with caution as considerable variations exist not only between countries but between companies operating in national markets.

One of the most useful indications of supply chain efficiency is stock levels. It was shown in Figure 1 that the efficient consumer response programmes in the US would ultimately lead to stock holding levels of 61 days. Table 2 shows the current situation in four European countries for total channel stock of ambient products. All countries hold considerably less stock than in the United States. Further analysis of where the stock is held, however, shows the differences between the UK and the other European countries. The UK is much further down the experience curve in logistics management. Regional distribution centres (RDCs) are large, invariably composite in nature and are progressively becoming transshipment centres as

TABLE 1
SALES BENEFIT OF EFFICIENT SPACE MANAGEMENT

Space Description	Current Size (sq. feet)	Sales Per Sq. Ft/Week ($)	Sales/Week ($)	Efficient Space Management Improvement	Freed Space (sq feet)	Increased Sales/Week ($)
Selling Space	27,500 (75%)	8.75	241,000	Same Volume in 10% Less Space	2,750	24,062
Non–Selling	9,100 (25%)	0	0	Reduced Need to 20% of total store	1,780	15,575
TOTAL	36,600	*	241,000	*	4,530	39,637 or 16% of Sales

* Assumes average sales per square foot.

Source: Kurt Salmon [1993].

TABLE 2
TOTAL CHANNEL STOCK AMBIENT PRODUCTS (DAYS)

TOTAL CHANNEL STOCK (Days)

Country	Italy	France	UK	Germany
Supplier	12	14	11	14
RDC	19	20	11	22
Store	9	9	7	11
TOTAL	40	43	29	47

Source: Walker [1994].

TABLE 3
ATTITUDES TOWARDS SUPPLIER-RETAILER COLLABORATION IN SPECIFIC COUNTRIES

SPAIN	GERMANY	ITALY	FRANCE	UK
• Little reciprocal knowledge	• Very positive: ready to go	• First SRC attempts	• Very high conflict due to "squeeze" and push	• Very advanced
• Little trust	• Leaders will drive	• Some reciprocal knowledge	• Some leaders block SRC	• Determined to continue towards strategic SRC

• Busy with other priorities:
  – growing
  – Infrastructures
	• Trust derived from 'common goal'	• Some mistrust, lot of fear	• High professional potential	• Reciprocal knowledge and trust

• Poor basis of information	• Agreement on key rules	• Need for:
		  – set of rules
		  – a catalyst
			• Need for an industry catalyst	• Good infrastructure and technology

• Need for catalyst to start SRC		• 'Let's do easy things first'		

Source: GEA [1994].

TABLE 4
THE RELATIVE PROSPECTS FOR EDI IN SPECIFIC COUNTRIES

RELATIVE PROSPECTS for EDI

Factor	United Kingdom	France	Germany	Italy
Prerequisites	Excellent	Poor	Poor	Poor
Shapers	Excellent	Moderate	Poor	Poor
Inhibitors	Low	High	Moderate	High
Accelerators	High	Low	Moderate	Moderate

Source: Walker [1994].

TABLE 5
SALES BY TRADING FORMAT OF THE LARGEST EUROPEAN GROCERY RETAILERS (%)

	Hyper-markets	Super-stores	Super-markets	Local/ Convenience Stores	Speciality Stores	Limited Line Discount Stores
UK						
J Sainsbury	6.9	93.1				
Tesco		100.0				
Argyll		79.9	20.1			
Asda		100.0				
Kwik Save						100.0
FRANCE						
Promodès	40.0		38.1	21.8		0.04
Carrefour	95.1					4.9
Leclerc	N/A		N/A			
Intermarché	N/A		N/A	N/A		N/A
Casino	61.7		36.1	2.3		
GERMANY						
Rewe BH	10.6		32.6	23.3		33.4
Aldi						100.0
Tengelmann		9.0	44.6			46.4
Asko	54.3		45.7			
Spar Handels	18.7	26.5	33.5			21.3
BELGIUM						
GIB	4.6		57.7	37.2	0.6	
Delhaize le Lion			81.8	13.4		4.8
HOLLAND						
Ahold			85.3	14.7		

Source: Burt and Sparks [1994].

more stock is cross docked and minimal stock is held in store and at RDCs. In the other three countries a high proportion of stock is held in RDCs and in store. These countries are similar to the US in that retailers forward buy and RDCs are cheap 'sheds' used to hold this, and other promotional stock in the intensely price competitive markets of continental Europe.

DISCUSSION

It is clear that the adoption of supply chain management by companies varies markedly within and between countries. Fernie [1994] identifies eight factors which tend to explain these differences although these can be classified into two types, those based on *relationship*, and those on *operational factors*.

Building Relationships

It is generally agreed that to achieve greater profitability throughout the supply chain, collaboration is required between suppliers and retailers to achieve cost reductions and improve sales. In Western Europe the initiative for forging relationships has come from the retailers as they have become more responsive to their domestic markets and take responsibility for elements of the value-added chain which were once the sole prerogative of the manufacturer. The growth of private brands, in particular, has enabled suppliers to work closer together with retailers in product development. Clearly the initial challenge to manufacturer brand domination led to conflict rather than collaboration but as penetration of private labels in many product categories has increased over the last ten years, greater collaboration between partners has ensued.

One significant feature of the GEA [1994] research was that there is no overriding panacea for supplier–retailer collaboration. Their case studies show a range of examples between partners of equal and unequal power which have all resulted in considerable shared benefits to the participants. A common theme running through the research is that reciprocal trust and product stability encourages collaboration, especially when evidence becomes available of practical results that can be achieved. Nevertheless, much remains to be achieved in supplier–retailer collaboration, especially when competition is strongly based on price cutting and promotions or there is a lack of consensus in industry about a set of codes of conduct. GEA [1994] show in Table 3 that attitudes towards collaboration varies markedly in the largest countries surveyed in the research. Spain and Italy are at the early stages of the learning curve, French companies required an industry catalyst, Germany is at the 'take-off' stage and the UK companies are most advanced.

The key factor which inhibits or accelerates collaboration in the supply chain is the adoption and implementation of information technology. The sharing of information and ultimately the integration of business functions of partners through the transmission of documents via EDI will facilitate greater collaboration. Much of the evidence from both sides of the Atlantic suggests that the enabling technologies are available but similar factors are cited for the adoption of EDI, notably a lack of industry standards, an insufficient critical mass of counterparts, the cost for small vendors and a degree of management inertia to new technology [Bamfield, 1994; Uniform Code Council, 1993; Machel, 1993; GEA, 1994].

Walker [1994] identifies four types of factors which influence the use of EDI in the UK, France, Germany and Italy (Table 4). He categorises these factors into prerequisites (essential for EDI to occur), shapers (organisations which influence EDI development) and inhibitors and accelerators (factors such as management and industry commitment). As can be seen from Table 4, the UK stands out as the leader in EDI usage. In Italy, by contrast, all of the factors work against adoption of EDI; the problem of availability of standards, cost of telecommunications, a lack of management commitment and insufficient critical mass of participants leave the Italians at the beginning of the adoptive curve. Walker [1994] maintains that the competitive French market was cited as an inhibitor to developing commitment to collaboration whereas in Germany the cost of EDI and the difficulties in restructuring organisations appear to be the main inhibitors.

Although much of the discussion on building relationships has focused upon suppliers and retailers, the partnerships between distribution companies and their clients are also worthy of comment in that the quality of service by providers of the logistics support function can impinge upon overall supply chain performance. In addition to being the leader in IT adoption, the UK has been at the forefront of fostering partnerships with professional distribution companies. Such developments go back over 25 years to the deregulation of transport markets in 1968 and the technological innovations in the handling and distribution of products around this time. Companies such as Tibbett and Britten and Christian Salvesen traditionally delivered on behalf of suppliers to thousands of retail outlets. BOC Distribution Services was created in response to a partnership relationship with Marks & Spencer when the latter company began to diversify into chilled products. These companies, in addition to NFC and the Transport Development Group, have provided dedicated distribution services to retailers. What this means is that during the 1970s and 1980s, grocery retailers centralised their distribution, in effect taking control of the supply chain away from manufacturers. This necessitated the construction of large, strategically positioned RDCs, some which were specially designed composite warehouses where products of all temperature ranges were housed under one roof. Contractors were often the instigators of new designs in warehouse and vehicle-developments, and they began to operate many of these new RDCs for retailers. Most of these contracts were long term (around five years) and 'dedicated', that is the site and vehicles were for the exclusive use of the retailer in question.

The approach in other countries differs markedly from that in the UK. Indeed, most commentators [Penman, 1991; Cooper et al., 1992; Fernie, 1994] have argued that the logistical support to stores is much more fragmented in the United States and mainland Europe than in the UK. Elsewhere, the tendency is to retain warehousing 'in house' and to contract out transport, often on a 'spot hire' basis. Cooper et al. [1992] dispute the cost effectiveness of an adversarial, lowest price approach in that it adds to administrative costs and does not enhance long-term partnerships.

Operational Factors

While the degree of collaboration by partners throughout the supply chain provides an explanation for why some countries are at a more advanced stage than others in supply chain efficiency, operational factors such as geographical spread of stores, cost structures and trading formats can determine the nature of logistical support to the retail operation.

In the United States and many of the continental Europe countries, the physical distances which have to be travelled between major urban centres encourages the holding of more in-store stock than in highly urbanised countries such as the UK and Benelux countries. Cooper *et al.* [1992] claim that the RDC concept has less applicability in France and Spain where the hypermarket is a major trading format. Here, the small number of widely dispersed sites cannot justify the additional costs of an extra link in the supply chain. Not surprisingly, geographical and other factors have a strong influence on the structure of logistics costs. The urbanised nations have higher land and property costs; therefore the maximisation of sales space in prime sites and holding stock in nearby RDCs was a major objective for UK and Dutch retailers, compared with their US, Spanish and French counterparts.

The relative costs of labour, capital and raw materials impinge upon the characteristics of distribution networks in different countries. Scandinavian countries developed warehouse automation because of high labour costs, whereas in the UK the high cost of capital in the 1980s encouraged inventory reduction and the construction of RDCs. While these sites were capital intensive and 'high tech' in terms of specification, the relatively lower land costs in France led to the development of 'low tech sheds' which often housed forward buy and promotional stock.

The UK, however, is somewhat unique in its development of composite warehousing. Even in the Netherlands, which is also highly urbanised, large RDCs exist but individual product categories are divided into cold or ambient streams for onward distribution to stores [Fernie, 1994]. This approach is also evident in the United States to the extent that when Safeway expanded initially in the UK, it developed a large site in the south-east of England along the lines of the mainland Europe model.

Part of the explanation for this difference in approach is that the UK grocery market has been dominated by one type of trading format, the superstore. Grocery retail operators in other countries tend to have a more diversified portfolio of trading formats and fascias. Table 5 shows the sales by format of the leading grocery retailers in five European countries.

Because the UK operators (except Kwik Save) have a small number of large superstores, strategically placed RDCs can supply these edge of town sites on a quick response basis. Other operators have an emphasis on hypermarkets (the French), supermarkets (Ahold), or a mixture of formats (German; Belgian companies). As mentioned earlier, hypermarkets are often stock holding points in their own right while the other formats require numerous product warehouses to serve hundreds, even thousands of stores.

CONCLUSIONS AND FURTHER RESEARCH

It has been shown that the logistical environment differs markedly between and even within countries. The amount of stock held in the grocery supply chain varies from over 100 days in the United States to 29 days in the UK, although relative performance of individual companies in specific product categories is better than these figures would indicate. Nevertheless, the main reasons why the United States and some European countries hold more stock than in the UK can be attributed to intense price competitive markets, conflict rather than collaboration between suppliers and retailers, commodity purchasing and holding of promotional stock and the slower development of information technology, especially EDI usage.

The UK is much further down the experience curve in logistics management than other countries; hence the future benefits of improved efficiencies throughout the supply chain are less than in Spain and Italy where savings of around three per cent of sales turnover can be achieved or in the United States where figures as high as 10.8 per cent can be realised. The key to success in achieving such efficiencies lies in greater collaboration between retailers and suppliers, especially in the areas of shared information and the adoption of EDI to enable these changes to take place. Nevertheless, no two countries are the same. Cultural tastes vary and so does the grocery product mix; geography is different as indeed are trading formats and elements of the distribution 'culture'. International marketers should take note of this forgotten element of the marketing mix; distributing grocery products requires a different approach between countries to take account of all the factors cited above.

Much of this paper has painted a broad picture of the current practices adopted by grocery retailers in the United States and parts of Europe. The GEA [1994] research did provide useful case studies of supplier–retailer collaboration to improve supply chain efficiency in different European countries. This is only the start of our understanding of a complex area of international retailing. More detailed research needs to be carried out of the nature of relationships between all companies involved in the grocery supply chain – retailers, manufacturers, wholesalers and distribution companies to gain a deeper insight into the evolving roles played by these operators in changing international markets.

REFERENCES

Alexander, N., 1994, 'Isoagora: retail boundaries within free trade areas'. Paper presented at the Fourth Triennial AMS/ACRA Conference, Richmond, Virginia, October.

Bamfield, J., 1994, 'Technological Management Learning: The Adoption of EDI by Retailers', *International Journal of Retail and Distribution Management*, Vol.22, No.2, pp.3–11.

Burt, S. and L. Sparks, 1994. 'Understanding retail grocery store format change in Great Britain: the continental European dimension'. Paper presented at the Fourth Triennial AMS/ACRA Conference, Richmond, Virginia, October.

Cooper, J., M. Browne and M. Peters, 1992, *European Logistics: Markets, Management and Strategy*, Oxford: Blackwell.

Dawson, J.A., 1993, 'The Internationalisation of Retailing', in R.D.F. Bromley and C.J. Thomas, *Retail Change*, London: UCL Press.

Fernie, J., 1992, 'Distribution Strategies of European Retailers', *European Journal of Marketing*, Vol.26, No.8/9, pp.35–47.

Fernie, J., 1994, 'Quick Response: An International Perspective', *International Journal of Physical Distribution and Logistics Management*, Vol.24, No.6, pp.38–46.

G.E.A., 1994, *Supplier–Retailer Collaboration in Supply Chain Management*, Europe, London: Coca-Cola Retailing Research Group.

Machel, P.G., 1993, 'Supply Chain Strategy in a Multinational Environment'. Paper presented at the IGD Conference, *Improving Supply Chain Effectiveness in the Grocery Trade*, London: IGD.

Peck, H. and M. Christopher, 1994 'Laura Ashley: The Logistics Challenge', in P.J. McGoldrick (ed.), *Cases in Retail Management*, London: Pitman.

Penman, I., 1991, 'Logistics – Fragmented or Integrated', *Focus*, Vol.10, No.9, pp.21–4.

Salmon, Kurt, 1993, *Efficient Consumer Response: Enhancing Consumer Value in the Supply Chain*, Washington, DC: Kurt Salmon.

Uniform Code Council, 1993, *Horizon Scan Project*, Dayton, Ohio: UCC.

Walker, M., 1994, 'Supplier–Retailer Collaboration in European Grocery Distribution'. Paper presented at an IGD Conference, 'Profitable Collaboration in Supply Chain Management', London: IGD.

The Planning Implications of New Retail Format Introductions in Canada and Britain

ALAN G. HALLSWORTH, KEN G. JONES and RUSSELL MUNCASTER

A recent retail internationalisation trend has been the arrival in Britain and Canada of COSTCO warehouse membership clubs (WMCs). Further investigation reveals similarities between those countries in terms of the responses of their planning systems to this newcomer. However, the wider picture must also include analysis of why so many other innovative new types of outlet are also internationalising. The trend can be seen as part of the interface between the spatial pattern of retailing and other legal matters. We therefore suggest that not just the planning system but also the legal aspects of trading regulation must be studied.

INTRODUCTION

One of the most active arenas for retail internationalisation in the last five years has been the US–Canada border. Canada has seen a dramatic influx of US retailers – prompting initiatives to assess the competitive effects and to formulate appropriate planning policy. Part of the problem for policy-makers has been that the process of cross-border activity has become intertwined with innovative retail formats. Of late, trends in the retail geography of Canada and Britain have thrown up remarkable similarities because those new formats are at last also appearing in Britain. This paper seeks to add some detail to the advance of COSTCO in both countries and reactions to it [see also Tigert, 1992]. Additionally, it is clear that the recent entry of Wal-Mart into Canada cannot be ignored. Even as the work is written up, the process is moving on and the *Sunday Times* of 13 November 1994, noted the possibility that Wal-Mart, the world's biggest retailer, was looking to move into Britain. Our aim is not to write specifically about internationalisation [see Pellegrini's recent work, 1994] nor to achieve an expression of the current market situation for discount retailers, but to try to contextualise some of the regulatory aspects of the process. Our notion of regulation covers not just planning but other aspects of market organisation.

This, incidentally, adds to existing work that shows how Britain and Canada can act as mutual role-models [for example, Hallsworth and Jones, 1991; Hallsworth 1991, 1992a].

First we briefly study the rise of warehouse membership clubs (WMCs) – especially COSTCO – and show how their entry to Britain and Canada has been effected. We then look at US legislation – specifically the Robinson–Patman acts – and argue that these have been important for the rise of innovative, US-based retailers. This leads us to discuss Wal-Mart before posing the suggestion that the planning systems of Canada and Britain have come under serious threat. We start, however, with WMCs and consider their recent growth.

THE RISE OF WMCS

The WMC can be seen as part of the ever-shortening life-cycle of retail formats. The WMC specialises in price discounts on bulk purchases of (usually) branded goods. The clubs have a membership fee and the implication is that their customers are 'trade' customers – much like Cash and Carry warehouses. A further key element is the charging of a membership fee, a practise that carries wider implications. Note, too, that the phenomenal domestic growth of the 1980s is slowing equally rapidly for WMCs such as COSTCO. This was confirmed by Morris [1993] who suggested that like-for-like sales increases over one trading year in some US COSTCO stores was, in 1993, likely to be only 3 per cent–5 per cent in comparison with over 10 per cent in each of the previous five years. A further straw in the wind was that Price Club, founded in San Diego in 1976, merged with Washington-based COSTCO on 16 June 1993 to found Price–Costco – a clear sign of fears of market saturation. Another to detect increased trading pressures was Bidlake [1992] who suggested that the need to maintain levels of growth in a sector that comprised four stores and $275 million turnover in 1980 but 500 stores and $28 billion turnover in 1991 puts operators under extreme pressure. Johns [1992] suggested that one response was that the warehouse clubs were increasing their appeal to the ordinary shopper rather than the business customer – a key problem for conventional retailers. Indeed, the idea that COSTCO in particular was moving towards a more retail type of operation was made some years ago by Johnson [1988] who even then regarded a full 25 per cent of the sales mix at COSTCO to be aimed at opportunistic retail-type purchasing. These estimates seem to be reflected in the first British COSTCO – with preliminary survey results of users indicating 80 per cent of patrons to be 'trade' users.

COSTCO IN BRITAIN

A High Court decision of 27 October 1993, not to set aside a planning decision allowing COSTCO to open a 142,000 sq. ft (gross) store in Thurrock, Essex, served to refocus attention on the significance of legal matters in retailing [see Blomley, 1988; Blomley and Clark, 1989]. Front page headlines were made because it was a consortium of the 'big three' UK food superstore retailers (Tesco, Safeway and Sainsbury) that had tried – but failed – in a joint bid to overturn the *sui generis* planning consent awarded to COSTCO. Exceptionally, COSTCO was given permission to build on land designated for commercial and industrial rather than retail uses. Thus did it start out on its attempt at 'organic' growth via a policy of new store openings on controversial sites. The judge accepted COSTCO's argument that they genuinely did operate a members-only 'club'in requiring members to pay a modest fee to join. Conversely, the COSTCO practice of not necessarily selling goods for re-sale was what attracted the opposition of rival retailers. Indeed, COSTCO were expected to generate turnover of £53 million *per annum* from the store of 12,881m² (gross) floorspace – but from where so much demand emanate if not from the existing retail sector? It is also clear that a planning decision in respect of COSTCO was resolved by use of arguments relating to the nature of its trading operations rather than to traffic, locational, impact, or other more usual planning reasons. The threat to the UK superstore operators appeared to be clear for they were already under pressure for their high land-cost strategies [Shiret, 1992; Wrigley, 1992a; Hallsworth and McClatchey, 1994]. COSTCO represented a new entrant in their sector and one that could compete in size terms yet 'build on cheaper land designated for commercial and industrial use' [*Supermarketing*, 1993]. Small wonder that the British retailers wanted COSTCO and rival WMCs to compete on a level playing field of equal land costs. Note that COSTCO was by no means an innovator in respect of operating a membership club in Britain. By adopting a low profile, 'cash and carry' operations such as MAKRO had been trading in Britain for some years. They adopted sites more clearly of a warehouse nature and downplayed any aspects of their trade that might take place with purchasers who were not intending to re-sell the goods.

Much was made in the court proceedings of the fact that many of COSTCO's customers were owners of small businesses. The vague *implication* was that most goods would be bought by businesses for business uses. Yet it would be equally true to state that many of the shoppers at rival supermarkets such as Tesco or Sainsbury or Safeway are also owners of small businesses – after all, the self-employed sector in Britain rose by 1.3 million between 1979 and 1988. The real difference is not between different types of end-user but in the fact that COSTCO's membership system allows it to target the potential high spenders. It does not in any way necessarily follow that COSTCO makes a discrimination between sales for later re-sale and sales for home use. However, in the Thurrock case, the draft judgement stated: 'there is no reason to suppose that these clubs are in any way a sham designed to get round statutory or other restrictions' [Draft judgement, 1993: 3]. This is an interesting conclusion since, at almost exactly the same time, Sampson and Tigert [1993] were stating: 'The evidence, however, is overwhelming. WMCs are primarily retailers' [Sampson and Tigert, 1993: 99]. Indeed, Sampson and Tigert [1994] have recently expanded upon the work by making reference to seven different response strategies to WMCs. On this list, response number six notes: 'In Canada, several supermarket chains have sought remedy through legal action. They have petitioned the Ontario Municipal Board to overturn or halt the zoning applications by WMCs as primary retailers and to limit their zoning applications to land zoned for retail stores' [Sampson and Tigert, 1994:53].

Interestingly, because the judge in the Thurrock case refused leave to appeal, it seems unlikely that Britain will see a re-run of the debates in other countries where WMCs have interfaced with the planning system. Other local Borough Councils are, however, using powers under Town Planning legislation in order to control what COSTCO can sell. The position is now further confused because new Department of Environment (DOE) PPG6 planning guidelines – issued just days after the Thurrock judgment – suggest that in the future such applications must indeed be regarded as retail in nature. This situation has still to be thoroughly tested in Britain. There are few situations in other countries where WMCs have faced serious 'statutory or other restrictions' – but one such is the Province of Ontario. It is clear that COSTCO's opponents in Ontario viewed the claim to be simple wholesale clubs as a sham – and sought to prove it.

WAREHOUSE CLUBS IN ONTARIO

In Canada during 1993 there were several instances of local retailers (most notably Loblaws – part of the Weston empire) and local councillors, trying to take the WMCs through the courts. The arguments surfaced most often in Ontario, not least because of its British-type planning controls. Accordingly, the contrast between Britain and Ontario provides a useful case study of planning responses in the face of retail innovation. It also confirms that COSTCO has consistently sought a trading 'edge' over its rivals through seeking lower-cost sites. This process is as true in Britain as in Canada. In Provinces other than Ontario, however, the US-based bulk discounters

FIGURE 1
LOCATIONS OF THE MERGED PRICE–COSTCO STORES IN CANADA (AS OF 1993)

found it easier to move onto lower-cost sites since planning controls were not so strict. Some evidence of the strictness of Ontario (up to 1993) can be gleaned from Price–Costco locations in Canada which are shown in Figure 1. In comparison with the other heavily-populated Provinces (Quebec, British Columbia and Alberta) Ontario, in 1993, had one COSTCO outlet per 1,053,777 of the 1988 population. The figures for the other three Provinces are, respectively, 665,300, 429,857 and 402,333, and it is of note that the ranking by population size is close to the ranking by strictness of planning laws.

Legal issues arose in the town of Ancaster, Ontario (near Hamilton) where Price Club obtained a site zoned 'prestige industrial' and a permit on 2 June 1992, to build a large warehouse club. Note that the approach was again via 'new-build' organic growth – a policy certain to bring it into contact with the planning process. On 3 June 1992, Loblaws and others appealed the decision to the Ontario Municipal Board (OMB). The OMB functions much as the planning appeals section of the DOE in Britain. The main argument used in the Ancaster case was that the items likely to be sold were retail items that should properly be sold from sites where retail planning factors applied. The town of Ancaster, which backed the development, attempted a compromise by defining a 'specialised wholesale' function for the site that included wholesaling proper but also direct sales to the public. Ontario Court proceedings focused on the quasi-legal distinction between wholesale and retail functions. Clearly, the warehouse clubs aim in part to sell to the public, precisely the constituency of ordinary retailers. Another example is drawn from the town of Markham, Ontario where Loblaws appealed on 26 March 1993, on the obscure grounds that building permits and site plan approval were obtained in the wrong order [OMB, 1993]. It thus exemplifies the efforts that protagonists go to find interesting technicalities in the law; and the preparedness of the warehouse clubs to be seen as retail when it suits them. It is clear that where land-use planning legislation exists that has to be adhered to by some retailers, then those same retailers will quickly resort to the law to ensure that those who serve the same market are treated equally.

Other examples exist of Loblaws applying to have WMCs stopped because of adverse impact they may have on existing centres – precisely the remit of British Planning Policy as laid out in the new PPG6 of July 1993 [DOE, 1993]. One example of such an approach by Loblaws was reported thus in the Toronto *Globe and Mail* in respect of a COSTCO proposal for Brampton, Ontario, where it was alleged that 'Putting the store there would 'upset the commercial hierarchy'and cause supermarket closings in the area' (*Globe and Mail*, 26 July 1993:B3). It is apparent that established British and Canadian retailers tried to use *all* available legal measures to attempt to forestall unwelcome competition. Retailers make expensive locational decisions in the light of their perception of the national context for retailing. If predatory locational behaviour is outlawed they may locate in what they view as sub-optimal locations. If the law later changes they may then be disadvantaged.

COSTCO AND MARKET REGULATION IN THE USA

A most interesting feature of COSTCO, then, is not simply that they have been involved in planning skirmishes both in Canada and England but that they can themselves be seen as a product of changing regulatory practices noted above. Many of the crucial changes in the US regulatory environment as they directly affect retailing have been thoroughly discussed by Wrigley [1992b: 733–5, 737–41] and merit some consideration. In particular, the 1936 Robinson–Patman Act brought in legislation to protect the small trader and was thus 'an attempt to protect and privilege one particular sector of the industry' [Wrigley, 1992b:734). The outlawing both of predatory behaviour and of the ability to trade on volume discounts meant that there were not inherently any great advantages in very innovative store sizes or formats. Stagnant retail groups often worked to operate supermarkets within the limits of the prevailing legislation. Vitally for COSTCO, however, the climate of the 1980s was to sweep away many anti-trust restraints, and under the Reagan administration prosecutions under this type of legislation fell away. This is an important watershed in policy for, as has subsequently been argued [Clark and Wrigley, 1993], those whose locational strategies had been based on the expectation of continued protection may be very vulnerable because of their attendant 'sunk costs' – if and when the rules change. Such changes have now negatively affected the cost base of some long-established retailers – magnified by Government inactivity in the face of corporate mergers.

THE SIGNIFICANCE OF ROBINSON–PATMAN

Those Robinson–Patman Acts of 1936 [Hallsworth, 1990,1992b] were clearly a talisman for retailer–supplier relationships in the United States. Under Robinson–Patman, US retailers were prohibited from seeking advantageous pricing deals with suppliers: a prohibition that did not apply in Britain. Accordingly, it was not until Robinson–Patman withered on the vine [Wrigley, 1992b:738, Table 7] that such deals were feasible for US retailers. In Wrigley's arguments – accepted here – the relative size and importance of British retailers testifies to this phenomenon. We also wish to note the likely effect of 'flexible production' technologies since the last decade has seen an explosion of 'retailer exclusives'. These are variants on standard manufacturer brands (lawnmowers, refrigerators, etc.) that show slight differences of badging, colour, and so on. If totally standard products were supplied at different prices to different US retailers then this might infringe Robinson–Patman. The subtleties of difference in the 'exclusives' may be just enough to evade prosecution. New 'flexible' production techniques now allow variants to be produced at only marginal extra cost.

AND SO TO WAL-MART

Graff and Ashton [1994] have recently outlined the continued spectacular growth of Wal-Mart, the diversified US retail chain. They describe Wal-Mart's origins in rural USA and its unusual and remarkable organic-reverse-hierarchical growth [Graff and Ashton, 1994:24]. This policy thrived because one very price-competitive Wal-Mart location could draw the life-blood from several surrounding communities. Christopherson [1993] also noted this ability of Wal-Mart to use prices to draw customers from a wide area and has described this [Christopherson, 1993: 282] as the 'Wal-Marting' of America [see also [Brennan, et al., 1991]. By the end of January 1993 Wal-Mart had 1,880 discount stores and 256 Sam's Club warehouses and were turning over $55.5bn per annum. Many sources have suggested that the pressure on US discounters to move abroad stems in large part from the highly-competitive trading of Wal-Mart. Our purpose in considering Wal-Mart alongside COSTCO is to note the radically different way in which they entered Canada. Indeed, part of Wal-Mart's spectacular US growth has been based on its apparent ability to find the funds to purchase existing stores from rivals. Wal-Mart made a major acquisition as early as 1981 when it purchased the Big K chain and moved away from its earlier, and unique, locational policy.

WAL-MART AND CANADA

On 14 January 1994 Wal-Mart paid an undisclosed sum to Woolworth for 120 of its 142 Canadian Woolco stores. Wal-Mart took over fully on 1 March 1994, at which time the merged Price–Costco had 29 Canadian outlets with $Can 3 billion in turnover. The key point is that by acquiring most of Woolco's 12.2m sq. ft of *existing* space Wal-Mart forestalled the legal planning battles faced by COSTCO in Ontario. US experience demonstrates that forestalling Wal-Mart's future organic growth is not easy: if one community refuses Wal-Mart, another nearby may accept – leaving the prospect of downtown dereliction as real as before. When any format appears that will affect more than one municipality then its strongest ally is the community that breaks ranks. This is indicative of the pressure that Wal-Mart can exert in the USA and the possible incentive for COSTCO to 'move on'. We do not seek here to address the very widest issues of retailer internationalisation [see, for example, Kacker, 1985; Williams, 1992; Alexander, 1990; Laulajainen, 1991] but still this leaves unresolved at least four further key aspects of Wal-Mart's entry into Canada and possibly Britain.

One is cash-flow. There are Canadian and British examples of companies brought low by expanding via buying job-lots of stores only to fail to repay the attendant debt. With some stores poorly situated, the remedy is not always found in increased sales. For Wal-Mart to make a big presence quickly in any new country it will always have to find a group like Woolco that is willing to sell out. Wal-Mart must also take on the costs of transforming the acquired stores into a successful sector of the overall Wal-Mart portfolio.

Secondly, will Canadians take to Wal-Mart? Many retail analysts still see Canada as essentially rather 'British' and are sceptical of potential success of the Wal-Mart version of the soft-sell. The perceived 'Britishness' of Canada is not, however, borne out by current statistics. Canada is a rapidly changing and 'multi-cultural' society [Muncaster, 1994; Davies, 1994]. Toronto claims to be the most cosmopolitan city in the world and sceptics may be mis-reading the situation. Certainly Wal-Mart did so – by commencing their Quebec campaign with advertisements solely in English. Note, too, that in 1995 the possible secession of Quebec was, again, a key dimension.

Thirdly, will the rather more restrictive Canadian retail environment allow Wal-Mart to expand, redesign and even re-build the stores it has obtained from Woolco? This is especially a problem with those stores that occupy locations in high-rent malls.

Fourthly, Wal-Mart has been able to use its strong purchasing power in the liberalised, post-Reagan, USA to exert better prices from suppliers (so good that it has had to appeal an Arkansas court predatory-pricing verdict). Will Wal-Mart be able to provision its stores so readily from Canadian suppliers – or has the NAFTA debate rendered the problem redundant [*London Journal*, 1994]?

DISCOUNTERS IN A WIDER CONTEXT

Pulling together all the above influences we see that the 1980s in the United States offered an ideal opportunity to WMCs such as COSTCO, Wal-Mart's own 'club' chain 'Sams', and assorted other discounters. The peculiar hybrid status of COSTCO could confound competitors in the unlikely event of planning issues being raised. COSTCO, then, is a product of its time: of the era of Reaganomics in the USA. It is too early to tell if the effect on the British and Canadian retail scene is to be equally dramatic. What is certain is that rival Wal-Mart will be a key part of the equation.

PLANNING SYSTEMS UNDER THREAT?

We have studied in some detail the origins of COSTCO and Wal-Mart because they represented a radical shift in retail styles – born of deregulation. Hardly surprising, then, that they caught out the established planning order just as it was learning to cope with RSCs. Wal-Mart, of course, avoided any planning battles in Canada through its stratagem of taking over existing retail outlets – and may yet do likewise in Britain. Should Wal-Mart attempt its US policy of relocating to nearby, larger, sites – or onto the edge of small communities – then the battles might surface. This is a classic problem for retail planning which is too often slow and reactive [see Guy 1994 for a recent view on British retail planning]. We now suggest that the innovative, freestanding retail format typified by COSTCO is, indeed, a threat to the established order of planning. We start first with the situation in Britain.

Much as in 1972, when the British planners failed to anticipate the French hypermarket invasion, so COSTCO provided an unwelcome shock. Planners are by now familiar with large freestanding stores – it has been the membership aspect of COSTCO that has caused the problems. Admittedly, the High Court proceedings were not a planning inquiry – merely a challenge to a prior planning decision. Yet many local planners were clearly happy to ignore PPG6 advice that COSTCO are indeed retailers. Why should this be so? To understand recent British retail trends it is useful to think of decentralisation taking place in three waves – first foodstores, then freestanding non-food 'sheds' then Regional Shopping Centres [Schiller, 1986]. One must conclude that COSTCO is best seen as a 'second wave' type of centre [Lord and Guy, 1991; Hallsworth, 1994], like retail warehouses. In this typology of three waves of British retail decentralisation the second wave centres have had the easier ride. The third wave centres – Regional Shopping Centres (RSCs or malls) – have come to be seen as posing the greatest threat to existing town centre developments, and have been staunchly resisted. The first two waves are now accepted as less threatening and only where 'cumulative impact' could cause town centre damage should they be resisted. Second wave or 'hybrid' retail forms have faced least resistance for two further reasons. One is that issues of social equity (can the poor reach the stores?) are less significant than with first-wave foodstores. Secondly, in a recession, any new-build and thus new tax income is welcomed by municipalities. Indeed, for over a decade,

Conservative central government has been starving local democracy of its funding base [Hallsworth, 1993]. A major new freestanding store can be a tax windfall for a city, the more so if the developer can be persuaded to build on publicly-owned land. The pragmatic approach, then, is to say yes rather than no – *a pressure that helped Wal-Mart to thrive in the USA.*

Turning now to the position in Ontario, we find that it is, if anything, rather less clear. Following a landmark decision by the OMB of 22 December 1993 in respect of its Brampton 112,000 sq. ft proposal at Highway 410 and Steeles Avenue, COSTCO appears to have a clear field. The OMB seemed to be more concerned to punish Loblaws for a vexatious appeal (and COSTCO for resisting) than to clear up the true nature of such operations. This may have been pressured by a feeling that, in a recession, backlogs at the OMB were impeding economic growth. Again we see that non-retail, wider economic factors have come to intrude. If a clear planning signal emerged at all from the OMB it was found on pp.96–7 [OMB, 1993] where 'excess competition causing actual blight' would be regarded as against the public interest. The OMB followed with precisely the point so summarily dismissed in Britain when Tesco, Safeway and Sainsbury were rebuffed – why should COSTCO get the economic advantage of locating on cheaper industrial lands when rivals paid top prices for adjacent retail sites? Called as an expert witness, Douglas Tigert was critical of the practice and raised it as a 'level-playing-field' issue [OMB, 1993: 105–6]. One might feel that the proper role of planning would be to identify highest and best uses for sites and then hold that line. Not so. The Tigert protest was also dismissed with these words: 'If Loblaws, COSTCO or anyone else can legally organise their affairs to reduce their business expenses, that's their business'. This can only be read to mean (as in Britain) that land-use zones are not *absolute* but subject to negotiation. The implications are profound and are best seen in the context of the new retail formats that are emerging in Canada.

NEW RETAIL FORMATS IN CANADA

US retailers have begun to flood north across the 49th parallel and it is important to note that the US invaders are the retailers currently seen as the newest, most dynamic, market leaders and it is possible to relate this to our arguments on market regulation. We suggested that the sea-change generated by deregulatory 'Reaganomics' specifically put newer chains at an advantage. They began to show steep market growth – and would have been pressured by shareholders and their advisors to keep the growth rate high [see Hallsworth, 1995, forthcoming, for a British analogy]. As market growth slowed, mere organic growth was certainly not fast enough for Wal-

Mart. They moved into rapid, take-over-driven expansion – including Canada's Woolco stores. For COSTCO, the growth also came to be driven by merger with Price-Club (it instantly created a group with 195 WMCs and turnover of $US 16 billion) and a faster push into markets further overseas. The theme of growth and saturation abounds in the trade literature on these groups. Price-Club was forced into a merger with COSTCO because they had, according to *Business Week* 'refused to expand much beyond their California base' [*Business Week*, 12 July 1993:122]. By the time they reached distant Ontario their market dominance was lost.

The point we stress is that all the deregulation-induced growth sectors in US retailing would have hit the possible saturation problem at the same time. We would have expected a US invasion into Canada – and it can be seen to have happened. Recent research suggests some powerful effects and Lyon Consultants [1993] were asked to prepare a report on the public interest aspects of new format retailing for the Ontario Ministry of Municipal Affairs. Not the least of their findings [see Sampson and Tigert, above] was 'These warehouse operations may have wholesale components, but are fairly described as retail enterprises and should be treated as such' [Lyon Consultants, 1993:7].

A key point to stress is that whilst COSTCO are especially interesting because of their 'hybrid' nature, many of the other newcomers are, as it were, 'full frontal' retailers. Recent developments in the Ontario market reveal both foreign retailers currently trading from 'new formats' (IKEA, COSTCO) but also established Canadian Chains that have been forced to react (Canadian Tire, Grand and Toy). Among the new format retailers are optical outlets, sporting goods, office equipment and toys. Jones *et al.* [1994] suggest that a whole new level has been added to the retail hierarchy of the Greater Toronto Area. Small wonder that the planning system is in disarray. It is possible to suggest that, in their haste to effect a quick and easy entry into the Canadian market, Wal-Mart may initially have hamstrung themselves on location. They have a heavy commitment to existing Woolco locations, many of which are situated in malls. They, therefore, have to try to make a success of locations in which Woolco itself performed badly enough to justify the management selling the chain. However, only a few of the 'new format' retailers, by definition, will be suited to such mall locations. The new format retailers seek freestanding new locations, often highway-oriented 'power centres' where many such outlets will come to congregate. Already we have seen that whilst planning systems in many Provinces now readily recognise the impacts of full-blown RSCs, they find it difficult to assess the impacts (singly or collectively) of new retail formats in new locations. There would seem to be parallels here with the British experience of 'retail parks' and 'retail warehouse parks'

[Bernard Thorpe and Partners 1985; Brown, 1989; Bromley and Thomas, 1989]. These hybrid forms have led a leakage away of trade from established centres but are not of such a high profile as RSCs. Accordingly, they have had by far the easiest ride in terms of success in finding non-standard retail locations [Schiller, 1986; Hallsworth, 1994].

TABLE 1

LEADING RETAIL CHAINS IN THE USA AND CANADA– BY APPROXIMATE 1993 TURNOVER

Top Five US Retailers

		Sales ($ billion) 1993
1	Wal-Mart	68
2	K-Mart	34.6
3	Sears	29.6
4	Kroger	22.4
5	J. C. Penney	19.6

Top Five Canadian Retailers

		Sales ($ billion) 1993
1	Hudson's Bay Co.	8.6
2	Sears Canada	4.0
3	Canadian Tire Corp	3.5
4	F. W. Woolworth Co.	2.8
5	Dylex Ltd	1.9

Figures relate to Publicly-Traded Companies only and hence exclude T. EATON Co. in Canada

Source: CSCA Ryerson Toronto.

CONCLUSIONS

When innovative retail formats appear there is an immediate temptation to conclude that the key issues are ones of micro-location and planning regulation. Our researches show, however, that the WMC trend in Canada and Britain stems from much deeper roots. Whilst the general context is one of price-competitiveness in a recession, it is impossible to ignore the pressures that were building in the United States under Reaganomics. The trend to deregulation – assisted by flexible production techniques all combined to offer advantages to any new retail formats that did not have locational sunk costs. When the CUFTA and NAFTA agreements presaged foreign expansion (just as Canadian cross-border activity was slowing) so the major moves into Canada began.

Note, too, that whilst localities were concerned with local effects and local planning matters there was also a wider agenda – in both Canada and

Britain. There is a strong feeling that the delays imposed by the appeals by Loblaws and others were seen as politically unacceptable on a wider canvas. It was felt that recession-hit Canada needed new inward investment and that reactionary forces were inhibiting this. Growth and new-build won out over established planning practice and the retail hierarchy. In Britain, the hegemonic political agenda is to beat inflation. Any business format that appears to be price-competitive is welcome – whatever the effects on others who have chosen to abide by extant planning rules. The overall picture is one where retail-related regulation at the highest, national, level can always be made to change. When this happens, aggressive new formats emerge and in turn they challenge more locally-embedded systems of regulation, such as planning systems. Ultimately, if new formats emerge strengthened, they can go on to influence the retail system in other countries. This is the clear message emerging from COSTCO and from Wal-Mart.

ACKNOWLEDGEMENTS

The authors wish to thank the editors and two anonymous referees for their helpful comments on earlier drafts, and Brian Beharrell, Silsoe College, for observations on recent activities by COSTCO in Britain.

REFERENCES

Alexander, N., 1990, 'Retailers and International Markets: Motives for Expansion', *International Marketing Review*, Vol.7, No.4, pp.75–85.

Bernard Thorpe and Partners, 1987, *Retail Warehouse Parks*, London: Bernard Thorpe and Partners.

Bidlake, S., 1992, 'Warehouse Attraction', *Marketing*, 19 March, Vol.23.

Blomley, N., 1988. 'Law and the local state; enforcement in action', *Transactions, IBG*, Vol.13, No.2, pp.199–210.

Blomley, N. and G.L. Clark, 1990, 'Law, Theory and Geography', *Urban Geography*, Vol. 11, pp.433–46.

Brennan, D.P, P.M. Flottemesch and K.S. Rowekamp, 1991, 'Analysis of the impact of discounters on retailing in small towns and alternative responses for retailers and community leaders', *Research Study University of St Thomas*, Minnesota.

Bromley, R. and C. Thomas, 1989, 'The impact of shop type and spatial structure on shopping linkages in retail parks', *Town Planning Review*, Vol.60, pp.45–70.

Brown, S. 1989, 'Form and function in an unplanned retail park; evidence from the Abbey Trading centre', *Area*, Vol.21, pp.137–144.

Business Week, 1993, 'Costco', 12 July, p.122.

Christopherson, S. 1993, 'Market rules and territorial outcomes; the case of the United States', Vol.17, No.2, *International Journal of Urban and Regional Research*, pp.272–84.

Clark, G.L. 1989, 'Remaking the map of corporate capitalism; the arbitrage economy of the 1990s', *Environment and Planning A*, Vol.21, pp.997–1000.

Clark, G.L. and N. Wrigley, 1993, 'SUNK COSTS: a framework for economic geography paper presented to annual meetings', *Association of American Geographers*, Atlanta, Georgia.

Davies W.K.D. (ed.), 1994, *Canadian Transformations*, Canadian Studies in Wales Group, University of Wales, Swansea.

Department of the Environment, 1993, 'PPG6 Town centres and retail developments', London: HMSO.

Draft Judgement, 1993, 'R v Thurrock BC and Ors ex p Tesco Stores Ltd and Ors', unpublished.

Globe and Mail, 1993, 'COSTCO, Loblaw tangle in turf war', 26 July, pp.B1–B3, Toronto.

Graff, T.O. and D. Ashton, 1994, 'Spatial Diffusion of Wal-Mart: Contagious and reverse hierarchical elements', The Professional Geographer, Vol.46, No.1, pp.19–29.

Guy, C.M., 1994, The Retail Development Process, London: Routledge.

Hallsworth, A.G., 1990, 'The lure of the USA; some further reflections', Environment and Planning A, Vol.22, pp.551–8.

Hallsworth, A.G., 1991, 'Regional Shopping Centres in Canada and the UK', Service Indusries Journal, Vol.11, No.2, pp.219–32.

Hallsworth, A.G., 1992a, 'Canadian role-models for retail developments', Canadian Journal of Urban Research, Vol.1, No.2, pp.135–44.

Hallsworth, A.G., 1992b, The New Geography of Consumer Spending, London: Belhaven (Halstead).

Hallsworth, A.G. and Ken G. Jones, 1991, 'Planners'attitudes towards retail development in Canada', Proceedings 6th World Conference on Distributive Trades, pp.535–42, The Hague, Netherlands.

Hallsworth, A.G., 1993, 'Land-use planning and regulations in Britain and Canada – some associations with local democracy', Proceedings, Applied Geography Conferences, Vol.16, pp.117–22.

Hallsworth, A.G., 1994, 'Decentralization of retailing in Britain – the breaking of the third wave', The Professional Geographer, Vol.46, No.3, pp.296–307.

Hallsworth, A.G., 1995 forthcoming, 'Stock market influences on retail restructuring'in N. Wrigley and M. Lowe (eds.), Retailing, Consumption and Capital: Towards the New Economic Geography of Retailing, London: Longman.

Hallsworth, A.G. and J. McClatchey, 1994, 'Interpreting the Growth of Food Superstore retailing in Britain', International Review of Retail, Distribution and Consumer Research, Vol.3, No.4, pp.315–29.

Jones, K., W. Evans and C. Smith, 1994, New Formats in the Canadian Retail Economy, CSCA, Ryerson Polytechnical University, Toronto, Canada.

Johns, E., 1992, 'State of the industry: marketing strategies come to warehouse clubs', Chain Store Executive, Vol.68, No.8, pp.32a–33a.

Johnson, J.L., 1988, 'What it takes to be top rank', Discount Merchandiser, Vol.28, No.11, pp.20–7.

Kacker, M.P., 1985, Transatlantic Trends in Retailing, London: Quorum.

Laulajainen, R., 1991, 'Two Retailers Go Global', International Review of Retail Distribution and Consumer Research, Vol.1, No.5, pp.607–26.

London Journal of Canadian Studies, 1994, special edition on NAFTA, Vol.4.

Lord, J. and C. Guy, 1991, 'Comparative retail structure of British and American cities: Cardiff (UK) and Charlotte (USA)', International Review of Retail Distribution and Consumer Research, Vol.1, pp.391–436.

Lyon Consultants, 1993, New Format Retailing and the Public Interest, report prepared for ministry of municipal affairs, Ontario, Canada.

Morris, K., 1993, 'Life among the cannibals', Financial World, Vol.162, No.9, p.60.

Muncaster, R., 1994, 'Current trends in Canadian Retailing', in A. Terasaka and S. Takahashi (eds.), Comparative Study on Retail Trade Tradition and Innovation, pp.213–18, Ryutsu Keizai, University, Japan

Ontario Municipal Board, 1993, Case files, OMB, Canada.

Pellegrini, L., 1994, 'Alternatives for growth and internationalisation in retailing', International Review of Retail Distribution and Consumer Research, Vol.4, No.2, pp.121–48.

Sampson, S. and D. Tigert, 1993, 'Warehouse membership clubs: are they wholesalers or retailers and who is at risk?', Proceedings, 7th Annual Conference on Research in the Distributive Trades, pp.97–101, Stirling, September.

Sampson, S. and D. Tigert, 1994, 'The impact of warehouse membership clubs : the wheel of retailing turns one more time', *International Review of Retail Distribution and Consumer Research* ,Vol.4, No.1, pp.33–60.

Schiller, R., 1986, 'Retail decentralisation: the coming of the third wave', *The Planner*, Vol. 72, No.7, pp. 13–15.

Shiret, T., 1992, 'Putting a price tag on the property of food retailers', *Credit Lyonnais Laing*, Appold St, London.

Supermarketing, 1993, 'Are the floodgates now open?', Vol.1097, pp.14–15.

Tigert, D.J., 1992, 'Warehouse Clubs', *Babson College Retail Research Report*, No.6.

Williams, D., 1992, 'Retailer Internationalisation: An Empirical Inquiry', *European Journal of Marketing*, Vol.26, No.8/9, pp.8–24.

Wrigley, N., 1992a, 'Commentary. Sunk capital, the property crisis, and the restructuring of British food retailing', *Environment and Planning A*, Vol.24, pp.1521–7.

Wrigley, N., 1992b, 'Antitrust regulation and the restructuring of grocery retailing in Britain and the USA', *Environment and Planning A*, Vol.24, pp.727–49.

Retailing in Canada and the United States: Historical Comparisons

DAVID J. BURNS and DALE M. RAYMAN

Although Canada and the United States are comparable in many ways, the retail environments of these two countries are not identical. This paper explores the evolution of the retail environments of both countries to identify the sources of these differences and provide prospects for the future. It appears that the differences in retail environment observed have their origins in population differentials and differing cultural philosophies of the countries. Although the retail environments of Canada and the United States have been converging for some time, it is unrealistic to expect that the differences will disappear.

INTRODUCTION

The similarities between Canada and the United States and their citizens are extensive. Because of their relatively close proximity to each other and the similarity of their histories, the cultures of these two countries are remarkably parallel. Indeed, 'there are few distinguishing characteristics between the individuals living on either side of the imaginary boundary separating our two nations' [McCready, 1972:17]. This cultural similarity extends to many of the social institutions existing in these countries. For instance, the retail environments present in these two countries have also been strikingly similar.

The similarity which exits between Canada and the United States, however, is not total – the cultures and, similarly, the retail environments of these two countries are clearly not identical. Instead, the retail environments found in both countries vary in a number of material ways. The purpose of this paper is to explore the development of the retailing environments in Canada and the United States. This analysis will be conducted in order to provide an understanding of the formation of differences in retail environments which exist between similar countries and to provide an understanding of the issues which may hinder the merging of their respective retail industries. First, the histories of these two countries and the consequent effects on their retail environments will be examined. Second, the retail environments of Canada and the United States as they presently exist will be investigated. Finally, the prospects for the future will be discussed.

HISTORICAL BACKGROUND

Located in the western hemisphere, Canada and the United States, and their respective retail environments, are of relatively recent vintage. In fact, the retail environments of these two countries as they are known today, developed subsequent to the Civil War in the United States (the mid-1860s). Prior to that time, the relatively small populations of both countries, and the lack of large population centres (in the early parts of the nineteenth century, only twelve cities in the United States had a population in excess of 5,000 [Mayfield, 1949]), lack of intracity transportation services, and lack of significant discretionary income among the working class, acted to restrict most retailing activities to small, single-outlet, necessity-oriented specialty stores. At that time, excluding factors related directly to population or climatic differences, there were little significant differences between the retail environments of the two nations.

The coming of the industrial revolution in many western countries during the mid-nineteenth century produced conditions which were favourable for the expansion of retail industry. It was this expansion, however, which prompted divergence in the development the retailing environments of Canada and the United States.

Industrial Revolution

The industrial revolution was, in the words of Roscher [Gellately and Roscher, 1901], the ally of retail trade. The industrial revolution provided the prerequisites necessary for the evolution of the contemporary western retail environment [Simmons, 1964]. The industrialisation process required concentrations of large numbers of individuals in single geographic areas (cities) and the development of intracity transportation systems (such as trollies and bicycles) to transport individuals to the newly formed factories (and subsequently, to large retailers). Furthermore, a direct outgrowth of the industrialisation process was the growth in discretionary income which became available to a large percentage of the population.

The urbanisation of the populations in the soon-to-be industrialised nations had profound effects on the affected societies [Shaw, 1992]. The appeal of the better ways of life promised by the industrialisation process led to a significant migration of individuals from an agriculturally-based, subsistence life style to factory-based city life. This process saw the 'representative [person] turn town dweller' [Court, 1954:232]. In this new-found life style, individuals could no longer be responsible for meeting their needs through their own efforts. For instance, it was usually impossible for these new city dwellers to grow a majority of their own food (the amount of open land necessary to provide for the fulfilment of these needs usually was not available in the cities). Many individuals, therefore, found that they were increasingly forced to satisfy many of their daily needs via retailers [Benson, 1992a].

As the result of the industrial revolution, the social and economic environments of affected areas became ripe for the development of large new retailing enterprises, many of which still play significant roles in the retailing industry of Canada and the United States today, such as the department store.

The industrialisation process, however, affected Canada and the United States differently. Whereas the United States was at the forefront of the industrialisation movement, Canada industrialised late and unevenly [Benson, 1992a]. The reasons for this disparity lie in two areas. First, the industrialisation of the United States was significantly advanced by the war effort. The American Civil War produced a need to develop large amounts of armaments quickly, a factor which became a driving force in the industrialisation of the United States. Canada, however, was not involved in this war, nor did it encounter a similar war during this time period. Hence, the Canadian industrialisation process did not have such a pivotal push.

The Canadian industrialisation process was also hampered by the country's demographics. The significantly smaller population of Canada and the greater geographic dispersity of that population made the population concentrations necessary for industrialisation more difficult to obtain. In fact, during the latter half of the nineteenth century, industrialisation, and the accompanying urban growth, only occurred in three provinces, British Columbia, Quebec, and Ontario [Benson, 1992a]. Indeed, by the end of the nineteenth century more than one-half of the residents of British Columbia and Ontario could be classified as urban dwellers, while less than a third of the residents of the Maritimes and only one-quarter of the residents of the prairie provinces could be classified as urban dwellers [Artibise, 1982].

This difference in the rate of the industrialisation experienced by the two countries had a direct impact on the nature of their respective retailing environments.

Department Stores

One of the first and most significant retailing fruits of the industrial revolution was the department store [Smith, 1956]. The department store was a large retail establishment which was actually an arcade, but with all of the 'shops' under one ownership [Taubman, 1987]. The industrial revolution provided all of the necessary prerequisites for the development of these stores. Given this conducive environment, once introduced, department stores were an immediate success. Indeed, department stores appeared virtually overnight in most of the major cities in the United States. The success of department stores came from their ability to better satisfy customer needs than the existing retailers at that time. For instance, department stores were able to provide a one-stop shopping experience. Furthermore, department stores were generally the low-cost shopping alternative. In part due to the efficiency possible through the large size of these establishments, department stores were often able to provide better value than many of the existing specialty stores. The fixed-price philosophy employed by many department stores only served to enforce this image. By the end of the nineteenth century department stores were clearly the dominant form of retailing in the United States.

Department stores, however, appeared substantially later in Canada than in the United States. For instance, Timothy Eaton, the founder of Eaton's department store and regarded as the pioneer of the Canadian department store industry [Bliss, 1987; Santink, 1990], opened his first store in 1869 – a stop which became a full-fledged department store in 1883 [Bliss, 1987]. Eaton's sales grew from a mere $1.6 million in 1891 to $125 million in 1921 [Drummond, 1987]. Although this growth was impressive, the growth of Eaton's and other Canadian department stores occurred several decades after that in the United States [Benson, 1992b].

Furthermore, the diffusion rate of department stores in Canada was slower than that in the United States. Although the department stores quickly diffused across Canada, the pace was much slower than that experienced in the United States. As a result, department stores were relatively slow to dominate the Canadian retailing scene [Benson, 1992b]. It has been estimated that department stores accounted for only 7.7 per cent of expenditure by Canadians as late as the late 1920s [Heywood, 1941] – a figure which was significantly lower than that experienced by department stores in the United States at a comparable stage in their diffusion.

Through this time period then, the retail environments of Canada and the United States were fairly similar, differing primarily in timing with the retail environment of Canada trailing that of the United States by several decades. During this era there was relatively little cross-retailing between Canada and the United States (comparatively few American firms had outlets in Canada, and vice versa). The growth of department stores, however, did result in a sizeable increase in foreign sourcing, particularly from suppliers in Europe [Benson, 1992b].

Chain Stores

A chain store system is a group of stores characterised by centralised ownership and control, and whose stores are highly homogeneous. In the United States, chain stores presented a significant competitive challenge to traditional department stores during the early parts of this century [Darby, 1928]. Guernsey noted that chain stores represented 'the most serious menace yet faced by the present type of department stores and independent stores' [Guernsey, 1929:2]. Indeed, following their birth, chain stores made immediate significant inroads into American retailing. In 1924, chain stores (including grocery stores) accounted for 8 per cent of retail business, whereas only five years later they accounted for 10 per cent of retail stores and 28 per cent of retail business [Guernsey, 1929].

The primary advantage which chain stores possessed over existing department stores was their greater efficiency which resulted from meticulous attention to operating costs, advances in distribution, and the increased economies of scale [Darby, 1928; Palmer, 1930]. In effect, chain stores provided a similar challenge to traditional department stores as traditional department stores presented to independent stores in the previous century (higher efficiency and lower prices).

A further advantage held by chain stores over department stores consisted of superior management expertise [Darby, 1928]. 'Department stores [were] victims of too much tradition and a lack of imagination or business curiosity' [Emmet, 1930:34], a condition reflected in their competitive behaviour. Competition between department stores tended to consist of adding more and more services, involving 'a constant striving for super-quality and "class" without considering cost' [Emmet, 1930:37]. As a result, even with significant increases in pricing, 58 per cent of department stores were unprofitable in 1929. Chain stores, meanwhile, competed primarily on the issue of price and proved to be very successful in doing so. (It should also be noted that chain stores typically specialised in merchandise which was standardised, generally packaged, and which could achieve high rates of turnover [Palmer, 1930]. These products were made possible through the same industrial revolution which had earlier spawned the department store).

Chain stores also made their appearance in Canada, but again at a later time than they did in the United States. 'Indeed, the development had reached considerable proportions in Europe and the United States before chains appeared in Canada in the form of branch systems of large United States variety and drug companies' [*Report of the Royal Commission on Price Spreads*, 1935:213]. Moreover, similar to the situation with department stores, the advent of chain stores in Canada did not have the same effect as their advent in the United States. The chain stores 'did not exert real influence [in Canada] until well into the 1920s', however, 'changes were there, but not in the extent that is often assumed' [Benson, 1992b: 196].

The slower diffusion of chain stores in Canada and their lesser impact on Canadian society was caused in part by differences in national philosophies between Canada and the United States. Traditionally, the United States had based itself on the idea of being a 'melting pot' with residents uniting to form one distinct new culture, whereas Canada has been based on the idea of a 'mosaic' with residents maintaining their own distinct cultures within an 'overall' culture of Canada. The residents of Canada then, have generally maintained stronger ties to their home cultures, resulting in the existence of distinctly different sets of wants and needs of across different Canadian residents. The national philosophy of Canada, therefore, produced an environment which was less conducive to the 'cookie cutter' approach which is common in many chain operations. This situation in turn, tended to preserve a demand for small specialty retailers in Canada – retailers which have the capability to address the various Canadian subcultures.

Discount Stores

The twentieth century also saw the development of another significant competitive challenge to the department stores in Canada and the United States – the discount retailer. Interestingly, discount retailers possessed many of the same strengths which the chain stores and department stores exhibited when they were first entered the retail scene many years earlier. Specifically, further advances in distribution, increased use of self-serve, and increased economies of scale permitted discount retailers to offer significantly lower prices than their department store and chain store competition.

Discount stores had their origin in the United States during the Great Depression (1930s), although much of their growth occurred immediately subsequent to the Second World War. The increasing price consciousness resulting in part from a widespread lack on income during the Great Depression provided for an environment which was conducive for the formation of these stores. Department stores, however, viewed discount retailers as potentially formidable competitors and they attempted to use their economic power to thwart this new retailer. Indeed, some department stores even expanded their real estate holdings in the CBDs where they had stores in order to prevent discount retailers from locating in the CBD, the primary retail space at that time [Grossman, 1970].

In part in response to these actions, in part in response to the high operating costs associated with locating in the CBD, and in part to the large sizes of many of these stores, discount stores typically located in other sections of town, often in high traffic areas some distance from the CBD (in the suburbs). These suburban locations, however, proved to be choice locations with the increasing reliance on the automobile for transportation (CBDs were not designed to handle automobile traffic [Jonassen, 1955; Reilly, 1929; Taubman, 1987]) and the suburbanisation of American cities [Burns, 1994]. Indeed, this migration from the central cities to the suburbs was in no way uniform. The younger, more affluent population was that group of individuals which was most likely to make the move – a group which quickly became regular customers of the new discount retailers.

The growth of discount stores in the United States was also fostered by the existence of re-sale price maintenance, or fair trade laws. Fair trade laws often made it impossible for retailers in the United States to discount much manufacturer-branded merchandise. Discount retailers were able to avoid the impact of such laws by stocking primarily private-labelled merchandise which could be priced significantly lower than the manufacturer-branded competition at other retailers.

Given a significantly different retail environment in Canada from that in the United States at this time, discount stores did not make their first appearance in Canada until 1960, nearly thirty years after their first appearance in the United States [Moyer and Snyder, 1967]. There are several reasons for this late movement into Canada. The first reason can be found in the slower rate of suburbanisation which was characteristic of Canada. Discount retailers locating in the suburbs did not always find themselves locating in the midst of young, affluent customers as was the case in the United States.

A more important issue, however, was the strict zoning laws which were more common in Canada. Canada made a stronger commitment to the maintenance of CBDs as viable retail entities – a commitment which often involved restricting retail activity in the suburbs where feasible. This philosophy can apt be seen in the following statement which addressed smaller towns.

> If a community has no heart, it has no soul; and its heart should beat faster at the core. For here is the glory of the past, the symbol of stability, the structures that our fathers and their fathers erected, the visual reminder of another time that gives every small town a sense of community [Holdsworth and Berton, 1985:vii].

Finally, the lack of fair trade laws in Canada removed one of the initial advantages which discount stores possessed over their competition in the

United States. In Canada, department stores could conceivably selectively compete on price by discounting some manufacturer-branded merchandise, an option which was not available to their counterparts in the United States. Discount stores in Canada evolved from variety chains as in the United States, but the evolution was of a more gradual nature, often without the distinct transformations as was more common in the United States. Until recently, the top Canadian discounter was Canadian-owned Zeller's, followed by American-owned Woolco (although Woolco stores were once present in the United States, they found that they could not compete in that marketplace), and American-owned Kmart. The appearances and practices of these stores were conspicuous in their dated appearance *vis-à-vis* discount stores located in the United States. Indeed, discount retailing in Canada today is not nearly as mature as that in the United States [Jones, Evans and Smith, 1994].

Summary

In conclusion, it appears that, although the retail environments existing in Canada and in the United States were similar, significant differences exist. New trends in retailing, such as the rise in department stores and chain stores, tended to arrive in Canada at a later time than the United States, and the effects of the new trends in retailing tended to be of a lesser magnitude than in the United States. Given the different environment in Canada, it appears that smaller local specialty stores in that country have exhibited a stronger 'staying power' than similar small retailers in the United States.

These historical differences in the retailing environments of Canada and the United States appear to have their bases in a number of issues. First, as discussed above, the industrialisation process of Canada lagged behind that of the United States and tended to progress unevenly. As a result, the 'modern' retailing environment tended to form more quickly and evenly in the United States. Second, as also discussed above, with customer demand as the driving force in the formation and the character of a retailing environment, the significantly smaller and more fragmented population of Canada (when compared to that in the United States) tended to make Canada a less attractive site for retail development, also causing development in the retailing environment in Canada to lag behind that in the United States. Indeed, many of the retail firms which introduced and diffused many of elements of the evolution of the retail environment in Canada were American firms expanding into Canada due to diminishing growth opportunities in the United States (e.g., chain stores and discount stores).

RETAILING IN CANADA AND THE UNITED STATES TODAY

In more recent times, the relative differences between the retail environments found in Canada and those found in the United States have persisted.

First, although the magnitude of these differences have declined, cultural and demographic differences still exist between Canada and the United States. Recently, the 'melting pot' philosophy of the United States has been questioned. Increasingly, the 'mosaic' philosophy, the traditional philosophy held in Canada, is being accepted in the United States under the name of multiculturalism. Canada, however, has experienced a significantly higher immigration rate than has the United States, which has tended to further the cultural diversity in Canada. Indeed, over half of the residents in Canada's largest metropolitan area, Toronto, Ontario, were born in a country other than Canada. It can still be expected, therefore, that smaller specialty retailers in Canada will continue to be formidable competitors in many areas of retailing, more so than in the United States.

Furthermore, although several large population centres have developed in Canada which would rank favourably in size with the larger population centres in the United States, the population of Canada is still significantly smaller (approximately one-tenth the size) than that of the United States. In many areas in Canada, therefore, smaller specialty stores can be expected to continue to prosper to a greater extent than similar retailers in most areas of the United States.

Climatic differences, resulting from the geographic differences of the two countries, have also led to differences in the retail environments of the two countries. Generally, the climate found in most of Canada is colder than that found in much of the United States. This difference in turn has resulted in differences in shopping customs between the residents of the two countries. Nowhere is this more apparent than in the location of supermarkets in the two countries. In the United States, supermarkets are found almost exclusively in free-standing locations or in community and neighbourhood shopping centres. In Canada, however, it is common to find supermarkets as tenants of enclosed regional shopping malls in Canada [Moyer and Snyder, 1967]. (Attempts by several supermarket chains to locate in enclosed shopping malls in the United States in the 1960s were met with total failure.)

Finally, Canada traditionally has not had, nor has it fostered, the 'entrepreneurial zeal' which has been valued so in the American culture [McMurdy, 1994]. With a few exceptions (i.e., Simpson's and Eaton's [Benson, 1992b]), much of the change which has occurred in the Canadian retailing environment has been the result of a slow acceptance of the ways of other counties (e.g., the United States), which has in turn been adapted to the Canadian environment.

The Coming of Free Trade

In spite of the continuation of the social, geographic, and demographic differences between Canada and the United States, the passage of the US – Canada Free Trade Agreement (and more recently, NAFTA) would lead one to expect that the retail environments of Canada and the United States will become more similar in the future. Although this is true, the effect of the coming of free trade was greatly magnified by another environmental factor – the Canadian national GST (Goods and Services Tax).

The GST was enacted in Canada as a means to begin to address the perennial Canadian governmental budgetary problems. The GST rate is a 7 per cent national sales tax which was added to retail sales in addition to the already high provincial sales taxes. In essence, Canadian consumers quickly found themselves facing significantly higher-priced consumer goods. These sudden higher prices provided Canadian consumers with an incentive to explore new shopping options which may avoid this tax. One obvious alternative consisted of cross-border shopping in the United States [Sullivan and Lavoie, 1994].

Since the majority of the Canadian population lives within two hundred miles of the US border, many Canadians found it relatively easy to shop in the United States. In doing so, they found a relatively attractive shopping environment. What they found was lower prices (even after accounting for an adverse exchange rate), more choice, and better customer service [Symonds, 1994]. They found an American retail industry which was generally much more competitive and efficient than the retail industry in Canada, offering substantial benefits which could not be obtained domestically [Chatterjee, 1991; Symonds, 1994]. More importantly, however, they gained first-hand exposure to American retailing alternatives. Indeed, the magnitude of the cross-border shopping phenomenon was so great that retail sales in Canada dropped 15 per cent in real terms from 1988 to 1992 [Symonds, 1994].

The effect of the passage of the US–Canada Free Trade Agreement was thus that it opened the Canadian retail market to American retailers – retailers to which many Canadians had already gained exposure. As a result, the number of American retailers which have entered the Canadian market have mushroomed over the past few years. Such dominant American retailers as Wal-Mart, Home Depot, Gap, and Price–COSTCO are just a few of such examples. Generally, these retailers have found a very favourable market. Stephen Bebis, president of Home Depot Canada, estimates that

Home Depot Canada was initially able undercut competitors' prices by 30 per cent [Symonds, 1994]. As a direct result, there was a significant decline in cross-border shopping – significantly fewer Canadians were making the trek to the United States to shop [Chatterjee, 1993].

United States-based retailers entering the Canadian retail market found another ally as well. In a shopping centre industry which is overbuilt and a number of existing centres in the state of being under-anchored, Canadian leasing agents are looking longingly to the United States for the prospect of new anchor stores and specialty retailers [Anon., 1990]. American retailers, therefore, found that suitable locations were, in many instances, relatively easy (by Canadian standards) to obtain.

PROSPECTS FOR THE FUTURE

Clearly, the influx of retailers from the United States will affect the domestic, Canadian-based retailers [Fox, 1994]. John Winter, a Canadian retailing consultant, predicts that by the late 1990s 'half of the Canadian retailers you see up here now may not be in business' [Symonds, 1994: 72]. Although all of this change can not be blamed on the influx of retailers from the United States (the number of retailers in the United States is likewise expected to significantly decline during the same time period), retailers from the United States have played their part.

The net effect on the Canadian retail environment is the introduction of a level of competition, volatility and change which had not previously existed [Jones, Evans and Smith, 1994]. In many instances, the existing Canadian-based retailers have been forced to adapt through the development of new, more-efficient distribution systems and the introduction of new retail formats. Such changes can be seen at a number of Canadian-based retailers, such as Canadian Tire, Consumers Distributing [Symonds, 1994], and Lewiscraft [Jones, Evans and Smith, 1994], to name a few.

Although most American retailers have been successful in their initial entry into the Canadian market, this does not imply that the Canadian retail market has simply become a subsidiary of that market in the United States. Indeed, the differences which have existed between the environments in these two countries still exist. Although the movement of United-States-based retailers into Canada has resulting in a 'seismic change' [Fox, 1994] in Canadian retailing, it does not represent the 'Wal-Martisation' of Canada [McMurdy, 1994]. The cultural, geographic, demographic, and political differences between the two nations will continue to affect the respective retail environments.

CONCLUSION

In the present economic environment, where world trade is clearly on the upswing resulting in part from a lowering of various trade barriers on a global scale, the internationalisation of retailing can be expected to continue at a rapid pace. The purpose of this paper was to explore the retail environments of two highly similar, closely located countries, namely Canada and the United States. In this instance, the retail environments of these two countries have been in the process of converging for some time. This convergence, however, has primarily taken the form of the retail environment of the United States permeating that of Canada instead of vice versa. This convergence, as it is occurring today, is not necessarily the result of the stronger economic power inherent in the United States. Instead, the higher levels of competitiveness and efficiency which have existed in the retail environment of the United States (a difference which is at least in part cultural in its origins [McMurdy, 1994]) has been the driving force.

Within this environment, however, it is unrealistic to expect a total convergence of the retail industries of these two countries. The cultural, geographic and demographic differences between Canada and the United States can be expected to be continuing forces in the continued differentiation between the retail environments found in these two countries.

REFERENCES

Anonymous, 1990, 'Canadian Centers: Overbuilt, Underanchored', *Chain Store Age Executive*, Vol.66, No.3, pp.34, 37–8.

Artibise, A. F. J., 1982, 'The Urban West: The Evolution of Prairie Towns and Cities to 1930', in R.D. Francis and D.B. Smith (eds.), *Readings in Canadian History: Post Confederation*, Toronto: Holt, Rinehart and Winston.

Benson, J., 1992a, 'The North American Scene: Canada', in J. Benson and G. Shaw (eds.), *The Evolution of Retail Systems c.1800–1914*, Leicester: Leicester University Press.

Benson, J., 1992b, 'Large-Scale Retailing in Canada', in J. Benson and G. Shaw (eds.), *The Evolution of Retail Systems c.1800–1914*, Leicester: Leicester University Press.

Bliss, M., 1987, *Northern Enterprise: Five Centuries of Canadian Business*, Toronto: McClelland and Stewart.

Burns, D. J., 1994, 'Suburban Regional Shopping Malls: Downtown Revisited, Or It's Déjà Vu All Over Again', in H. Timmermans (ed.), *Recent Advances in Retailing and Service Sciences*, Edmonton: European Institute of Retailing and Services Studies/Canadian Institute of Retailing and Services Studies.

Chatterjee, A., 1991, 'Cross Border Shopping: Searching for Solution', *Canadian Business Review*, Vol.18, No.4, pp.26–8, 31.

Chatterjee, A., 1993, 'The Cautious Canadian Consumer', *Canadian Business Review*, Vol.20, No.3, pp.34–6.

Court, W. H. B., 1954, *Concise Economic History of Britain from 1750 to Recent Times*, Cambridge: Cambridge University Press.

Darby, W. D., 1928, *Story of the Chain Store*, New York: Dry Goods Economist.

Drummond, I. M., 1987, *Progress Without Planning: The Economic History of Ontario*, Toronto: University of Toronto Press.

Emmet, B. 1930, *Department Stores: Recent Policies, Costs and Profits*, Stanford CA: Stanford University Press.York: Reinhold.

Fox, J., 1994, 'Wal-Mart's Canadian Venture Reshaping the Country's Retail Landscape', *Discount Store News*, Vol.33, No.12, pp.67–78.

Gellately, R. and W. Roscher, 1991, *The Politics of Economic Despair*, London: Sage.

Grossman, L. H., 1970, *Department Store Merchandising in Changing Environments*, East Lansing MI: Bureau of Business and Economic Research, Michigan State University.

Guernsey, J., 1929, *Retailing Tomorrow: Practical Retailer's View of the Future of His Profession*, New York: Dry Goods Economist.

Heywood, P.K., 1941, 'Tested Retail Selling Policies', *Commerce Journal*, pp.33–9.

Holdsworth, D. and P. Berton, 1985, *Reviving Main Street*, Toronto: University of Toronto Press.

Jonassen, C. T., 1955, *The Shopping Center Versus Downtown*, Columbus OH: Ohio State Bureau of Business Research.

Jones, K., W. Evans and C. Smith, 1994, 'New Formats in the Canadian Retail Economy', *Journal of Shopping Center Research*, Vol.1, No.1, pp.161–208.

Mayfield, F.M., 1949, *The Department Store Story*, New York: Fairchild Publications.

McCready, G.B., 1972, *Canadian Marketing Trends*, Georgetown Ontario: Irwin–Dorsey.

McMurdy, D., 1994, 'Baffling Bentonville', *Macleans*, Vol.107, No.18, p.36.

Moyer, A.S. and G. Snyder, 1967, *Trends in Canadian Marketing*, Ottawa Ontario: Dominion Bureau of Statistics.

Palmer, J.L., 1930, 'What are Chain Stores?' in D. Bloomfield (ed.), *Selected Articles on Trends in Retail Distribution*, New York: N. W. Wilson.

Reilly, W.J., 1929, *Methods for the Study of Retail Relationships*, Austin TX: University of Texas Press.

Report of the Royal Commission on Price Spreads, 1935, Ottawa Ontario: King's Printer.

Santink, J. L., 1990, *Timothy Eaton and the Rise of His Department Store*, Toronto: University of Toronto Press.

Shaw, G., 1992, 'The European Scene: Britain and Germany', in J. Benson and G. Shaw (eds.), *The Evolution of Retail Systems c.1800–1914*, Leicester: Leicester University Press.

Simmons, J.W., 1964, *The Changing Pattern of Retail Location*, Chicago: University of Chicago Press.

Smith, P.E. 1956, *Shopping Centers: Planning and Management*, New York: National Retail Merchants Association.

Sullivan, P. and D. Lavoie, 1994, 'Why Canadians Cross-Border Shop', in H. Timmermans (ed.), *Recent Advances in Retailing and Services Science*, Edmonton: European Institute of Retailing and Services Science and Canadian Institute of Retailing and Services Science.

Symonds, W.C., 1994, 'Invasion of the Retail Snatchers', *Business Week*, No.3370, pp.72–3

Taubman, A. A., 1987, 'Challenging Myths that Plague Retail Development', *The Real Estate Finance Journal*, Vol.3, No.1, pp.61–4.

Consumer Behaviour Convergence in the European Union

BARRY J. DAVIES and MALENE FLEMMER

This paper examines and contrasts the attitude to food shopping in Denmark and Spain in both grocery products and white goods used to store and prepare foods. The focus is on the underlying dimensions used by consumers in Copenhagen and Madrid to select food and electrical stores to patronise. The attributes studied are drawn from prior research and are consistent across the two product categories. The research concludes that there is a relatively meaningful set of attributes, which is limited in size, that consumers may employ to make judgements. The salience of individual attributes was shown to vary with the sector under consideration. Contrasts are evident between the attribute ranking given by Danish and Spanish consumers. Particular attention is paid to the manner in which consumers distinguish between 'service' and 'personnel' in making their store selection. The work is set in the context of the retail internationalisation literature, where it is held that there is a convergence of consumer tastes in different international markets that facilitate operators developing stores overseas. Some evidence is produced to support this idea, though the need for additional cross-cultural and longitudinal studies to test this idea further is recognised.

INTRODUCTION

In his review of the literature on the motives for retailer internationalisation, Williams [1992:271] writes of 'motives stemming from an *internationally appealing and innovative retail concept* due to the existence and convergence of certain international market segments' (emphasis in the original). There are eleven citations which contribute to this strand of the literature. This paper focuses on the source of this motive – the existence and convergence of certain international market segments. This singular motive is a combination of two conceptually separate, though linked, ideas. The first is the idea that there are certain segments which exist internationally, i.e., where the similarities between those within the segment outweigh differences associated with the nationalities of segment members. The second is the idea that (by implication) a degree of convergence is to be found between the requirements of segments in differing national markets. The link arises after 'convergence': by definition, an international segment can then be said to exist – though not all 'international market segments' must arise through the one process of convergence.

UK retailers themselves have identified [Alexander, 1990:185] 'problems of fundamental consideration to retailers, location, service provision and issues of cultural differences' as being of major concern in the process of 'internationalisation' within the EU. Food retailers showed themselves to be, comparatively, the most willing to adapt their format and merchandise to 'local' conditions [Alexander, 1990]. The views amongst the respondents at that time were such that the EU's 1992 programme would not reasonably be expected to 'create an homogeneous market ... the problems uppermost in retailers' minds are based on an appreciation of the issues raised by regional diversity' [Alexander, 1990:186]. However, Burt [1989] argued that a degree of convergence within the EU could be identified amongst consumers in terms of a number of personal factors. Schmidt and Pioch [1994] point out that the 'Euro-consumer' has not yet arrived, but that European consumers may be separated by factors other than national boundaries.

This paper examines the requirements of consumers with respect to food retailing and some associated products in two of the EU's member states: Denmark and Spain. The research was carried out in the capitals of those states. What the paper does not explore is the extent to which geographical and anthropological notions are connected with 'internationalisation'. When should 'regional diversity' be distinguished strictly from 'national diversity'; when should 'nation' be conceptually separated from 'state'; when do issues of culture and language override those of politics, are concerns that are not directly addressed here. However, the choice of the two locations does reflect the view that capital cities may be atypical of their nation, but in ways that are comparable from state to state. Capital cities may be thought of as more advanced, more cosmopolitan, less provincial, more adventurous, than their territories. The two states are seen as strongly contrasted in terms of their culture and language: the one Nordic and Scandinavian, the other Mediterranean and Romance; contrasted in geography and climate and contrasted in forms of economic and infrastructure development.

THE RESEARCH APPROACH

After the selection of the two countries for contrast (based on the features indicated above and the availability of linguistic skills and cultural familiarity amongst the researchers), the choice was made of the food retail sector for investigation. This sector was chosen as the food consumption patterns of Danish and Spanish consumers differed markedly in terms of, for example, purchases of frozen foods, convenience meals, outlets patronised and so on, on the basis of national statistics and commercial market research reports. As some food purchase patterns were thought to be related to the availability of white goods – freezers, microwaves – white goods were included as the second sector for investigation.

The focus for investigation was the shopping behaviour of the two groups in respect of the two sectors. As resource constraints militated against fully national surveys, the research was concentrated in the respective capital cities. Face-to-face intercept interviews were selected as the chief method of data collection, on the basis of the criteria advanced in Hague [1992:29]. The shopping behaviour was to be investigated descriptively, using the structured questionnaire. Data from the two groups were then to be contrasted. Whilst there was insufficient previous data on which to formulate precise hypotheses about shopping behaviour in the two groups, a number of propositions were developed which the research would test.

THE PROPOSITIONS

- Denmark and Spain differed on a number of relevant dimensions. This would be reflected in differences between the capital cities.
- Differences would not only manifest themselves in overt elements of shopping behaviour for food and white goods, such as frequency of shopping trips, locations visited, goods purchased, but also in consumer attitudes towards underlying phenomena such as retail store image.
- The determinants of image (store attributes) presented in the literature would be meaningful to respondents in both locations equally.
- Store attributes would be differently ranked both as to sectors and between countries.

METHODOLOGY

Research Literature

The extensive literature on retail store image was reviewed. The most relevant papers for present purposes were those of Stephenson [1969], which related specifically to food store patronage motives; Lindquist's [1974] review of the literature, and the list of store attributes developed from it; Kunkel and Berry's [1968] study on departmental store image and their determination of attributes; Hirschman *et al.*'s [1978] study which examined variation in the importance ranking of attributes, market to geographical market; Alonso and Múgica's [1986] pioneering study of food store image in Spain and Azpiazu's [1992] discussion of attributes (criteria) used by consumers in outlet selection. This review resulted in the selection of eleven attributes (which coincided with others used previously):

1. Personnel
2. Quality of the merchandise
3. Price of the merchandise items
4. Location of the store
5. Merchandise range
6. Service
7. Atmosphere
8. Clientele
9. After sales service
10. Physical facilities
11. Waiting time at checkout

Research Instrument

A questionnaire was designed (in English) which contained items related to all the facets of the study, including overt shopping behaviour and attribute ranking in respect of the two sectors (food and white goods) under study.

Engstrom and Larsen's [1987] criticism of providing the attributes for consumer to rank was considered. However, as guidance was given on context through the identification of store type – food and electrical stores – the need to allow 'user situation' (as identified by Engstrom) to determine the attributes would be offset. The concern had arisen as prior studies had investigated, on occasion, store attributes in general, with no or little specification of the shopping situation.

The questionnaire had 27 questions, and was presented in three sections relating to white goods, grocery products and demographic information. The particular structure and wording were influenced by prior research [Schwedler, 1989; and Alonso and Múgica, 1986]. Initial pre-testing revealed difficulties for respondents in dealing with the large number (11) of attributes. Several options for question format were tested, including the use of interval scale responses to individual items: some additional items (such as cleanliness, credit facilities and opening hours) were also tested.

The use of Likert-type scales in pre-test did not produce data with sufficient discrimination as many respondents tended to rate a large proportion of attributes as 'very important'. Some respondents also found it difficult to distinguish between attributes such as 'personnel' and 'service'. After four separate pre-tests, six attributes were chosen (items 1–6 above) and a ranking method, supported by open questions where appropriate, selected. This version of the questionnaire was then piloted with a sample of thirty English shoppers. The questionnaire was then, after the successful pilot, translated into Danish and Spanish. The questionnaire was not back-translated into English, because of the available language skills. It was, however, sent for comment to colleagues at the Department of Retailing, Danish Business School and the Department of Marketing Research, University of Complutense, Madrid, to whom we are grateful for their assistance.

The definitions of the six selected attributes were based on respondents' understanding, obtained early in the pilot work. Generally, other than in an element of overlap between service and personnel, little confusion or difficulty was encountered in understanding of the attributes. The definitions were:

personnel: either an established, personal relationship (when speaking of a small store) and/or the technical knowledge possessed by staff.

quality of merchandise: the presence of well-known brands and the overall perception of the standard of goods in the shop.

price of merchandise: a view of whether the relative level of charge for a given item of merchandise is high or low compared with other retailers and/or an overall perception of value for money.

location of store: proximity of the outlet to home, place of work or other retailers and/or its accessibility in terms of both distance and time/convenience elements.

merchandise range: the width (number of different merchandise categories) and depth (number of examples within a particular category) held in stock.

service: the availability of ancillary features, such as home delivery, repairs, refund policy and/or the expression of a clear wish to achieve customer satisfaction by personnel, 'read' through their actions and attitudes.

Sparks [1990/91] points out that retailers regard service as a series of physical services or facilities, whilst customers regard service as an intangible element embodied in the personnel. This research suggested that consumers may hold to both definitions, though for a particular individual, one would tend to predominate. Service and personnel are thus both included as attributes, but a supplementary open question – 'What do you associate with service?' – was asked of all respondents in order to explore this issue a little further.

Sampling

The intended sample size was 400 respondents in each country, using a proportionate sample design, based on gender and age within the population. A quasi-random sampling procedure was used. Intercept interviews were commenced at a pre-set time. The first person to pass the interviewer was approached, with substitution; a short break (two minutes) after each completed interview was then allowed, and the procedure repeated. At the end of five hours of sampling, proportions were reviewed, and respondents then sought for any strata which appeared (proportionally) under-represented in the next one and a half hours of interviewing. Sampling then became quasi-random again.

The interviewing points were rotated through selected postcode locations in Copenhagen and locations based on census information in Madrid. The locations were selected on the basis of presence of major shopping facilities and a wide mix of local residents. Four areas were used in Copenhagen, and seven in Madrid.

In the event, 307 respondents were interviewed in Denmark and 363 in Spain. Fieldwork was carried out in Winter 1992 and Spring 1993. The fieldwork in Copenhagen was adversely affected by weather, and insufficient time was available to complete all the desired interviews in Madrid. Whilst the obtained samples are smaller than those intended, they conform to the desired gender and age characteristics in the main.

RESULTS

The data gathered in the questionnaire were in the form, largely, of frequency counts and rankings. Analysis was carried out using descriptive statistics and non-parametric tests (such as chi-square, Kolmogorov-Smirnov two sample test, Kendall's coefficient of concordance) and analysis of variance techniques. The analysis was performed using SPSS PC+ 4.0 and SPSSX.

As expected, Danish and Spanish consumers reported differing overt shopping behaviours. Buying patterns for food products such as frozen vegetables, prepared meats, meat, prepared fish, fish, ice cream, bread/dough products all varied significantly between the two groups. Differences also emerged which can be related to cultural factors, such as the length of the midday break, and the proportion of women in employment.

The households in Madrid had significantly less storage space for frozen foods then their Danish counterparts, which impacted some of the frequency of purchase data. There appeared to be no significant correlation between microwave ownership and ready-meal purchase (gamma coefficient) in either group. Income level and purchase of food types was related in both samples, but in different ways. For example, in Copenhagen, those in higher income groups had an increased propensity to purchase ready meals: the reverse was true in Madrid. Males in both countries seemed ready to over-claim the extent to which (in households with two or more adults) they assisted with shopping activities (33 per cent versus 7 per cent according to females in Denmark, and 40 per cent versus 1 per cent in Spain).

These results tended to confirm elements of the propositions that differences known to exist between the countries would be reflected in the pattern of shopping behaviour exhibited. The other major element in the propositions related to the attributes that contributed to store image. The data relating to this are discussed here in greater detail.

Respondents were asked to rank the chosen six attributes when selecting an outlet (1 = most important, 6 = least important), using prompt cards. Several cards bore the attributes in randomised order, and the use of the cards was rotated through the two survey exercises.

TABLE 1
FOOD ATTRIBUTES

	Denmark			Spain		
Attribute	*Mean*	*Median*	*Mode*	*Mean*	*Median*	*Mode*
Quality	2.44	2	2	1.77	1	1
Price	2.24	2	1	2.33	2	2
Service	4.79	5	5	4.76	5	5
Merchandise Range	3.17	3	3	3.49	3	3
Store Location	3.11	3	3	3.59	4	4
Personnel	5.18	6	6	5.00	5	6

TABLE 2
CONCORDANCE AND X^2 VALUES – FOOD

	Spain		Denmark	
Attribute	*Mean Rank*	X^2	*Mean Rank*	X^2
Quality	1.78	304.4	2.45	144.1
Price	2.34	252.2	2.25	181.3
Service	4.79	242.3	4.81	341.1
Merchandise Range	3.49	146.0	3.18	80.1
Store Location	3.57	36.4	3.12	42.3
Personnel	5.03	333.5	5.19	370.1
Coefficient of Concordance (Sig. = 0.000 for all)	0.48	–	0.43	–

TABLE 3
COMPARISON OF ASSIGNED RANKS – MADRID AND COPENHAGEN

	FOOD		WHITE GOODS	
Attribute	K-S 'Z'	2-Tail Prob.	K-S 'Z'	2-Tail Prob.
Quality	3.60	0.002	1.41	0.038
Price	1.65	0.000	0.59	0.877
Service	1.09	0.188	1.71	0.006
Merchandise Range	1.35	0.053	1.78	0.004
Store Location	1.85	0.008	1.47	0.026
Personnel	1.01	0.255	0.32	1.000

TABLE 4
MAN-WHITNEY U-TEST SCORES

	FOOD		WHITE GOODS	
Attribute	Corrected Z-Score	Sig.	Corrected Z-Score	Sig.
Quality	-7.93	0.000	-3.28	.010
Price	-1.61	0.107	-0.97	0.330
Service	-0.18	0.859	-2.23	0.026
Range	-3.13	0.002	-4.75	0.000
Location	-4.07	0.000	-2.06	0.398
Personnel	-2.07	0.038	-0.55	0.583

TABLE 5
SERVICE ASSOCIATIONS (FOOD)

Percentage of Responses

	Copenhagen	Madrid
Personnel	47.9	43.8
Product features	15.0	11.6
No queue	6.5	3.9
After Sale	4.6	5.5
Easy Access	3.6	3.3
Home Delivery	1.6	7.4
Opening Hours	0.3	1.7
Cleanliness	0.3	4.7
Other	2.6	0.6
Don't know	2.0	5.8
Nothing	15.6	12.1

Food Store Responses

The modal and mean scores for the attributes are shown in Table 1. In general, the frequency distributions of ranks were highly skewed towards rank 1 or 2 for price and quality; for service and personnel, skewed towards 5 and 6, with merchandise range and location centred on 3 and 4. For all attributes in both samples, chi-square tests showed significant differences from the rectangular distribution. Table 2 shows the calculated values.

The Kolmogorov–Smirnov two sample test, which is sensitive to any differences between the distribution observed in samples, was used to test for the difference (if any) in the pattern of ranks assigned to each attribute by the two samples. (Table 3). Price, quality, location and range (the four highest ranked attributes) show significant differences between the two groups sampled. In general, using all measures of central tendency, the switching of price and quality and of location and merchandise range in order of preference between the two samples is consistent.

Respondents showed themselves able to discriminate between the attributes, and were able to provide rankings for them. The additional, open question had been provided to probe attitudes to service, as some prior work suggested this could be confused with personnel by shoppers. Our results show that, whilst there is a strong association between the two, they remain distinguishable in some way.

The consistency of the assigned rankings for the attributes amongst the sample was tested using Kendall's coefficient of concordance, W, which may take values between 0 (no agreement amongst judges) and 1 (perfect agreement) in terms of assigned ranks. Table 2 shows the obtained values.

The responses to the supplementary open question – 'What do you associate with service?' – are given in Table 5. The Mann–Whitney U-test was performed to examine differences, if any, in the sum-of-ranks assigned by the two groups. (See Table 4.)

These figures suggest that the two samples differed significantly with respect to the rankings assigned to quality, location, range and personnel. Price seems to be rated similarly (though it is edging towards significant difference) and service was rated in the same way. Examination of the distributions shows similarities and differences being exhibited in two ways: the preponderance of assigned ranks within a sample varied, though the pattern was similar; or the pattern of ordering was different, even though the proportion selecting the first, second choice, etc. categories was similar.

TABLE 6
WHITE GOODS

	Denmark			Spain		
Attribute	Mean	Median	Mode	Mean	Median	Mode
Quality	1.98	2	1	1.68	1	2
Price	2.14	2	1	2.21	2	1
Service	3.65	4	4	3.50	3	3
Merchandise Range	3.70	4	5	4.25	4	5
Store Location	4.57	5	6	4.51	5	6
Personnel	4.78	5	6	4.81	5	6

TABLE 7
WHITE GOODS

Chi-square Values

Attribute	Denmark	Spain
Quality	271.4	350.8
Price	221.9	247.4
Service	103.9	114.3
Merchandise Range	40.6	93.4
Store Location	186.5	141.3
Personnel	186.9	242.1

(Sig = 0.000 for all)

TABLE 8
SERVICE ASSOCIATIONS (WHITE GOODS)

Percentage of Responses

	Copenhagen	Madrid
After Sales	51	62
Personnel	41	28
All others	8	10

TABLE 9
ATTRIBUTE SUMMARY

	FOOD		WHITE GOODS	
	Denmark	Spain	Denmark	Spain
Most Important				
	Price	Quality	Quality	Quality
	Quality	Price	Price	Price
Some Importance				
	Location	Range	Service	Service
	Range	Location	Range	Range
Least Importance				
	Service	Service	Location	Location
	Personnel	Personnel	Personnel	Personnel

TABLE 10
FOOD ATTRIBUTES

Importance Rankings (1 = Most Important)

Attributes	Alonso and Mugica	Current Study
Quality	1	1
Cleanliness	2	•
Price	3	2
Product Range	4	3
Store Location	5	4
Quick Service	6	5
Personnel	7	6
Offers	8	–
Opening Hours	9	†
Atmosphere	10	–
Home Delivery	11	*

• 4.7 per cent of respondents mentioned this in open question
† 1.4 per cent of respondents mentioned this in open question
* 7.4 per cent of respondents mentioned this in open question
– Not included in closed questions and not mentioned in open responses

Electrical Store Responses

The data for white goods are shown in the tables, in respect of the same six selected attributes.

The pattern of ranks assigned was again highly differentiated. Price and quality were again dominant, but service and range took on far greater importance than for food outlet selection, with location and personnel being relegated. As with food stores, the assigned ranks were not rectangularly distributed. Table 7 shows the results of the chi-square tests. Each of the selected attributes was compared using the K-S two sample test, as to differences between the samples with respect to the ranks assigned. The test results are shown in Table 3. Range and service are significantly different in the pattern of rank assignment between the two cities, as are also (though less markedly) quality and location. Both price and personnel, however, show a similar distribution of ranks. The exploratory question related to service produced a much more concentrated set of responses in respect of white goods in both countries (Table 8).

As the replies were from an open-ended question, they can be further categorised. Sixty per cent of the Danish 'personnel' responses specifically mentioned technical expertise and 17 per cent referred to 'friendliness'. In Spain, the situation was reversed – only 25 per cent of personnel responses concerned expertise but 67 per cent alluded to friendly staff. The sum of assigned ranks for attributes used in electrical store selection was also explored using the Mann–Whitney test (Table 4). Merchandise range and quality are shown to have different ranks assigned between the two groups (highly significantly), whilst service also differs significantly. Price, location and personnel seem to be drawn from samples having the same sum of ranks for each attribute.

In summary, it seems that the attributes fall into pairs with respect to their importance to consumers in purchase situations. The respondent groups differed both from one another in many instances in the rankings typically assigned, and in respect of the apparent salience of attributes between the merchandise categories under investigation.

DISCUSSION

The data show that the selected attributes are meaningful as components or contributors to store image and outlet selection – the low non-response rates and discrimination applied in assigning ranks support this view. Each sample produced a relatively consistent set of attribute rankings. The assigned ranks, however, differed significantly between the two groups.

The data and analyses support the contention of Hirschman *et al.* [1978] that whilst consumers decide on store patronage and form retail images in all markets (defined geographically), the weighting attaching to a particular attribute varies between geographical locations. They further contend that knowledge of the major dimensions in one market does not serve to determine the major dimensions in a second. The research reported here does not support that contention. Pre-testing and piloting in the UK, and the open ended question responses in Copenhagen and Madrid suggests that the list of variables may well be similar. Alonso and Múgica's [1986] study of store attributes in Spain identified the attributes of food stores (in order of importance) shown in Table 10, where they are contrasted with the ranks assigned by respondents in the current study. The relative consistency between studies is heartening.

In general, we feel that the results presented here, relating to food and electrical store choice, support the view that there is probably a relatively consistent set of store attributes (in different sectors) used by consumers in making store choices. In support, there is the direct data; the correspondence between this work and earlier work in Spain and the observation that the derived set of attributes results from a number of chiefly US sources. What is clear is that the relative importance attached to a particular attribute by shoppers in a geographical market is likely to be relatively consistent within that market, but that shoppers elsewhere may weight the same attributes differently in respect of a particular store type, whilst within a market attributes vary in importance between store types.

These results lend credence to the view that retail operators may need to vary the particular offer to suit given locations – and that this need was uppermost in the minds of retailers [Alexander 1990] within the UK in respect of EU expansion. However, it may be that there are some segments in markets that are sufficiently alike across national markets as to make this a modest degree of needed modification, if any. Discount grocery formats, or fashion formats such as Benetton, may be examples of this: relatively modest (if any) variation in format and merchandise across national market boundaries. An alternative explanation of the same phenomenon may be that a particular purchase situation in respect of such formats outweighs national differences.

The consistency shown in the white goods attribute rankings (relatively speaking) may allow the tentative suggestion that stores selling particular types of merchandise may require less adaptation of offer internationally. The caveat is that there is other (weaker) evidence here to show that a choice of factor that is ostensibly the same may conceal some inter-national differences. Such a position would be consistent with the most powerful motivator for retail internationalisation unearthed in Williams' [1992] study viz. 'the broad global convergence of markets based upon lessening cultural distinctions and increased similarity in consumer lifestyle' [Williams, 1992:275] that seemed apparent to his UK respondents. We would not agree with his proposition that retailers do not appeal to 'the mass heterogeneous market but often pursue a concentrated market strategy to homogenous market segment' [Williams, 1992:275]. The balance of evidence, such as it is, suggests that between-nation differences in a given sector are likely to be larger than within nation differences unless it can be shown that an international segment does in fact exist. The consequence is that, within a national market, many large retailers do pursue a mass heterogeneous market – or at least succeed in attracting one.

It may be argued that, despite the evident contrasts between Copenhagen and Madrid, the two capitals share in some European characteristics that override local variation. Wider comparative studies would provide some evidence to address this point: though given the US location of much previous work in this field, an Asian, African or Latin American perspective would be useful. The other major element implicit in Williams' [1992] analysis of the motives for retailer internationalisation is the time dimension of 'convergence'. Longitudinal studies, as well as comparative studies, are also required to assess within-market changes over time.

Until wider studies – in terms of both locations and types of outlet – are available, the position consistent with current knowledge appears to be that there are partial consistencies within outlet categories across national markets, but too little to treat, say, the EU as one market. The attributes that consumers internationally use to understand retail store offers are drawn from a relatively limited repertoire, but there may be differences in national interpretation of those attributes. Internationalising retailers still need to attend to the variations that exist between markets nationally, unless they can determine that any offer to consumers they make appeals to a homogeneous market segment – a situation that is likely to arise only in a minority of cases.

REFERENCES

Alexander, N., 1990, 'Retailing Post – 1992', *Service Industries Journal*, Vol.10, No.1, pp.172–87.

Alonso J., and L.L. Múgica, 1986, 'Customer Store Image in Spain: an Empirical Study on Food Stores', *International Journal of Retailing*, Vol.1, No.2, pp.3–11.

Azpiazu, J., 1992, '"El 'Nuevo" Consumidor Espanol: Imagen de los establecimientos y captacion de clientas la conducta de patronazgo', *Distribucion y Consumo*, Vol..4, pp.26–30.

Burt, S., 1989, 'Trends and Management Issues in European Retailing (Section 1: the European Consumer)', *International Journal of Retailing*, Vol.4 (4), pp.1–97

Engstrom, H., and H.H. Larsen, 1987, Husholdningernes Butiksvalg – Indkobsabfaerd for Daglig-Varek. Erhvervsokonomisk Forlag.

Hague, P., 1992, *Industrial Market Research Handbook*, London: Kogan Page.

Hirschman, E., B. Greenberg and D. Robertson, 1978, 'The Intermarket Reliability of Retail Image Research: an Empirical Examination', *Journal of Retailing*, Vol.54, No.1, pp.3–12.

Kunkel, J., and L.L. Berry, 1968, 'A Behavioural Conception of Retail Image', *Journal of Marketing*, Vol.32, No.4, pp.45–51.

Lindquist, J., 1974, 'The Meaning of Image – A Survey of Empirical and Hypothetical Evidence', *Journal of Retailing*, Vol.50, No.2, pp.29–38.

Schmidt, R., and E. Pioch, 1994, 'The Elusive Euro-consumer', *Consumer Policy Review*, Vol.4, No.1, pp.4–9.

Schwedler, M., 1989, Nyt Liv, Nye Spisevaner.

Sparks, L. 1990/1, 'Retailing in the 1990's: Differentiation through Customer Services?' *Irish Marketing Review*, Vol.5, No.2, pp 29–45.

Stephenson, P.R., 1969, 'Identifying Determinants of Retail Patronage', *Journal of Marketing*, Vol.3, No.3, pp.57–60.

Williams, D.E., 1992, 'Motives for Retailer Internationalisation: Their Impact, Structure and Implications', *Journal of Marketing Management*, 8, pp.269–85.

The Internationalisation of Retailing in the Czech and Slovak Republics

TOMÁŠ DRTINA

Czech and Slovak retailing has, in the past, had low amounts of selling space, inconvenient retail structures and the consumer in an inferior role. After the fall of the communist regime, a period of fundamental economic transition began. Privatisation has entirely changed the ownership structure and the retail network has become very fragmented. Now a re-concentration process has been started. These developments go hand in hand with changes in the quality of retail supply, and are supported by the influx of foreign retail chains.

HISTORY

The 40-year socialist period is sometimes described, with a typical bitter Czech sense of humour, as 'a long, hard and distressing road from capitalism to capitalism' [Krásný, 1992]. Although tremendous changes have occurred since the fall of the communist regime, the old regime still strongly influences the contemporary patterns of society, the economy and the everyday life of people in the countries of Central and Eastern Europe. Nevertheless, the gap is narrowing between East and West. Distribution is also experiencing convergence.

Before the Second World War, Czechoslovakia belonged to the developed European countries and the development of retail network did not remarkably differ from its western neighbours. After taking power in 1948, the communists disrupted this evolution. As early as the beginning of the 1950s, the private sector was virtually liquidated as a 'necessary condition for successful development' of the economy. Along with the state sector, co-operatives were allowed to exist, although their role was limited. They operated mainly in the country and they were closely controlled by the state.

In accordance with the concept of a centrally planned economy, retailing was degraded to the role of apportioning goods, where central direction was intended to minimise distribution costs. The intention was that the distribution system created should avoid 'useless competition'. Distribution could be carried out only by a limited number of trade enterprises, usually monopolistic, within one branch and one region.

The margins for both state and co-operative distribution activities were centrally fixed at a very low level, about three times lower than usual in developed market economies. Furthermore, volumes to be sold, as well as price levels charged were fixed by state institutions. Consequently one product had the same price both in the town where it had been produced and 500 kilometres away. Likewise the price was the same in an exclusive shop in the centre of Prague and in a dirty supermarket somewhere on the outskirts.

As for the increase of selling space, the so-called population needs were calculated and accordingly space extensions were planned. However, they were always very small. Investment in retailing was not considered to be of significance. As a consequence of this mistaken approach, which was adopted in most East European countries, the retail network was limited in its market coverage and especially lacking in the provision of large-scale outlets. The best level of supply within the former Soviet bloc was achieved in East Germany, Czechoslovakia and partly also in Hungary (where private businesses were not completely banned and could thus play a positive role). The amount of selling space per inhabitant in these countries was only around 0.3 m², roughly only a third of the level to be found in developed economies [Krásný and Drtina, 1989; Krásný, 1991] – see Figure 1.

FIGURE 1
SELLING SPACE (m²) PER 1,000 INHABITANTS (1989)

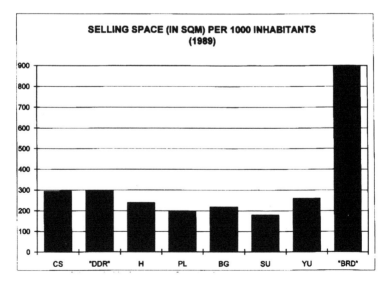

Note: Only so called 'main assortments' mentioned.

The revolutions of 1989 and 1990 saw the fall of communist regimes: however, it has been anything but easy to change radically the structure and development of the entire economic system. The Czech Republic, Poland, Hungary and Slovakia have been the most successful countries of eastern Europe in transforming their economic framework, although, of course, a lot still has to be done.

ECONOMIC TRANSITION

What conditions had to be fulfilled in order to introduce a free market system within the Czech and Slovak distribution systems? From 1 January 1991, practically all price subsidies, with some exceptions such as energy, have been abolished and price levels are no longer determined 'from above'. The course of this price liberalisation can be perhaps given as a text-book example of links between supply and demand. Only during the first ten days of January did food prices increase by 32 per cent. Consumers reacted unambiguously, immediately reducing their purchases and consumption. Retailers responded by setting prices at lower levels, until a market balance was established [Drtina, 1991]. Nowadays, a monthly price increase in the Czech Republic does not exceed 0.7 per cent in foodstuff and 0.9 per cent in non-food products, which is the lowest percentage level of all the transitional countries.

From January 1991, foreign trade has been fully liberalised. Furthermore, the so-called inner convertibility of the Czechoslovakian crown has been introduced, enabling Czechoslovakian enterprises free access to Western currencies. Sets of important legislative regulations have been passed, along with a new Business Code. A VAT system was introduced in January 1993 in the Czech Republic, with a rate of 5 per cent on food and 23 per cent on non-food products. In January 1995, the rate on non-food items was reduced to 22 per cent.

However, all these steps would hardly make sense if the question of privatisation had not also been addressed in a similar fashion. There have been several privatisation routes in Czechoslovakia. First, a restitution of the property nationalised after 1948 has been established for the original owners or their heirs. Second, the so-called 'small privatisation' started in February 1992, with a framework in which outlets were offered at public auctions. Foreigners were prohibited by law from participating in the first round of bidding, but were not barred from buying out the winning local bidder. Some foreigners have used this opportunity. The third way has been the 'large scale privatisation', through which big state enterprises have been privatised in various ways, such as through the direct sale to Czechoslovakian companies or to foreign investors, through management buy-out, or through transformation into a joint-stock company with some shares sold to the public at a symbolic price through investment coupons.

FIGURE 2
DEVELOPMENT OF DISTRIBUTION STRUCTURES IN THE CZECH AND SLOVAK REPUBLICS
USING THE EXAMPLE OF FOODS

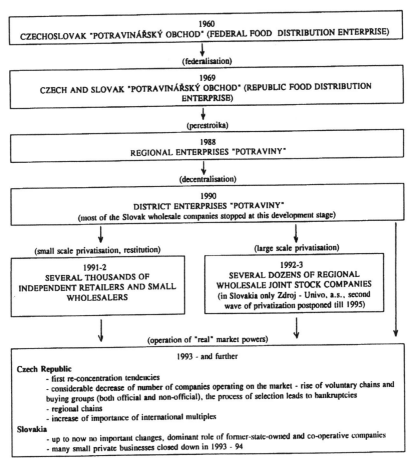

RETAIL DISTRIBUTION

Development of distribution structures in the Czech and Slovak Republics can be partly explained by using the example of food products (see also Figure 2). During the socialist period, most shops were named according to the goods offered, thus, they mostly carried the name POTRAVINY

(FOOD). In the 1960s, there was one state-owned Czech enterprise, called 'Potravinársky obchod' (Food Trade). This company was responsible for the distribution of food throughout the whole country, both retail and wholesale. After a federal law had been approved in 1968, it split into two enterprises – the Czech Food Trade and the Slovak Food Trade (1969) [INCOMA Praha, 1991].

Perestroika brought further decentralisation. In 1988, 12 regional POTRAVINY or PRAMEN enterprises were established and in 1990 several district enterprises were also set up. Most of the Slovakian wholesale companies remained at this development stage.

Following all necessary enabling laws, the setting of guidelines for private entrepreneurial activities, price liberalisation and in particular, privatisation itself, massive changes have occurred in the distribution system. Within a framework of public auctions (small privatisation) more than 11,000 outlets have been privatised and, through restitutions, a further 7,000 former state outlets have come into private hands. The number of co-operative stores has fallen from 18,000 to 7,000, mostly due to restitution and through the renting or selling of these shops to private entrepreneurs. Approximately 10,000 co-operative *horeca* outlets were privatised. Also, tens of thousands of new outlets, mostly small ones, have opened. All these steps were very desirable from the general political point of view, they nevertheless saw the atomisation of retail distribution. This trend was not as marked in Slovakia.

In 1991, and especially in 1992, the Czech retail network, and partly the Slovakian one, became enormously fragmented as a result of periods of restitution and public auctions. The former socialist monopolies lost their power. Only some of them succeeded in keeping at least some shops. Most of the wholesale divisions of the enterprises were privatised as part of a large-scale privatisation scheme in 1993 and 1994. This upheaval resulted in a completely different retail scene. The increase in the number of active retail and wholesale companies was enormous. Czech and Slovak entrepreneurs discovered a market niche after the breakdown of the old distribution channels. The boom in private business can be measured by the number of private enterprises registered, nearly 1.5m by the end of 1992. Approximately one-sixth of them dealt with distributive trades, although about 50,000 were active in retailing. In the Czech Republic, the number of wholesale companies registered increased from some 450 in 1990 to 19,500 in 1993, while a further 40,000 entrepreneurs have announced that trading is one of their activities [Czech Statistical Office information].

By the end of 1992, retail companies with less than 25 employees accounted for 66 per cent of sales in the Czech Republic and 67 per cent in Slovakia [Czech Statistical Office information]. For consumer good suppliers, both producers and wholesalers, this meant a drastic change in their clientele. It is now much harder for them to reach the final consumer. While in the past they sold their products only to a few distribution companies, now they have to face hundreds or even thousands of them. Producers have had to develop their own market support teams. There has been a tremendous growth in the number of sales representatives, sales promoters and field managers.

In contrast to the radical organisational and ownership changes, there has not been a radical change in the physical structure of distribution outlets. This is the result of inertia within the investment process. While thousands of new outlets have appeared, the large outlets are mostly formed by reconstructing warehouse facilities, revitalising old shops which were closed, and utilising space on the ground floor of panel block housing. The absolute increase in the number of food shops is linked with buoyant demand, compared with the non-foods sector, and also with certain legal measures, such as the protection of food outlets privatised during the small privatisation process. Unfortunately, the average size of outlets remains low – only about 90 m² of selling space. In spite of the enthusiasm of Czech and Slovak entrepreneurs, their financial backing is not substantial enough to support the development of large-scale retail facilities. Consequently, foreign investors have an important role [Baker, 1991]. Their influence is considerable due to the fact that those ambitious and dynamic Czech and Slovak retailers who wish to develop their retail operations observe these foreign competitors and try to copy their operations.

Due to the rise in new operations, the Czech and partly the Slovak retail scene is beginning to mirror western patterns. Consequently, customer attitudes to the quality of retail services have become more positive. While in spring 1990 only ten per cent of households said they were satisfied with retail facilities, two years later 67 per cent were satisfied [Drtina, 1992a]. Research into shopping habits and consumer attitudes towards the retail network raises some interesting issues. Primarily, consumers are interested in the quality of merchandise and a pleasant and professional quality of service. Thereafter, they indicate the importance of a wide selection of merchandise and lower prices.

Under pressure from market forces, the situation in Czech and Slovak retailing has altered considerably since 1994. A phase of selection is under way – only the strong can survive. In the Czech Republic, the number of companies operating in the market is declining, which is leading to concentration in the retail sector. Numerous small companies have gone bankrupt and some former state enterprises have been liquidated. The importance of multiples, especially international multiples and regional chains, is increasing. Voluntary chains and buying groups operate in the market in both an overt and hidden way. Franchising has become a hot topic of the day. In Slovakia, the changes have not been considerable until now – former state-owned and co-operative companies still play a dominant role. Retailers and wholesalers have begun to realise that is very difficult to survive as an independent enterprise. VEGA is a good example of the new voluntary integration of food wholesalers. This group had 40 members at the beginning of 1995 and turnover is estimated to represent about one quarter of the Czech market share.

Later changes have also manifested themselves in the significant decline of canteen catering. Its share is now estimated to be around 2 per cent of food sales. Retail outlets have taken on new forms. Discount stores and Cash & Carry (C&C) operations are of growing importance. C&C wholesalers often serve the final consumer, and thereby operate as discount operations. Furthermore, sales have risen in greengrocers, kiosks and tobacco shops. New distribution channels have appeared, including petrol stations and home delivery of foods. However, their turnover is still very low. The Dino Warehouse Club in Bratislava is representative one of the most modern examples of wholesale/discount retailing in Slovakia. Likewise, the first out-of-town facilities and the first specialised large-scale non-food outlets have been launched to provide do-it-yourself merchandise, furniture and carpets.

There are no 100 per cent reliable data available on the numbers of outlets. A rough survey based on INCOMA estimates is presented in Table 1.

TABLE 1
NUMBER OF RETAIL OUTLETS IN THE CZECH REPUBLIC AND SLOVAKIA (1994)

Food stores (incl. C & C)	17 000	8 000
of which supermarkets over 400 m²	300	60
Mixed stores (department stores and co-operative shopping centres)	9 500	3 500
Non-food stores	22 000	8 000
Restaurants (incl. other catering)	21 000	7 000
Kiosks	2 500	1 800
Petrol stations	800	350
Distribution points in total	72 800	28 650

Source: INCOMA Praha.

The position of the biggest Czech and Slovak retail companies corresponds with the atomised structure of the market. The biggest Czech retailer (KMart) had a retail market share of less than 1 per cent in 1993 and the biggest Slovak retailers (KMart and Zdroj Košice) had only slightly above 1 per cent [Anon., 1994]. In some western countries, the corresponding figure may be between 20 per cent and 30 per cent. Similarly, the top five Czech retail companies accounted for only 3 per cent of the market, and the Slovak top five only 5 per cent of the market. In some western countries, the corresponding figure may be between 50 per cent and 70 per cent. In future years we can expect the position of retail chains to be much stronger, especially through the development of foreign multiples.

INTERNATIONAL RETAILERS

The role of foreign retailers is becoming increasingly important. During the early 1990s hesitation and fear was generated by an ambiguous regulatory system and an unfriendly bureaucratic system, and low purchasing power prevailed [Drtina, 1992b]. However, by 1993 foreign retail and wholesale companies were beginning to exert a market presence. Their market share is increasing rapidly. The biggest increase, however, is expected to come in the second half of the 1990s, with the development of large shopping centres. This will lead to higher levels of concentration and integration. International know-how, links to foreign suppliers and sufficient capital resources for large investments are held to be the main benefits.

While in 1992 KMart was the only foreign company within the top 10 Czech retailers, in 1993, Spar and, in 1994, Ahold's daughter company, Euronova, joined this prominent group. The growth of Delvita (a division of Delhaize le Lion), BILLA and Plus Discount (Tengelmann) is making those companies increasingly important in the market. In Slovakia, KMart is still the only big international company on the retail market.

It is worth considering the main foreign retailers in the Czech and Slovak retail markets [INCOMA Praha, 1994]. Without any doubt, the biggest foreign investment has come to Czechoslovakia from outside Europe. The American KMart, operating in the United States as a huge network of hypermarkets, decided in the early 1990s to expand its activities into Europe. Czechoslovakia was chosen as a location. Privatisation of the state-owned network of department stores PRIOR also offered opportunities for foreign interests. KMart started negotiations with the Czech government and succeeded in winning a majority stake in 13 large department stores – 6 in the Czech Republic (in Prague – 9,000 m², Brno, Liberec, Plzen, Pardubice and Hradec Králové) and 7 in Slovakia (Bratislava – 15,000 m², in Nitra, Zilina, Košice, Banská Bystrica, Prešov and Stará Turá). The Americans promised to import into Czechoslovakia the same amount of merchandise as the company sourced in Czechoslovakia and exported overseas. In the beginning, a rather long time period was spent in market observation and the training of personnel. In 1993 KMart started to refurbish their biggest department stores. The first of them has been completed in Prague – the flagship (called 'Máj', currently 11,000 m² of selling space) is also the headquarters of KMart Europe. KMart not only holds the biggest foreign investment in Czech and Slovak retailing, but is at the same time the biggest retail company in both countries with sales of CEK 4.5bn (c. US$ 150m) and SLK 2.6bn (c. US$ 90m). But KMart are not satisfied with that. They realise they need to introduce a system of centralised buying. Moreover, for the coming years, investments in new locations are planned.

The second largest foreign investment scheme has been managed by the Dutch group Ahold. They belonged to the first group entering the Czechoslovakian market, however they were not as successful as KMart in the beginning. In 1990 they had already started intensive negotiations with the Ministry of Trade and with state enterprises dealing with food retailing. Although the Ministry of Privatisation blocked a big part of their plans, they did not give up their efforts. In June 1991, their Czechoslovakian subsidiary, EURONOVA, launched their first supermarket called 'Mana' in Jihlava, and by the end of 1992 another 14 outlets were opened, mainly in the South Moravian region, an area with a relatively lower purchasing power. In early 1994 they succeeded in acquiring 12 supermarkets in Northern Moravia and by the beginning of 1995 they operated some 35 supermarkets, mostly under the 'Mana' fascia. Mana shops are very popular with customers, not just because of the modern selling concepts, common to most of Albert Heijn's outlets, but also for a friendly atmosphere. Ahold put special emphasis on the quality of personnel, from top managers to shop assistants. EURONOVA's headquarters is in the second largest Czech city of Brno. Both C&C stores (in Jihlava and Uherské Hradiště) and the new discount line Sesam (their first outlet was in Olomouc) are managed from Brno. Top managers at EURONOVA hope to enlarge their network of supermarkets to 200 by the end of 1995. Some of the new stores will be operated on a franchise base. In the Czech Republic, EURONOVA is among the top five retailers; however, expansion plans in Slovakia have been frozen.

SPAR (from Germany and Austria) is the third largest international retail developer. Its innovative concept fits neatly into present conditions in Czech and Slovak retailing. Its expansion has been organised from two centres near the Czech border, from Passau in Germany and Linz in Austria. The German and Austrian operations own 49 per cent of SPAR Czechoslovakia, while 2 per cent is owned by SPAR International in Amsterdam. There were plans to cover all regions in both Republics with around 1,000 licences and to reach a 20 per cent market share by the end of 1994; however, these proved to be too ambitious. Fast growth is partly limited by a dependence on supplies and control structures from abroad, although there are three local wholesale bases – in Sušice, Ceské Budejovice and Brno.

Nevertheless, about 100 independent retailers, some of them in Slovakia, used the 'Spar' logo on their shops by the beginning of 1995. This number is increasing slowly. The Austrians are preparing construction of the first INTERSPAR supermarkets in Ceské Budejovice, Prague and Plzen.

DELVITA is a subsidiary of the Belgian supermarket chain Delhaize le Lion and manages one of the best examples of a western-style operation. DELVITA runs 11 supermarkets in Prague and is now expanding to other regions. The first 'green field' supermarket was opened in Beroun. Further take-overs of one-time state-owned outlets are awaited. Since 1994, DELVITA has had its own centralised buying system.

Tengelmann (Germany) has launched its discount outlet, Plus, in the Czech Republic. Fifteen Plus Discounts are already in operation. They are mostly in Prague but are also to be found in Mladá Boleslav, Louny, Most, Ústí nad Labem and Kladno. The company has its own distribution centre situated on the outskirts of Prague. At least ten more shops are planned for 1995. Plus Discounts now distribute, after learning from their own mistakes, a high share of local products and have had considerable success because consumers like outlets of this type.

At the same time as Tengelmann, another German discounter, Norma, entered the Czech market, but it has not developed as rapidly. Norma currently operates two discount shops in Prague and in the West Bohemian town of Rokycany. Only a small proportion of the merchandise is locally produced. Norma plans to open its own distribution centre in Prague in 1995.

The Austrian operation BILLA opened its first supermarket in Brno and now operates eight outlets in the Czech Republic, including two large hypermarkets in Prague that were acquired from SYP. Foreign items are a major part of its range of merchandise. BILLA is also active in the Slovak towns of Trnava, Bratislava and Trencín. Further outlets are planned and a wholesale distribution centre will be established in Brno.

Kathreiner AG (Germany) has obtained a 15-year lease on a department store in the centre of Prague. It operates under the fascia Krone, 80 per cent of which belongs to Kathreiner and 20 per cent to the Czech company Mercurius. Kathreiner also plans to start building its own hypermarkets on 'green field' sites.

The discount outlet Rema 1000 is a joint venture between the Scandinavian discount chain Reitan and the Czech enterprise Koospol. Six discount stores were opened in 1994 in Czech towns and one in Central Slovakia. Plans have been announced to expand in cities with over 10,000 inhabitants. Wholesale deliveries are guaranteed by Propo, another Koospol subsidiary.

The year 1994 brought a heavy offensive from Julius Meinl (Austria).

Meinl shops existed in Czechoslovakia before the Second World War and now the Austrians intend to return to their traditional market. Initially, they co-operated with the successful Czech company Pronto Plus. Later, they decided to purchase 10 supermarkets, most of which were in Prague. All the refurbished stores are of a good standard and Meinl seeks further expansion.

Mobile outlets of Family Frost/Eismann (100 vans) distribute ice cream and frozen products every week to half of the Czech districts. In 1995 they intend to enlarge their area of activity to the rest of the country.

Two Delta discount stores in Northern Bohemia and a Diska supermarket, both belonging to the German Edeka, have recently opened in Plzen. Another German chain, Rewe, plans to launch a voluntary chain for retailers and also its own penny discount store. The company's ultimate aim is to recruit 1,500 independent retailers; however, it did not meet its initial target of 150 shops in 1994.

Some foreign retailers are successful in wholesaling. Lekkerland is the best example. The Germans established a joint venture with a dynamic local food wholesaler OK FOODS. They are strong, especially in the Prague market, amongst non-standard customers such as petrol stations, key accounts, department stores and so on. The Czech–German joint venture called Drinks is a market leader in beverages. The Dutch–Czech joint venture Bonmart operates a C&C store in Prague and the Dutch–Slovak joint venture Maxa has another store in Bratislava. Besides the companies mentioned, many other international multiples are observing the market and are searching for good locations and/or potential partners. For example, Intermarché, Leclerc (France), Makro SHV (Netherlands), Globus, Famila (Germany) and Marks & Spencer are all monitoring the market.

Some foreign retailers have not been successful, Spanish grocery group SYP Supermercado being the best example. SYP operated the two largest hypermarkets in the Czech Republic. Both stores were located in the densely populated block-housing areas of Prague. Problematic siting of the outlets, a poorly conceived merchandise selection, occasional arrogance towards suppliers and, last but not least, a lack of experience with large-scale outlets were the main reasons for poor consumer interest and disappointing sales. In early 1994 all SYP outlets were sold to BILLA.

Non-food retail activities of foreigners should not be forgotten in this overview. There is a whole spectrum of them, especially in the Czech Republic. Hundreds of brand names have appeared in the branches of both exclusive and discount textile and clothing shops. Bata, the Canadian shoe producer and distributor of Czech origin, owns more than 30 outlets all over the country. Salamander, Humanic, Leiser, Rieker, Herto or Bama can also be seen on Czech streets. The voluntary groups of Garant Schuh and Nord-West-Ring have also been formed. However, Reno had to withdraw from the market because its discount concept was not acceptable to Czech consumers.

The furniture and do-it-yourself sector has been addressed by foreign operations with some vigour: IKEA, Europa-Möbel, ASKO, Obi, Baumax-X, Götzen, and the new specialised large-scale outlets of Bauhaus. The German retailers DM and Rossmann have launched their discounter drugstores. Sportswear and electronics operations have also entered the market. For instance, individual retailers apply for membership of PORST, active in the Czech Republic and in Slovakia, as well as other buying groups or franchisers.

In the beginning, some foreign supermarket operators assumed that they could achieve large profits by applying western formulas, including merchandise ranges. Nothing could be further from reality. Czech and Slovak consumers have certain standards and one has to combine one's own experience and abilities with the knowledge of the local market. For instance, most consumers want to see local products in their supermarkets and only buy foreign goods as a supplement to vary their selection. Those retailers who can find an optimum balance are the most successful in the market.

PROSPECTS FOR RETAILING IN THE CZECH AND SLOVAK REPUBLICS

In the second half of 1990s, retail multiples, especially the foreign multiples, will increase their market share through the development of chains of discount shops, supermarkets and hypermarkets. Independent retailers, especially in foods and *horeca* keepers, will have to find their place in a highly competitive market. Their survival will depend on either strict specialisation or co-operation within buying groups, voluntary chains or franchise systems. Such purpose-built groupings will occupy a big part of the market, both in retail and in wholesale. Integration of big and medium-sized Czech enterprises into companies with a strong financial background will occur more frequently.

Large-scale retail outlets (over 400m²) will increase in number, either through new constructions on 'green-field' sites (hypermarkets, specialised non-food outlets, shopping centres) or by redeveloping storage and production facilities. Their number in the Czech Republic will exceed 1,000 in the second half of 1990s. Smaller, wide assortment shops (under 400m² selling area) will decrease in number, although their role in the next five years will still be very important. A certain percentage of them will be rebuilt into discount shops and stores with narrow specialisation.

Specialised shops will raise their standard of quality, orienting themselves to richer segments of the market and to tourists and customers with well-defined needs. Small mixed shops will certainly decline in number, because they will not be able to compete either on price, or on quality or on range in the non-food sector. By the end of 1990s their number could decrease by 5,000–6,000. The future prospects for kiosks are similar. Petrol stations will experience restructuring. The total prospective capacity of the Czech market is said to be about 1,500 outlets, and the Slovak around 800. The sales of basic consumer goods sold by petrol stations are expected to grow. *Horeca* outlets will profit through growing tourist expenditures. Their number soon will soon stabilise and the quality of services will improve.

Both republics will come closer to western distribution patterns within the next three to five years. The current retail organisation will probably be replaced by a concentrated structure dominated by international companies. Internationalisation will become the key factor of future retail development. The Czech Republic is already at the top of the list for foreign retail investment among post-communist countries. The development in the Slovak Republic is expected to be delayed for another two or three years.

REFERENCES

INCOMA Praha, 1994, 'Nejvetší obchodní podniky v CR a SR', *Moderní obchod*, April, pp.12–14.
Baker, M., 1991, 'The Future of Distribution in Czechoslovakia', *The Business Network Newsbulletin*, December, p.2.
Czech Statistical Office – various sources.
Drtina, T., 1991, 'De veranderende Tjechoslowaakse detailhadel', *Detailhandel magazine*, November, pp.22–4.
Drtina, T., 1992a, 'New Developments in East European Retailing', Paper at the EDPG Conference in Monte Carlo, October.
Drtina, T., 1992b, 'CSFR: Handel öffnet sich Europa', *Dynamik im Handel*, December, pp. 38–40.
INCOMA Praha, 1991, *Le Commerce Intérieur Tchécoslovaque*, Prague: Incoma, p.110.
INCOMA Praha, 1994, Food Distribution in the Czech Republic, Prague: Incoma.
Krásný T. and T. Drtina, 1989, Mezinárodní srovnání vývojových tendencí maloobchodní síte, Praha: VUO, p.40.
Krásný, T., 1991, 'Der Einzelhandel in Osteuropa', *Der Verbund*, January, pp.10–12.
Krásný, T., 1992, 'Retailing in Czechoslovakia', *Retailing in Eastern Europe, International Journal of Retail & Distribution Management*, Vol.20, No.6, pp.30–3.

Developing a Framework for the Study of the Internationalisation of Retailing

GARY AKEHURST and NICHOLAS ALEXANDER

INTRODUCTION

By the late 1980s it became *de rigueur* to include the word international in the titles of new journals, new research units and even established conferences. The three most important issues in retailing had become internationalisation, internationalisation and internationalisation.

In the next ten years international retailing will increasingly become a tautologous phrase. As retailers develop international operations, the study of retailing will be fundamentally international in nature. If the last ten years have seen the international retailing literature lifecycle pass through a time of rapid growth, the next will see a period of maturity as the lacunae in this subject area are considered. Beyond that horizon, it will be increasingly difficult to see the dividing line between the study of international retailing and retailing.

FUTURE AGENDA

In establishing an agenda there are six basic questions which should be asked.

What is the internationalisation of retailing?

The term is used liberally in the literature, but it is used loosely and activities are assumed. The word 'internationalisation' is as poorly defined as it is understood: '...as soon as one starts thinking about it, it becomes elusive. Does the word identify a clear area of firms' strategies, does it draw a clear border between a given set of actions and the remaining alternatives open to the firm? The answer is probably no' [Pellegrini, 1994: 121]. Pellegrini is correct in his statement. This is not a satisfactory condition. Any subject area must have a clearly defined vocabulary on which to draw. Without a sufficiently robust lexicon, a subject will dissolve into repetitive, disparate and unprofitable research programmes. Retailing may be accused of this deficiency, a deficiency partly a consequence of the dynamic nature of the subject area. Thus efforts to define retail terms are an invaluable exercise. Baron, Davies and Swindley's [1991] systemised approach is to be lauded, therefore, but lexicographers are at the mercy of researchers who fail to establish or misuse definitions.

It is important to consider what is occurring during the internationalisation process. In so doing, it is necessary to appreciate if not understand those factors which define internationalisation [Alexander, 1994]; that is, the process needs to be understood both in terms of those factors which are shared by different retail structures and those factors which differentiate retail structures. This demands an understanding of the divergent and convergent processes which exist within the local, regional and global environment. Davies and Flemmer's article and Myers' article took up this theme in this volume. While we may see convergence on a regional, or in terms of these papers, a European basis, divergence may be occurring on a sub-national level. This raises questions as to how groupings, both socio-economic and geographical, should be perceived within an increasingly integrated yet inherently heterogeneous economic area. Thus it may be appropriate to differentiate between the regionalisation of retailing – where the region is seen to represent the global region – and the globalisation of retailing within an overarching explanatory framework of internationalisation.

Who are internationalising?

International retailers have been categorised on a number of bases. They have been categorised by operational approach [Hollander, 1970], geographical dispersion and operational cost and control [Treadgold, 1988], or strategically [Salmon and Tordjman, 1989]. Chen and Sternquist's study in this volume compares international Japanese retailers with other Japanese retailers who have not internationalised their operations, and thereby identify key determinants which will help to define international categories of retailer. Such studies will lead to a greater understanding of the internationalisation process, as will those which compare unsuccessful attempts at internationalisation with those which have succeeded. The process of withdrawal from international activity is an informative but underexplored area of research.

A greater understanding of those who internationalise may also be achieved through the approach adopted by Sparks in his essay in this volume. While an increasing amount of information concerned with individual company experience is emerging, an in-depth consideration of a retailer's experience is a valuable means of understanding more fully the process of internationalisation. In many respects, the example used by Sparks is not a classic route to internationalisation, but if the activities of other Japanese retailers are indicative, this may be a more important route in the future.

Sparks' article follows in a distinguished line of inquiry. Martenson's [1981] consideration of IKEA provides an example of the deep analysis which is possible in these cases. Likewise this approach has been given considerable academic weight by such as Wilson [1985] through his consideration of W.H.Smith. There is, however, a danger that individual studies will not attempt to place the company under consideration in a wider theoretical framework. While frameworks may have proved constraining within business studies and interesting lines of inquiry curtailed because of the need to return to normative or quantitative judgements, such individual cases should be judged in terms of what they contribute to an understanding of the wider environment, and care should be taken that they do not degenerate into something approaching an antiquarian exercise.

Why are retailers internationalising?

While the motivations which lie behind internationalisation have received consideration in recent years, much work remains to be done on this issue. Treadgold [1988: 8] has stated: 'For many ... retailers ... the principal motivation for expanding internationally has been the limited opportunities for sustained domestic growth.' Certainly, many retailers faced with 'saturation' in the domestic market may seek alternative growth opportunities in non-domestic markets, yet there are dangers in assuming that the primary reasons for internationalisation are push rather than pull factors. Indeed, empirical research has shown that push factors may not be the primary determinant of international development. Williams [1992: 278] has suggested that 'the major motives behind the RI of UK-based international retailers originate from a perceived internationally appealing and innovative offering and growth oriented and proactive motives'.

There is an important dichotomy in the literature to be reconciled. In part, the dichotomy may be the product of methodology, and in part it may reflect the time frame of research activity. Certainly, both reactive and proactive responses are observable in the internationalisation process. Alexander [1995a] has suggested that these views may be reconciled with reference to a framework whereby motives are conceptualised as proactive, reactive, expansive and autochthonic.

The international retail literature also needs to be reconciled with the broader business and economic research agenda. Whitehead [1992] has suggested the validity of this approach, while Dawson [1994] has indicated that caution should be exercised in this respect. Nevertheless, the strength of research in the area of manufacturing industry is not easily dismissed and due consideration should be given to this potentially stimulating vein of research endeavour.

Where are retailers developing operations?

Retailers, during the most recent period of international expansion, have concentrated their activities on the markets of North America, Western Europe and the Pacific Rim. This is changing. Drtina's paper raises the issue of retail development in markets which have operated under a completely different economic system. In the 1990s retailers are exploring opportunities in eastern Europe and China that would have seemed a very distant prospect ten years earlier. While studies of underdeveloped retail markets have appeared [Paddison *et al.*, 1990], considerable work remains to be carried out in this area. It has been noted that: 'To the analyst more familiar with retailing in the economically advanced nations, the first encounter with retailing in less-developed countries is something of an academic shock' [Paddison *et al.*, 1990: 3]. Such shocks are to be encouraged. Research in this area will be useful in challenging the assumptions made about developed retail structures.

Much work, however, still remains to be carried out on the internationalisation of retailing within developed retail structures. In this volume, Burns and Rayman explore the development of retailing within North America and the cross-border influences of Canadian and US retailing. Myers raises the question of market definition within the EU. The geographical development of retailers in Free Trade Areas, as opposed to nation-states, deserves consideration and conceptualisation. Davies and Fergusson explore the developing retail structure of the Pacific Rim. Further research is required to develop these lines of inquiry.

How are retailers developing operations?

The operationalisation of international retailers requires closer examination, especially the vehicles retailers use to access new markets and the positioning strategies they employ. Much is implicit within the literature where operational development is concerned, but much remains to be fully explored. The internationalisation of retail operations is investigated in this volume in the article by Bailey, Clarke-Hill and Robinson. While the article focuses on the issue of strategic alliances, it has wider implications for the conceptualisation of operational development which is closely linked with organisational development and culture [McGoldrick and Fryer, 1993]. Likewise, it is important to consider such operational issues as distribution and the impact of planning regulations on international expansion as, respectively, the articles by Fernie and by Hallsworth, Jones and Muncaster do in this volume.

From the perspective of marketing, McGoldrick and Ho [1992: 62] have indicated their surprise 'that so little research attention has been given to the image and positioning of retailers operating outside their home market'. In this volume, Davies and Flemmer's contribution addresses the need to understand the differences and similarities which exist across different markets. Drtina's study emphasises the differences which will exist in some markets. Simpson and Thorpe's essay in this volume identifies key determinants of success and explores the need to provide useful managerial tools.

When does internationalisation occur?

In the main, the retail literature does not dwell on this specific issue. The conditions under which internationalisation is taking place or has recently occurred are stated and then accepted as the conditions under which internationalisation occurs. This ahistorical approach seriously qualifies, even if it does not render void, some conclusions. Without understanding the historical processes which have brought about changes in international retailing, there is a considerable danger that conclusions will be time-specific and deeply flawed. This problem has been explored in the literature [Alexander, 1993, 1995b] and there are examples of the collation of time series data [Burt, 1991, 1993], as Davies' contribution to this volume shows. Such time series analysis will help in understanding factors which stimulate internationalisation. Nevertheless, there remain considerable opportunities for research in this area.

It is possible to take several approaches to the changing nature of the internationalisation process. That adopted by Sparks is one method. Likewise, in this volume, Burns and Rayman's approach contributes to an overall understanding of the processes which lie behind retail structural development over time. Care, however, should be taken when applying givens about the present to past events and processes. There is always a danger of interpreting the past with reference to the present rather than with reference to the past. When considering the context in which previous internationalisation activity has occurred, it is important to make 'the past our present' [Butterfield, 1931: 16]. If researchers fail to observe this fundamental requirement when considering the contextualised development of international retail activity, their conclusions are in danger of being deeply flawed at best, and void at worst.

CONCLUSION

An important aspect of the international retailing research agenda in the next ten years must be the consideration of the internationalisation process: that is, the internationalisation of the organisation and the internationalisation of retail structures and markets. There is a clear synergy between these research areas. Indeed, it will be necessary to construct an overall framework within which these related issues may be placed and methodological developments made. The studies in this volume are a major contribution to this developing and fascinating area of research.

REFERENCES

Alexander, N., 1993, 'Internationalisation: Interpreting the Motives', *International Issues in Retailing, ESRC Seminars: Research Themes in Retailing*, Manchester Business School / Manchester School of Management, 15 March.

Alexander, N., 1994, 'Isoagora: Retail Boundaries in Free Trade Areas', presented at *Retailing: Theories and Practices for Today and Tomorrow, The Fourth Triennial AMS/ACRA National Retailing Conference*, 22–24 Oct., Richmond, Virginia.

Alexander, N., 1995a, 'UK Retailers' Motives for Operating in the Single European Market', *International Review of Retail, Distribution and Consumer Research*, Vol.5, No.4, forthcoming.

Alexander, N., 1995b, 'The Whig Interpretation of Retailing', 7th Conference on Historical Research in Marketing and Marketing Thought, 25–28 May, Ft. Wayne, Indiana.

Baron, S., B. Davies and D. Swindley, 1991, *Dictionary of Retailing*, London: Macmillan.

Burt, S., 1991, 'Trends in the Internationalisation of Grocery Retailing: The European Experience', *International Review of Retail, Distribution and Consumer Research*, Vol.1, No.4, pp.487–515.

Burt, S., 1993, 'Temporal Trends in the Internationalisation of British Retailing', *International Issues in Retailing, ESRC Seminars: Research Themes in Retailing*, Manchester Business School / Manchester School of Management, 15 March.

Butterfield, H., 1931, *The Whig Interpretation of Retailing*, London: Bell & Sons.

Dawson, J., 1994, 'The Internationalization of Retailing Operations', *Journal of Marketing Management*, Vol. 10, pp.267–82.

Hollander, S., 1970, *Multinational Retailing*, East Lansing, MI: Michigan State University.

McGoldrick, P. and E. Fryer, 1993, 'Organisational Culture and the Internationalisation of Retailers', 7th International Conference on Research in the Distributive Trades, Institute for Retail Studies, University of Stirling, 6–8 Sept..

McGoldrick, P. and S. Ho, 1992, 'International Positioning: Japanese Department Stores in Hong Kong', *European Journal of Marketing*, Vol.26, No.8/9, pp.61–73.

Martenson, R., 1981, *Innovations in Multinational Retailing: IKEA on the Swedish, Swiss, German and Austrian Furniture Markets*, Gothenburg: University of Gothenburg.

Paddison, R., A. Findlay and J. Dawson (eds.), 1990, *Retailing Environments in Developing Countries*, London: Routledge.

Pellegrini, L., 1994, 'Alternatives for Growth and Internationalization in Retailing', *The International Review of Retail, Distribution and Consumer Research*, Vol.4, No.2, pp.121–49.

Salmon, W. and A. Tordjman, 1989, 'The Internationalisation of Retailing', *International Journal of Retailing*, Vol.4, No.2, pp.3–16.

Treadgold, A., 1988, 'Retailing Without Frontiers', *Retail and Distribution Management*, Vol.16, No.6, pp.8–12.

Whitehead, M., 1992, 'Internationalisation of Retailing: Developing New Perspectives', *European Journal of Marketing*, Vol. 26, No. 8/9, pp.74–9.

Williams, D., 1992a, 'Motives for Retailer Internationalization: Their Impact, Structure, and Implications', *Journal of Marketing Management*, Vol.8, pp.269–85

Wilson, C., 1985, *First with the News: The History of W.H.Smith 1792–1972*, London: Jonathan Cape.

Notes on Contributors

Gary Akehurst is at Southampton Business School, Business Development Research Centre, Southampton Institute, East Park Terrace, Southampton SO14 0YN.

Nicholas Alexander is in the Faculty of Business and Management, University of Ulster, Coleraine, Northern Ireland BT52 1SA.

Eithel Simpson is in the Department of Consumer Science and Retailing, Purdue University, 1262 Matthews Hall, West Lafayette, Indiana 47907-1262, USA.

Dayle Thorpe is in the Department of Logistics and Transportation, Stokley Management Center, University of Tennessee, Knoxville, Tennessee 37996, USA.

Jayne Bailey and **Colin M. Clarke-Hill** are at the School of Business, University of Huddersfield, Queensgate, Huddersfield, West Yorkshire HD1 3DH.

Terry M. Robinson is Principal Lecturer in Marketing, Teesside Business School, University of Teesside, Middlesbrough, Cleveland TS1 3BA.

Hayley Myers is in the Department of Management Studies, University of Surrey, Guildford GU2 5XH.

Leigh Sparks is at the Institute for Retail Studies, University of Stirling FK9 4LA.

Keri Davies and **Fergus Fergusson** are at the Institute for Retail Studies, University of Stirling FK9 4LA.

Yung-Fang Chen and **Brenda Sternquist** are in the Department of Human Environment and Design, Michigan State University, 204 Ecology Building, East Lansing, MI 48824-1030, USA.

John Fernie is at Dundee Business School, Dudhope Castle, Dundee DD3 6HF.

Alan Hallsworth is Director of the Service Industries Research Centre, University of Portsmouth, Portsmouth PO1 3HE.

Ken G. Jones is Director of the Centre for the Study of Commercial Activities (CSCA) at Ryerson Polytechnical University, Toronto.

Russell Muncaster is Professor of Geography at Wilfrid Laurier University, Waterloo, Canada.

David J. Burns is in the Department of Marketing, Williamson School of Business, Youngstown State University, Youngstown, Ohio 44555, USA.

Dale M. Rayman is in the Department of Business Administration, Tiffin University, Tiffin, Ohio 44883, USA.

Barry J. Davies and **Malene Flemmer** are in the Department of Retailing and Marketing, the Manchester Metropolitan University, Aytoun Building, Aytoun Street, Manchester M1 3GH.

Tomáš Drtina is at INCOMA Praha, Benešovská 21, 10100 Prague, Czech Republic.